T0332117

Hidden Link Prediction in Stochastic Social Networks

Babita Pandey
Lovely Professional University, India

Aditya Khamparia
Lovely Professional University, India

A volume in the Advances in
Social Networking and Online
Communities (ASNOC) Book Series

Published in the United States of America by
    IGI Global
    Information Science Reference (an imprint of IGI Global)
    701 E. Chocolate Avenue
    Hershey PA, USA 17033
    Tel: 717-533-8845
    Fax: 717-533-8661
    E-mail: cust@igi-global.com
    Web site: http://www.igi-global.com

Library of Congress Cataloging-in-Publication Data

Names: Pandey, Babita, 1976- editor. | Khamparia, Aditya, 1988- editor.
Title: Hidden link prediction in stochastic social networks / Babita Pandey
    and Aditya Khamparia, editors.
Description: Hershey, PA : Information Science Reference, 2020. | Includes
    bibliographical references.
Identifiers: LCCN 2018057677| ISBN 9781522590965 (hardcover) | ISBN
    9781522590996 (softcover) | ISBN 9781522590972 (ebook)
Subjects: LCSH: Computer network architectures. | Online social
    networks--Data processing. | Webometrics. | Prediction theory. |
    Intersection theory (Mathematics) | Stochastic analysis.
Classification: LCC TK5105.52 .H53 2020 | DDC 302.23/10151922--dc23
LC record available at https://lccn.loc.gov/2018057677

This book is published in the IGI Global book series Advances in Social Networking and Online
Communities (ASNOC) (ISSN: 2328-1405; eISSN: 2328-1413)

British Cataloguing in Publication Data
A Cataloguing in Publication record for this book is available from the British Library.

All work contributed to this book is new, previously-unpublished material.
The views expressed in this book are those of the authors, but not necessarily of the publisher.

For electronic access to this publication, please contact: eresources@igi-global.com.

Advances in Social Networking and Online Communities (ASNOC) Book Series

ISSN:2328-1405
EISSN:2328-1413

Editor-in-Chief: Hakikur Rahman, Institute of Computer Management and Science, Bangladesh

MISSION

The advancements of internet technologies and the creation of various social networks provide a new channel of knowledge development processes that's dependent on social networking and online communities. This emerging concept of social innovation is comprised of ideas and strategies designed to improve society.

The **Advances in Social Networking and Online Communities** book series serves as a forum for scholars and practitioners to present comprehensive research on the social, cultural, organizational, and human issues related to the use of virtual communities and social networking. This series will provide an analytical approach to the holistic and newly emerging concepts of online knowledge communities and social networks.

COVERAGE

- Knowledge as a Competitive Force
- Citizens' E-participation in Local Decision-Making Processes
- Organizational Knowledge Communication and Knowledge Transfer as the Focal Point of Knowledge Management
- Introduction to Mobile Computing
- Advanced Researches in Knowledge Communities
- Whole-Network Properties and Knowledge Communication
- Knowledge as a Symbol/Model of Development
- Communication and Management of Knowledge in R&D Networks
- Agent-Mediated Knowledge Management
- General Importance and Role of Knowledge Communities

IGI Global is currently accepting manuscripts for publication within this series. To submit a proposal for a volume in this series, please contact our Acquisition Editors at Acquisitions@igi-global.com or visit: http://www.igi-global.com/publish/.

Titles in this Series

For a list of additional titles in this series, please visit:
http://www.igi-global.com/book-series/advances-social-networking-online-communities/37168

Cognitive Social Mining Applications in Data Analytics and Forensics
Anandakumar Haldorai (Sri Eshwar College of Engineering, India) and Arulmurugan Ramu (Presidency Universiy, India)
Information Science Reference • ©2019 • 326pp • H/C (ISBN: 9781522575221) • US $195.00

Modern Perspectives on Virtual Communications and SocialNetworking
Jyotsana Thakur (Amity University, India)
Information Science Reference • ©2019 • 273pp • H/C (ISBN: 9781522557159) • US $175.00

Exploring the Role of Social Media in Transnational Advocacy
Floribert Patrick C. Endong (University of Calabar, Nigeria)
Information Science Reference • ©2018 • 307pp • H/C (ISBN: 9781522528548) • US $195.00

Online Communities as Agents of Change and Social Movements
Steven Gordon (Babson College, USA)
Information Science Reference • ©2017 • 338pp • H/C (ISBN: 9781522524953) • US $195.00

Social Media Performance Evaluation and Success Measurements
Michael A. Brown Sr. (Florida International University, USA)
Information Science Reference • ©2017 • 294pp • H/C (ISBN: 9781522519638) • US $185.00

Political Scandal, Corruption, and Legitimacy in the Age of Social Media
Kamil Demirhan (Bülent Ecevit University, Turkey) and Derya Çakır-Demirhan (Bülent Ecevit University, Turkey)
Information Science Reference • ©2017 • 295pp • H/C (ISBN: 9781522520191) • US $190.00

Power, Surveillance, and Culture in YouTube™'s Digital Sphere
Matthew Crick (William Paterson University, USA)
Information Science Reference • ©2016 • 317pp • H/C (ISBN: 9781466698550) • US $185.00

For an entire list of titles in this series, please visit:
http://www.igi-global.com/book-series/advances-social-networking-online-communities/37168

701 East Chocolate Avenue, Hershey, PA 17033, USA
Tel: 717-533-8845 x100 • Fax: 717-533-8661
E-Mail: cust@igi-global.com • www.igi-global.com

Editorial Advisory Board

Table of Contents

Detailed Table of Contents

Chapter 1

    Praveen Kumar Bhanodia, Lovely Professional University, India
    Kamal Kumar Sethi, Acropolis Institute of Technology and Research,
        India
    Aditya Khamparia, Lovely Professional University, India
    Babita Pandey, Babasaheb Bhimrao Ambedkar University, India
    Shaligram Prajapat, IIPS DAV, India

Link prediction in social network has gained momentum with the inception of machine learning. The social networks are evolving into smart dynamic networks possessing various relevant information about the user. The relationship between users can be approximated by evaluation of similarity between the users. Online social network (OSN) refers to the formulation of association (relationship/links) between users known as nodes. Evolution of OSNs such as Facebook, Twitter, Hi-Fi, LinkedIn has provided a momentum to the growth of such social networks, whereby millions of users are joining it. The online social network evolution has motivated scientists and researchers to analyze the data and information of OSN in order to recommend the future friends. Link prediction is a problem instance of such recommendation systems. Link prediction is basically a phenomenon through which potential links between nodes are identified on a network over the period of time. In this chapter, the authors describe the similarity metrics that further would be instrumental in recognition of future links between nodes.

Chapter 2

Social network and its corresponding website permits a client to make a profile, set up an authorized account to create a digital representation of themselves, to select other members of the site as contacts, make connections with them, communicate and engage with these users in different social activities, etc. So, social network includes details of persons, group details, their friends list, contact list, business, affiliations, personal data, personal preferences, and historical information. In this age of smart communication and technology, most of the time people are connected with mobile smart telephones in their work culture, home, office, or any other related places. As they are constantly associated with social systems for long time, they get new posts, messages, and current refreshed news readily available in a flash. This is the constructive part of social networking that individuals consistently remain refreshed with most recent news and innovation. This chapter presents an overview of social network design, various issues, and emerging trends that are evolved simultaneously with modern age. It also presents a detail study on application and impact of social network in modern society as well as exhibits an exhaustive review of security measures in social sites.

Expansion of online social networks is rapid and furious. Millions of users are appending to it and enriching the nature and behavior, and the information generated has various dimensional properties providing new opportunities and perspective for computation of network properties. The structure of social networks is comprised of nodes and edges whereas users are entities represented by node and relationships designated by edges. Processing of online social networks structural features yields fair knowledge which can be used in many of recommendation and prediction systems. This is referred to as social network analysis, and the features exploited usually are local and global both plays significant role in processing and computation. Local features include properties of nodes like degree of the node (in-degree, out-degree) while global feature process the path between nodes in the entire network. The chapter is an effort in the direction of online social network analysis that explores the basic methods that can be process and analyze the network with a suitable approach to yield knowledge.

Chapter 4

Position Independent Mobile User Authentication Using Keystroke Dynamics 64

Baljit Singh Saini, Lovely Professional University, India & Sri Guru Granth Sahib World University, India
Navdeep Kaur, Sri Guru Granth Sahib World University, India
Kamaljit Singh Bhatia, IKGPTU, India

In this chapter, a novel technique to authenticate a mobile phone user irrespective of his/her typing position is presented. The user is never always in sitting position while using mobile phone. Thus, it becomes very important to check the accuracy of keystroke dynamics technique while taking input in all positions but authenticating the user irrespective of these positions. Three user positions were considered for input – sitting, walking, and relaxed. The input was taken in uncontrolled environment to get realistic results. Hold time, latency, and motion features using accelerometer data were extracted, and the analysis was done using random forest and KNN classifiers. The accelerometer data provides additional features like mean of all X, Y, and Z axis values. The inclusion of these features improved the results drastically and played a very significant role in determining the user typing behavior. An EER of 4.3% was achieved with a best FAR of 0.9% and an FRR of 15.2%.

Chapter 5

Drug Prediction in Healthcare Using Big Data and Machine Learning 79

Mamoon Rashid, Lovely Professional University, India & Punjabi University, India
Vishal Goyal, Punjabi University, India
Shabir Ahmad Parah, University of Kashmir, India
Harjeet Singh, Mata Gujri College, India

The healthcare system is literally losing patients due to improper diagnosis, accidents, and infections in hospitals alone. To address these challenges, the authors are proposing the drug prediction model that will act as informative guide for patients and help them for taking right medicines for the cure of particular disease. In this chapter, the authors are proposing use of Hadoop distributed file system for the storage of medical datasets related to medicinal drugs. MLLib Library of Apache Spark is to be used for initial data analysis for drug suggestions related to symptoms gathered from particular user. The model will analyze the previous history of patients for any side effects of the drug to be recommended. This proposal will consider weather and maps API from Google as well so that the patients can easily locate the nearby stores where the medicines will be available. It is believed that this proposal of research will surely eradicate the issues by prescribing the optimal drug and its availability by giving the location of the retailer of that drug near the customer.

Mobile ad hoc networks are infrastructure-less wireless networks; all nodes can quickly share information without using any fixed infrastructure like base station or access point. Wireless ad hoc networks are characterized by frequent topology changes, unreliable wireless channel, network congestion, and resource contention. Multimedia applications usually are bandwidth hungry with stringent delay, jitter, and loss requirements. Designing ad hoc networks which support multimedia applications, hence, is considered a hard task. The hidden and exposed terminal problems are the main which consequently reduces the network capacity. Hidden and exposed nodes reduce the performance of the wireless ad hoc networks. Access delay is the major parameter that is to be taken under consideration. Due to hidden and exposed terminal problems, the network suffers from a serious unfairness problem.

Deep learning approaches have been found to be suitable for the agricultural field with successful applications to vegetable infection through plant disease. In this chapter, the authors discuss some widely used deep learning architecture and their practical applications. Nowadays, in many typical applications of machine vision, there is a tendency to replace classical techniques with deep learning algorithms. The benefits are valuable; on one hand, it avoids the need of specialized handcrafted features extractors, and on the other hand, results are not damaged. Moreover, they typically get improved.

Due to the high mobility of vehicular nodes in VANETs, there are high chances of partitions in the network. In such a situation, the protocols developed for VANETs cannot work well and an alternative network known as DTN (delay tolerant network) is capable enough to deal with VANET characteristics. The network which does not need any immediate data delivery and can wait for time and delivery of data is known as DTN. The concept of hold and forward the message is exploited by DTN. In this chapter, the authors are providing characteristics, architecture, and applications of delay tolerant vehicular ad-hoc networks.

Chapter 9

Image classification is a technique to categorize an image in to given classes on the basis of hidden characteristics or features extracted using image processing. With rapidly growing technology, the size of images is growing. Different categories of images may contain different types of hidden information such as x-ray, CT scan, MRI, pathologies images, remote sensing images, satellite images, and natural scene image captured via digital cameras. In this chapter, the authors have surveyed various articles and books and summarized image classification techniques. There are supervised techniques like KNN and SVM, which classify an image into given classes and unsupervised techniques like K-means and ISODATA for classifying image into a group of clusters. For big images, deep learning networks can be employed that are fast and efficient and also compute hidden features automatically.

Chapter 10

In this chapter, the neuro-fuzzy technique has been used for the diagnosis of different types of diabetes. It has been reported in the literature that triangular membership functions have been deployed for Mamdani and Sugeno fuzzy expert systems that have been used for diagnosis of different types of diabetes. The Gaussian membership functions are expected to give better results. In this context, Gaussian membership functions have been attempted in the neuro-fuzzy system for the diagnosis of different types of diabetes in the research work, and improved results have been obtained in terms of different parameters like sensitivity, specificity, accuracy, precision. Further, for the comparative study, the dataset used for neuro-fuzzy expert system developed in this research work has been considered on Mamdani fuzzy expert system as well as Sugeno fuzzy expert system, and it has been confirmed that the result parameters show better values in the proposed model.

Preface

The tremendous growth of social networks has attracted lots of attention from academia as well as industry due to its use in various applications such as: friend recommendation, product recommendation, community detection, collaborations etc. In fact, the stochastic growth of the social network leads to various challenges in identifying hidden link such as: representation of graph, distinction between spurious and missing link, selection of link prediction techniques and network features, and type of network. The social networks are evolving into smart dynamic networks possessing various relevant information about the user. Link prediction in social network has gained momentum with the inception of machine Learning. The purpose of this book is to disseminate cutting-edge research results, highlight research challenges and open issues, and promotes further research interest and activities in identifying missing link in stochastic social networking. In addition to this this book also discusses about the application of various machine learning techniques and problems of various types of network such as: delay network.

BOOK OBJECTIVES

This book concentrates on the foremost techniques of Hidden Link predictions in Stochastic Social Networks. It deals, principally, with methods and approaches that involve similarity index techniques, matrix factorization, reinforcement models, graph representations and community detections etc. As well as, it will include the miscellaneous methods of different modalities in deep learning, agent driven AI techniques and Automata driven systems. This book will endeavour to endow with significant frameworks and the latest empirical research findings in the area. It will be written for professionals who desire to improve their understanding and developing automated machine learning systems for supervised, unsupervised and recommendation driven learning systems. As, the progressions of this field will help to intensify interdisciplinary discovery in e-commerce product recommendations, community detection, Facebook predictions and friend recommendations, credit score assignments. Anticipating linkages among information items is a crucial information mining undertaking in different application spaces, including recommender frameworks, data recovery, programmed Web hyperlink era, record linkage, and correspondence observation.

TARGET AUDIENCE

The target audience of this book will be composed of professionals and researchers working in the field of Artificial Intelligence and Social Networks in various disciplines, e.g. Online Book Store network, dynamic social network, complex networks, relational graph driven networks, Bayesian networks, predictive networks, researchers, academicians, advanced-level students, technology developers and Data Scientists. Furthermore, the book will provide insights and support executives concerned with recent Artificial Intelligence Systems that have magnetized much attention as advanced machine computing and devoted to use similarity techniques, predictive techniques, Automata, proximity measure, time series, matrix factorization, reinforcement learning, classification and clustering techniques.

ORGANIZATION

Chapter 1 describes the similarity metrics which further would be instrumental in recognition of future links between nodes. In social network the relationship between users can be predicted by measuring the similarity index between the users. Online social network is represented as a graph and the node in a graphs are user in social network. The link prediction formulates the association (relationship/links) between users. Social Networks such as: face-book, Twitter, Hi-Fi, Linkdln has provided a momentum to the growth of networks by adding millions of users. This growth in social network has motivated scientists and researchers to analyze the data and information of social network in order to recommend the future friends. Link prediction is problem instance of such recommendation systems. Link prediction is basically a phenomenon through which potential links between nodes is identified on a network over the period of time.

Chapter 2 discussed about the various application and Impact of Social Network in Modern Society. This chapter presents an overview of social network design, various issues and emerging trends that are evolved simultaneously with modern age. This chapter also exhibits an exhaustive review of various impact of social network on modern society. In current technological era, gadgets are easily available at cheap cost. Almost every people have the mobile phone they use theses mobile phones in their work culture and constantly associated with social systems for long time. Due to which every second they get new posts, messages and current refreshed news readily available in a flash. This is the constructive part of social networking that individuals dependably remain refreshed with most recent news and innovation.

In Chapter 3 we have analyse the online social network to explore the basic methods that can be process the network with a suitable approach to yield knowledge. The growth of online social networks is rapid and furious, daily millions of users are joining to it. The information generated from social network has various dimensional properties which provide new opportunities and perspective for computation of network properties. The social networks consist of nodes and edges whereas users are entities represented by node and relationships designated by edges. Processing of online social networks structural features yields fair knowledge which can be used in many of recommendation and prediction systems. The features exploited usually are local and global both plays significant role in processing and computation. Local features includes properties of nodes like degree of the node (in-degree, out-degree) while global feature process the path between nodes in the entire network.

Chapter 4 presents a novel technique to authenticate a mobile phone user irrespective of his/her typing position. The user is never always in sitting position while using mobile phone. Thus, it becomes very important to check the accuracy of keystroke dynamics technique while taking input in all positions but authenticating the user irrespective of these positions. Three user positions were considered for input – sitting, walking and relaxed. The input was taken in uncontrolled environment to get realistic results. Hold time, Latency and motion features using accelerometer data were extracted and the analysis was done using random forest and KNN classifiers. The accelerometer data provides additional features like mean of all X, Y and Z axis values.

Chapter 5 presents a drug prediction method in health care using big data and machine learning method. The Health Care System is literally losing patients due to improper diagnosis, accidents and infections in hospitals alone. The proposed model will act as informative guide for patients and help them for taking right medicines for the cure of particular disease. In this chapter, the authors are proposing use of Hadoop Distributed File System for the storage of medical datasets related to medicinal drugs. MLLib Library of Apache Spark is to be used for initial data analysis for drug suggestions related to symptoms gathered from particular user. The model will analyze the previous history of patients for any side effects of the drug to be recommended.

Chapter 6 present the analysis of access delay in Ad hoc wireless networks for multimedia applications. Mobile ad hoc networks are infrastructure less wireless networks; all nodes can quickly share information without using any fixed infrastructure like base station or access point. Wireless ad hoc networks are characterized by frequent topology changes, unreliable wireless channel, network congestion and resource contention. Multimedia applications usually are bandwidth hungry with stringent delay, jitter and loss requirements. Designing ad hoc networks which support multimedia applications, hence, is considered a hard task. The hidden and exposed terminal problems are the main which consequently reduces the network capacity. Hidden and exposed nodes reduce the performance of the wireless ad hoc networks. Access Delay is the major parameter which is to be taken under consideration. Due to hidden and exposed terminal problems network suffers from serious unfairness problem.

Chapter 7 presents the overview of Deep Learning. In last decade, the deep learning techniques have various wings in each area. It has been demanded by researchers for their work. The prediction and analysis report can be generated through Convolution Neural Network using Deep Learning approaches. In this chapter, we discuss some widely-used deep learning architecture and their practical applications. Nowadays, in many typical applications of machine vision there is a tendency to replace classical techniques with deep learning algorithms. The benefits are valuable on one hand it avoids the need of specialized handcrafted features extractors and on the other hand, results are not damaged, moreover they typically get improved.

Chapter 8 describes the architecture, protocols and application of delay tolerant networks in Vehicular Ad-Hoc Networks. Due to the high mobility of vehicular nodes in VANETs, there are high chances of partitions in the network. In such a situation the protocols developed for VANETs cannot work well and an alternative network known as DTN (Delay Tolerant Network)is capable enough to deal with VANET characteristics. The network which does not need any immediate data delivery and can wait for time and delivery of data is known as DTN. The concept of hold & forward the message is exploited by DTN. In this book chapter, the authors are providing characteristics, architecture, and applications of Delay Tolerant Vehicular Ad-hoc Networks. The technology/technical terms used in the book chapter are explained wherever they appear or at the Key Terminology & Definitions section. Apart from regular References, additional References are included in the References for Advance/Further reading for the benefit of advanced readers.

Chapter 9 presents a comprehensive review of digital image classification techniques. Image classification is a technique to categories an image in to given classes on the basis of hidden characteristics or features extracted using image processing. With rapidly growing technology the size of images is growing. Different categories of images may contain different types of hidden information such as x-ray, CT scan, MRI, pathologies images, remote sensing images, satellite images and natural scene image captured via digital cameras. In this chapter authors have surveyed various articles and books and summarized image classification techniques. There are supervised techniques like KNN and SVM, which classify an image into given classes and unsupervised techniques like K-means and ISODATA for classifying image into a group of clusters. For big images deep learning networks can be employed which are fast and efficient and it also computes hidden features automatically.

Chapter 10 presents an intelligent medical diagnostic system for diabetes. In this chapter the neuro-fuzzy technique has been used for the diagnosis of different types of diabetes. It describes the triangular and Gaussian membership functions and Mamdani and Sugeno fuzzy expert system. Various performance measures such as: sensitivity, specificity, accuracy, precision is computed and compared.

CLOSING REMARKS

In conclusion, we would like to sum up here with few lines that, the book is a small step towards the enhancement of academic research via motivating the research community and research organizations to think about the impact of Social intelligence, networking principles and its applications for augmenting the academic research. This book is putting insight on the various aspects of the academic social networking research and need of knowledge sharing and prediction of relationships through several links and their usages. This includes the research studies, experiments and literature reviews about social networking activities and to disseminate cutting-edge research results, highlight research challenges and open issues, and promotes further research interest and activities in identifying missing link in stochastic social networking. We hope that research scholars, educationalists and students alike will find significance in this book and continue to use it to expand their perspectives in the field of Social Networking and its perspective future challenges.

Babita Pandey
Lovely Professional University, India

Aditya Khamparia
Lovely Professional University, India

Acknowledgment

I would like to precise my gratitude to the many people; those who contributed, supported and guided me through this book by different means. This book would not have been possible without their guidance and the help.

First and foremost, I want to express heartfelt gratitude to my Guru for spiritual empathy and incessant blessings, to all teachers and friends for their continued guidelines and inspiration throughout the period of my studies and career. I wish my special gratitude to Dr. Babita Pandey my research guide; for her blessings and continuous inspiration.

I would like to thank IGI-Global, US publisher who gave me an opportunity to publish with them. I would like to express my appreciation to all contributors including the accepted chapters' authors, and many other contributors who submitted their chapters that cannot be included in the book. Special thanks to Ms. Mariah Gilbert, Ms. Jan Travers, Ms. Maria Rohde and Ms. Josephine Dadeboe from IGI-Global –team for their kind support and great efforts in bringing the book to completion. The encouragement of the Editorial Advisory Board (EAB) cannot be exaggerated. These are renowned experts who took time off their busy schedules to review chapters, provide constructive feedback, and improve the overall quality of chapters.

I would like to thank Dr. R B Mishra, Prof. Sandeep Garg, Prof. Kiran Pandey and all dear teaching and non-teaching staff-colleagues from our institute - LPU, Punjab. Special thanks to Dr. Babita Pandey i for motivating me for this book. Thanks to Prof. Shrikant Tiwari, Dr. Aman Singh, Dr. Devendra Pandey and Dr. Deepak Gupta for their kind support.

I would like to thank my dear friends Mr. Sanjay Kr. Singh and Mr. Mamoon Rashid for their continuous support and countless efforts throughout the process of publication of this book.

I express my personal and special thanks to my beloved father Krishna Kumar, mother Asha, my wife Shrasti, and other family members for supporting me throughout all my career, for love, the tremendous support and inspiration which they gave me in all these years.

Last but not the least: I request forgiveness of all those who have been with me over the course of the years and whose names I have failed to mention.

Aditya Khamparia
Lovely Professional University, India

Chapter 1

Similarity–Based Indices or Metrics for Link Prediction

Praveen Kumar Bhanodia
Lovely Professional University, India

Kamal Kumar Sethi
Acropolis Institute of Technology and Research, India

Aditya Khamparia
iD https://orcid.org/0000-0001-9019-8230
Lovely Professional University, India

Babita Pandey
Babasaheb Bhimrao Ambedkar University, India

Shaligram Prajapat
IIPS DAV, India

ABSTRACT

Link prediction in social network has gained momentum with the inception of machine learning. The social networks are evolving into smart dynamic networks possessing various relevant information about the user. The relationship between users can be approximated by evaluation of similarity between the users. Online social network (OSN) refers to the formulation of association (relationship/links) between users known as nodes. Evolution of OSNs such as Facebook, Twitter, Hi-Fi, LinkedIn has provided a momentum to the growth of such social networks, whereby millions of users are joining it. The online social network evolution has motivated scientists and researchers to analyze the data and information of OSN in order to recommend the future friends. Link prediction is a problem instance of such recommendation

DOI: 10.4018/978-1-5225-9096-5.ch001

systems. Link prediction is basically a phenomenon through which potential links between nodes are identified on a network over the period of time. In this chapter, the authors describe the similarity metrics that further would be instrumental in recognition of future links between nodes.

INTRODUCTION

The history of evolution of network structures had been studied by several mathematicians' long back. Eulars theorem of graph theory was first of its kind which we can say solved initially the problem of seven bridges given by Konigsberg (Biggs et. al. 1986). Since then the field of graph theory and research in this area was handled by mathematicians quite effectively. Knowledge retrieval and processing techniques now a days are pretty useful in crunching voluminous data captured via internet (Khamparia & Pandey 2016, 2017). Rule extraction

A social network is a network of people connected with each other resembling some kind of relationships in between over the internet, in other words we can say it is typically represents a social structure consists of social actors having association between these actors. These social networks are represented through graphs where the actors referred as nodes (users/individuals/organizations/cities, etc.) and association in between referred as edges also known as links (relationships/interactions/associations/ties). Earlier before the inception of internet the communication and cooperation between people was not convenient and fast but due to rapid development since then it has become so and the social networks have evolved quite significantly. The social networks now transformed into online social networks such as Facebook, Twitter, and LinkdIn, are now became an integrated part of human life. These (OSNs) online social networks are providing platforms for exchanging formal and informal information with each other. As a result of that huge database or voluminous data is getting piled up exponentially. the data incurred has obvious characteristics and attributes if exploited can generate useful information for further use to create certain recommendation system, lot many researchers are now paying attention to social network analysis for extracting valuable knowledge for better services to the society. The nature of these kinds of networks is quite dynamic with new edges and nodes are adding to the graph over the period of time. Comprehending and understanding the evolution of OSN is typically a complex challenge due to range of parameters. An instance of social network evolution could be easier problem to understand and link prediction (Liben-Nowell and Kleinberg, 2003) is one such instance where association between nodes is to be predicted. For example the questions to be answered can be how does the relationship between nodes changes with respect to time? What could be the factors affecting this relationship? What kind of influence nearby nodes can put on the relationship of associated nodes? Ultimately the problem here in this chapter is an effort to trace out the metrics involved in prediction of likelihood of future links between nodes.

The Graph

Any problem which is imitated mathematically can be analyzed and solved using computing facilities even when the scale of the problem is significant and difficult to understand and comprehend. The size of social networks is increasing exponentially and so is exploiting the data and information captured directly and indirectly by these networks. These networks created online and can be represented through a mathematical structure known as graph. It has a structured representation having set of vertices (nodes) V and set of links (or edges) and typically written as G=(V,E). As discussed above vertices (nodes) represents people and edges or links between them as relationships between people. edge or link is designated with letter e such that e belongs to E connecting set of two nodes from V. for example V = {a, b,c,d,e} and E{e1,e2,e3,e4, where E = ({e1= a,b},{e2=c,d},{e4=a,e}). In order to illustrate it further it says the graph is collection of five distant people named as a,b,c,d and e. a and b are friendly with each other, similarly c-d and a-e. It is illustrated diagrammatically.

Figure 1. Demonstration of nodes and links in graph

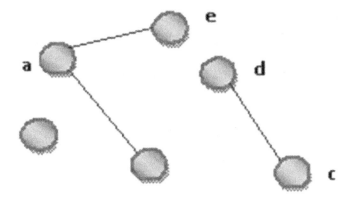

Sociologist usually call such diagrams as sociograms and in the field of research domain terms like network, social network, sociogram, graphs are interchangeable. The links in the network are undirected or bi-directed which means the exchange of information would be from both sides (ex: exchange of messages, emails, etc.) . In order to explore the graph theory is recommended in (Wilson, 1996).

The Link Prediction Problem (Hasan & Zaki 2011)

Let a social network is represented through a undirected and un-weighted graph G(V,E) at a specific time interval t, where V is the set of nodes and E refers to the set of links/edges between nodes. Link prediction is approximation of future links between nodes at time t' where t'>t, or missing links with in the network.

Let us understand the problem by taking an example of 7 random people, As shown below in 2(a and b) solid links between nodes shows existing edges/ links and relationships between the nodes at time t, dashed links exhibits probability of new link at the time interval [t,t']. For example Ashish and Ajay are friend to each other and a link is displaying association between these two. The relationship (friend) shown is a feature of link/edge, similar kind of association can be understood for Ajay and Shri, it is to be noted that the type of relationship (brother) is different than previous two . There is no link between Himanshu-Rohit, Ashish-Ashwin and other nodes too initially (time instance t) but at the next instance (t'=t+1) there would be probability that some kind of association or relationship occurs and link or edge would be established (dashed lines) which is to be predicted. Obviously it would be done by exploiting the available past structural information of the network.

Mathematically in terms of sets it can be understood as:

G(V,E)= Social Network Instance at time instance, V ={u,v,x…n}
e(u,v)ϵE = edge between nodes u and v belongs to set of edges E, showing interaction or association
G[t0, t1] = Given Subgraph at a timestamp between t0 and t1>t
G[t1,t2]=Subgraph inferring new edges used for testing purpose at a time stamp t1and t2>t1
Score(x_{uv})=score computed between the nodes u and v

Figure 2. (a) Network at time t. (b) Network at time t'=t+1

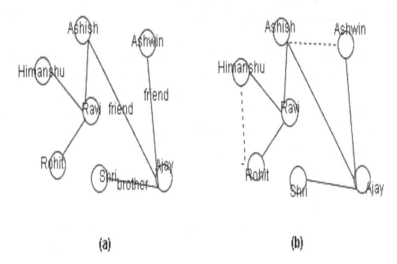

(a)   (b)

According to Liben-Nowell and Kleinberg the problem of link prediction (Liben-Nowell & Kleinberg 2003) has been formulated in three ways with respect to time.

The problem of link prediction is addressed by various researchers in different ways potential researchers having potential knowledge in mathematics and physics exploiting the structural features (nodes and edges) of the network whereas data scientists having potential skills in machine learning used to exploit the node and edge attributes information for the prediction of future links.

1. Addition of new links: Over the period of time new links will be added to the existing network
2. Removal of existing links: Over the period of time existing links may be removed due to noise or otherwise.
3. Addition and Removal of links: At time t+1 new links and exiting links added and removed simultaneously.

The chapter only discuss about prediction of new links which may appear in future within the network. The reason for the same is that mostly research is undergoing over the first type of link prediction and hence we would be having more data and methods available to exploit and correlate.

The General Method Adapted for Approximation of Link Prediction

Prediction of future links by processing the local features of nodes and edges a heuristic algorithm is used assigning a similarity matrix S containing score sxy between nodes x and y. This score could be used as a measure or index of similarity between the nodes. It is worth noting here that every pair of nodes x,y belongs to set of vertices V (x,y ϵ V) where $s_{xy}=s_{yx}$. The computed score for all the future links would be arranged in descending order, the links having the top score are most probable to exist in future (Hu, K., Xiang).

As it is obvious in any way we cannot predict the future links in a network, to verify the accuracy of the link prediction method's accuracy the sample network set is bifurcated in training(70% of the entire dataset) and test set(30% of the set), no information from the test set would be used for training the model. The accuracy of the prediction is evaluated by are under the receiver operating characteristic curve abbreviated as AUC.

Accuracy of the method can be defined as

$$AUC = (n' + 0.5\,'') / n$$

Suppose all the score which are generated from independent and identical distribution, accuracy of the method should be about 0.5. Hence degree by which accuracy exceeds 0.5 used to shows the performance of the method.

The Application of Link Prediction

Apart from application of Link prediction in social networks it has many other applications such as useful in finding protein-protein interactions (Airoldi et. al.2006); E-commerce recommendation systems where suggesting who will buy what on Flipkart, Amazon is another such kind of application where link prediction is applied. In the same fashion link prediction helps in identification of hidden groups or communities of terrorists or criminals. Many researchers are working on co-authorship networks wherein two researchers who are close to each other may collaborate and will be colleagues in area of common interest (Gao & Guan, 2012).

The Metric

The values computed from graphs structural features (node degree and distance) and contributing in description of the graph in some manner is referred as metric. A metric is typically used by researchers to analyze the social network which is basically a mathematical formula that computes the network features. For example degree and common neighbors are such two metrics generally categorized as monadic and dyadic respectively as illustrated by Wasserman S. and Foust K. in (Wasserman& Faust1994), all the traditional social network analysis metrics are summarized by Hanneman in (Hanneman, R. 2001)). Degree is supposed to be calculated for node, it is count of nodes connected to node whose degree is to be calculated which otherwise display the social existence of the node and its popularity in the social network. Common neighbors value normally calculated for pair of nodes referred as a dyad. Total number of common neighbors of dyad is basically count of mutual nodes that two nodes shares. This is illustrated as how many common friends two persons can have. These two metrics are basically common neighborhood based metrics which are supposed to exploit the node features (node analysis), moreover there are other neighborhood based metrics in practice such as Jaccaard Coefficient, Adamic Adar, etc described in later part of the chapter. The other type of metric used is distance(path) based metric used to involve shortest path computation between the nodes. For example Katz measure. This chapter is an effort to focus upon the metrics used for prediction of link in social network.

In order to understand the metrics properly let us explore few graph theory basics, it can usually be referred on the basis of direction of links of network, consequently:

Figure 3. Dyad and Triad demonstration

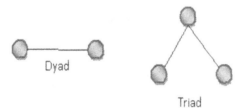

Figure 4. Links and Directions

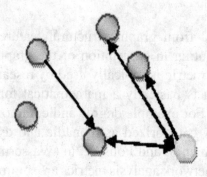

1. Metrics for links of bidirectional nature(incoming and outgoing links both)
2. Metrics for outgoing links
3. Metrics for incoming links
4. Metrics for undirected links

The bi-directed links represents in-degree, out-degree and in-out-degree for all the types of links. For the node shaded with different color has in degree of 2, out-degree of 3 and in-out degree 5.

The spectrum of notations and definitions used in these different ways includes set of shortest path, recency, distance and strength the detail description of graphical notations is illustrated in figure 5.

These are generally classified into three different categories:

1. Monadic metrics: It is computed over a single node for example node. It is typically defined for a node u_i at time instance t.
2. Dyadic Metrics: It is computed on pair of nodes for example common neighbors. It is mostly used for approximation of link prediction in social network.
3. Graph Metrics: This type of metric would be computed over the whole graph for example what is the size of the graph.

Figure 5. Graph notations used in definition and analysis of the network

Graph Notations	Illustration
G=(V,E)	A graph of nodes and links at a given time instance
V	Set of vertices in social network at a time instance. V={v1,v2,v3,v4,....vn}
E	Set of edges/links in social network at a time instance. E={e_{12},e_{23},e_{34},.... e_{ij}} the links are directed from v_i to v_j.
U	Set of bidirectional links in social network at time instance t. bidirectional links between nodes vi and vj can be designated as v_{ij} and v_{ji}
Max	Represents elements having Maximum value in a set. Max ({2,3,5,6}) = 6.
Min	Represents elements having minimum value in a set. Min({2,3,4,8})=2
Mean	Gives mean of a given set. Mean({3,4,6,2})=15/4=3.6
Γ(v_i)	Represents the set of neighboring nodes
Str(e_{ij})	Represents strength of edge/link from node I to node j. it can be a review of a movie given by viewer or number of messages exchanged between nodes
Rec(e_{ij})	It is typically the time elapsed since last message. It the message passed was in the last time instance the recency score would be 1.
Dist(v_i,v_j)	Represents the distance/path length (number of hopes to reach v_j from v_i) between node v_i and v_j. if the node unreachable in any way dist(vi,vj)=0 distance from node to itself would be undefined.
P(v_i,v_j)	It represents the set of all the shortest path between the nodes vi and vj.
P(v_i,v_j,v_x)	It is set of all the shortest paths from v_i to v_j via v_x
|Γ(v_i)|	Represents the set of common neighbor of node v_i

LINK PREDICTION METRICS

Monoadic Metrics

Degree of Node

The degree of a particular node in social network is typically total number of links it is having connected with other nodes. For example a node is connected with 5 different distant nodes than the degree of the node would be 5. In-Degree is the total number of links coming to the node/vertex. Out Degree of the node is the total number of links leaving a node/vertex. Similarly In-Out Degree is the total count of incoming and outgoing links/edges. The significant of degree of a node is such that degree distribution across the network can be obtained which could be used for further network analysis. The degree distribution is basically a kind of probability distribution of these degrees over the entire social network.

Mathematically it can be represented as

$$\text{Degree }(x) = \#\{\{x_{jj} : x_{jj} \in Un\}\} \quad \text{or} \quad \#(\Gamma(x_i))$$

Figure 6. Centrality score for Zachary's Karate Club Network (Zachary 1977)

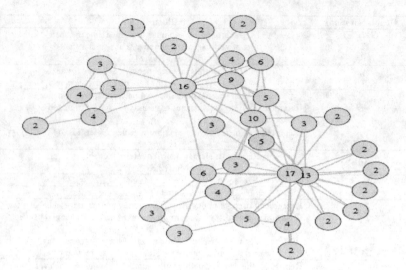

Degree Centrality

The degree of centrality is most primitive score or measure which says that a node with higher degree is more central. It determines the total number of links to a given node in the network. In an undirected graph it could be a count of links for a node, for directed type of networks it would count of in-degree and out degree determining the centrality score. The measures used to answer for social networks that how central a specific node is. In other words it gives us the most popular node in the network which is having maximum number of links. Usually centrality score is a kind of asset to any node of the network as it shows the level of activity and involvement of the node within the network.

More often in order to normalize or standardize the process of degree centrality measure as to compare the networks of different and varied sizes, the score is divided by the maximum possible in-degrees and interpret the results either by percentage or proportion: ($\#\Gamma(vi)/\#(V)-1$). As demonstrated below the degree centrality distribution in Zachary's karate social network.

Degree Eccentricity Centrality

It is basically a distance based measure where centrality of the nodes is measured on the basis of distance between the nodes. It is arguably a simpler notion when compared to closeness (Wang et. al. 2015). The eccentricity of a node in any connected network G is the maximum distance between two nodes within the network over all nodes of the network G. If the network is disconnected than the eccentricity for the nodes would be infinite. The maximum eccentricity of the network or graph is graph diameter (maximum hops required to reach to a node from other node in a given network) or network diameter and minimum would be graph radius or network radius (maximum hops required to reach to central node from any other node within the network).

Formally it can be stated as:

$$e_g(v) := \max\{dist_G(u, v) : u \in V(G)\}$$

Generally it has been said that Eccentricity is referred as the reciprocal of the eccentricity of a node because the reciprocal of the eccentricity value is quite easy to compute since it follows monotonicity rule (Matjaz K et.al. 2018).

Jordan Centrality

Hage and Harary (Hage, P. & Harary, F.,1995) implicitly introduced Jordan centrality which was derived actually from Jordan center of given network. Jordan center of a given network is referred as the set of nodes having minimum eccentricity, which means, set of all the nodes across network such that the greatest distance between nodes u and v, $(dist_{u,v})$ should be minimal. In other words we can say that it is the set of nodes having eccentricity equal to the radius of the network.

Jordan Centrality C_j formally can be written as:

$$C_j = \frac{1}{MAXd(x, y)}$$

where y is not equal to x

The authors have argued that identifying the nodes with the highest centrality value would offer worthy insights of a given social network.

Closeness Centrality

Closeness centrality yields how close a node to other nodes in a network is, it is determined by identifying the minimum path distances from the nodes. A node which is close to other nodes may easily and effectively interact with them without passing through many intermediaries nodes. In other words if two nodes are not connected directly then it should at least take minimum number of hops to reach other node to attain a higher closeness centrality.

Generally it measures the node to node mean path distance, it is worth mentioning here that geodesic distance is a shortest distance between two nodes. Then the mean geodesic distance for node v is:

$$Closeness(v) = \frac{1}{\sum_{i \neq v} d_{vi}}$$

The fartherness of node v is referred as summation of its distance to all the other nodes and closeness is defined as the inverse of the fartherness. It is standardized by dividing with the maximum possible value that is 1/(n-1). If in case of no path possible between node v and i then total count of vertices would be used in the formula in place of path length. It is to be noteworthy that more central the node is lower would be the distance to all other nodes. In a social network closeness centrality has significance in prediction of links between the nodes as the score calculated would endorse that the closer node obviously would have probability to have a direct link in future. The calculated computation of mean distance gives low values for the nodes situated near to the central nodes and higher values for them situated far away from central node which is quite opposite to other centrality metrics thus is not considered as centrality measure with respect to the previous ones. Therefore research community of the domain usually computer its inverse, known as closeness centrality.

Betweenness Centrality

The Betweenness centrality measure metric quantifies how many times a specific node would act as a intermediary node along the shortest path distance in between two distant nodes. It was introduced by Linten Freeman to quantify human's control in an ongoing communication between humans in a social network. The concept for the measure is such that the node having high probability of occurrence on a random chosen path distance in between two distantly parted nodes would have a high Betweenness.

The Betweenness centrality for a vertex v in a graph G (V, E) can be:

1. Compute shortest path distance between the pair of nodes(s, t).
2. Determining the fraction of shortest path distance passing through the node whose Betweenness centrality is to be calculated(for example node v)
3. Determining the sum of fraction of all of the pairs of nodes (s,t)

Formally it is represented as

$$Betweenness(v) = \sum_{s \neq v \neq t} \frac{\sigma_{st}(v)}{\sigma_{st}}$$

The metric can be further normalized or standardized by dividing with number of pairs of nodes not including v which for directed graph is (n-1)(n-2) and for undirected graph it is (n-1)(n-2)/2.

PageRank

PageRank algorithm has been introduced by Larry Page co-founder of Google and it is not just because it ranks the pages. According to this algorithm ranks are assigned to particular web pages and the ranks of the page would be an average of about 1. Typically the rank is depicted in the range of 1 to 10, 0 is supposed to be assigned to the least ranked web page and so forth for other web pages. For examples ranks of some websites are like www.google.com has 9/10 and www.amazon.com has 8/10. It is an algorithm which is based on link based object raking problem where the purpose is to assign a numerical value (Rank) to each one of the page exploiting the web link structure (Getoor, L., 2005). PageRank usually counts the number and quality of links to a web page as to approximate the importance of the website. The main objective behind is more important web pages of the websites are more likely to have incoming links from other websites.

The primitives of the algorithm or metric exploit the count and quality of backlinks or inlinks to specific web page or node. A back link of node P is a citation to P itself from another node. As demonstrated in above figure of a network links falling on node E are backlinks for the node and links

Figure 7. Social network

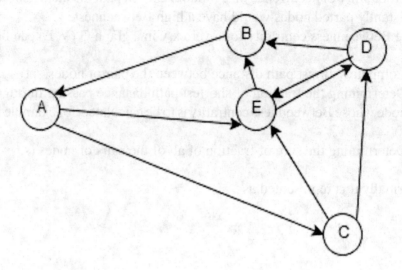

leaving the node are called as outlinks. Node A and node C are having single backlinks, similarly node B and node D are having two backlinks, and same way 3 backlinks are falling upon node E. As per the illustration of pagerank algorithm node E is found to be more potential and significant relative to other four nodes. Along with counts the measure also considers the quality of backlinks for setting up the priority value in order to make the method more reliable and accurate. Thus backlinks from node E will hold more importance than a backlink from node A. Node B is having higher rank than D since it is having back links from D and E.

Ranking of nodes in a given social network is not easy because the social network on which the method is supposed to be applied has relevant challenges like social networks are of dynamic nature, the frequency with which nodes of the network exchange information changes readily, the number of links of a particular node in the network will increase or decrease with respect to time and availability of relevant data and information. Moreover the major disadvantage with the simple approach is that the reliability of backlink cannot be trusted because there are fair chances that one can create fake reviews and spams as to increase the backlink counts. In order to overcome such spams, ranking of nodes generating backlinks will also be considered and the repetitive process so created makes it more reliable and accurate.

Figure 8. Symbols and notation for PageRank Algorithm

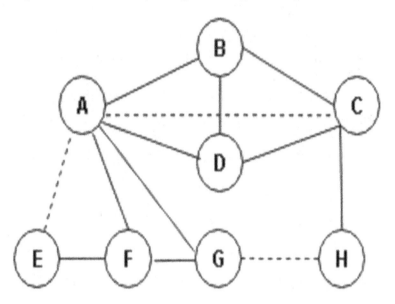

In order to formally define PageRank we will summarize the essential terminologies and notation used in defining PageRank mathematically (Figure 8).

As per illustration to compute rank of a node in a social network, suppose P_1, we have to see at all the other nodes which are linked to P_1 that is having backlinks to P_1. Let us say P_2 is a node having three outlinks (outgoing links to other nodes) in addition to one link going to P_1. the contribution of P_2 to P_1 in terms of rank would be 1/4th of its PageRank. The total of P_1 the summation of all values of nodes linked to it has to be obtained. In general if the node P_v is having n links to other nodes $\{P_u \mid u \in 1,2,3......n\}$, in this case the contribution of P_v will be only $\dfrac{1}{\deg(Pv)}$ th of the links it is having to the PageRank of node P_u and it can be written as:

$$PR(P_u) = \sum \frac{PR(Pv)}{\deg(Pv)^+}$$

Applying the formula to get the PageRank of node B

$$PR(B) = \frac{PR(E)}{2} + \frac{PR(D)}{2}$$

In the same fashion we can find the PageRank for all the nodes across the social network. For each node P_v we have to determing the number of outgoing links of P_v $(\deg(P_v)^+)$ and its PageRank $PR(P_v)$. for every node P_v first we have to determine the ratio of its calculated PageRank for the corresponding outgoing links count and then computing the sum over all of the nodes which are linked to a specific node of interest. Formally for the PageRank of P it can be defined as [15] (Brin, S., and L. Page.,(1998).

$$PR(P) = (1 - d) = d(\frac{PR(P_1)}{\deg(P_2)+} + \frac{PR(P_2)}{\deg(P_2)+} + \frac{PR(P_3)}{\deg(P_3)} + \cdots \cdots + \frac{PR(P_n)}{\deg(P_n)+}$$

where d is the damping factor which is used for representing a factor where the user is getting bored while browsing the web page and about to open a new web page. Typically the value for damping factor d is 0.85.Vice versa (1-d) would be the probability for the user not getting bored and will remain on the web page.

Dyadic Common Neighbor Based Metrics

Common Neighborhood

The CN is determined on the basis of number of common neighbors existing between two nodes where future link is to be predicted. The application of this approach was initiated on collaboration networks by Newman (M. E. J. Newman 2001). It provides a link prediction score for similarity by calculating the intersection of the sets of neighbors of the nodes to predict existence future link. As shown the nodes are the network entities (users, items, etc) and the edges representing the relationship between users. The dotted line represents future relationship/link which is to be predicted while solid lines are existing relationships. The Common Neighbors (CN) is calculated as follows:

Common Neighbors $(CN(x, y)) = \Gamma(x) \cap \Gamma(y)$

Figure 9. Common Neighborhood & Jaccard coefficient demonstration

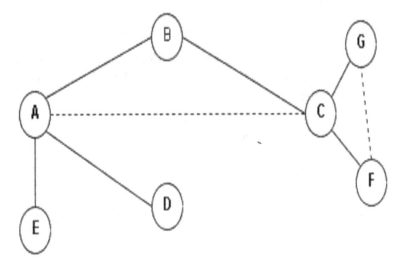

where $\Gamma(x)$ = (number of common neighbors to x) and $\Gamma(y)$ = (number of common neighbors to y)

As demonstrated in Figure 4, common neighbors of node A and node C that is CN (AC) = 1 and common neighbors between node F and node H is 1 thus the score between both pairs of node is 1 (CN (AC) = 1) and CN (FG) = 1). Likewise the score for all the non existing links of the social network at a time instance t is computed and sorted in an order. Links with high score have more probability to exist at t+1 time instance.

Moreover the weighted Common Neighbors (CN_w) would be determined as follows where $w_{(x,y)}$ is the number of interactions between the nodes x and y.

$$CN_{w(x,y)} = \sum_{ze(x)\cap\Gamma(y)}^{\infty} \left(\frac{w(x,z) + w(y,z)}{2} \right)$$

Jaccard Coefficient

It is another simple metric considered for link prediction which is a normalized form of common neighborhood technique, because it also considers the union of common neighbors of the two nodes between which future links is to be predicted. Thus the probability of predicting a link between nodes can be approximated by score obtained using formula given below:

$$JC_{xy} = \frac{\Gamma(x) \cap \Gamma(y)}{\Gamma(x) \cup \Gamma(y)}$$

Example: According to Jaccard Coefficient (JC) the score for prediction of a link between nodes AC (refer figure-4) would be JC (AC) = 1/6 = .166. Similarly score for link between node F and node G would be JC (FG) = ½ = 0.50. Hence probability of node F and node G to be linked at time t+1 instance is more than linking of node A and node C.

Adamic/Adar

According to Adamic and Adar the metric is designed to develop to consider the common neighbors between nodes which are not connected directly. Basically it considers all the common neighbors (common friend) existing between nodes and the number of nodes (degree of the node) connected to each common neighbor is also considered for computation of the score (Adamic and Adar 2003). Thus the probability of being a connection between the nodes of social network is determined by

$$AAxy = \sum_{ze(x) \cap \Gamma(y)}^{\infty} \frac{1}{\log|\Gamma(z)|}$$

where z is the set of common neighbors of nodes x and y

As shown in Figure 10 where dashed lines represent the future links while solid represents the existing links. The score between nodes A and C is AA (AC) = 1/log4 + 1/log2. Similarly the score for other links like AA (EF) is 1/log4 and AA (GH) is 1/log 5. Therefore if a neighbor node has more links better score or index value would be obtained.

Resource Allocation

The measures discussed above are usually neighboring node based, this measuring metric is basically based on resource allocation process that happens in networks. The approach considers nodes x and y which are not connected directly, suppose node x sends some kind of resource (message or data) to next node y via common neighbors used to play role of transmitters. it is assumed that these common nodes (so called transmitters) will have a

Figure 10. Adamic/Adar Demonstration

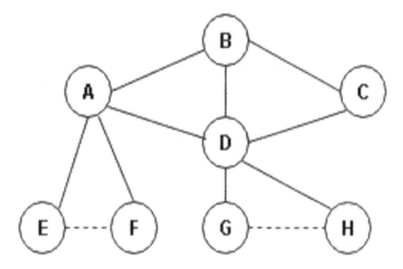

unit of information and distribute it equally between all of its neighbors here the similarity can be identified between the nodes by the score determined using the equation given below (Zhou & Zhang 2009).

$$RA_{xy} = \sum_{ze(x) \cap \Gamma(y)}^{\infty} \frac{1}{N(Z)}$$

It is noteworthy that index score $s_{xy} = s_{yx}$, accordingly refer figure, here the resource allocation score value between nodes A and C is determined as RA (AC) = 1/3 +1/3 = 2/3 = .66, similarly the score value between nodes G and H would be RA (GH) = 1/3 = .33. The probability of happening a link in near future between nodes A and C is more than nodes G and G. In the same fashion research allocation index score for non existing links between the nodes across the entire social network would be determined and the resultant score is sorted and arranged.

Salton index

This index was proposed by G. Salton and defined as the ratio between the common neighbor node and the square root of product of degree of node x and node y for which link has to be predicted in near future. Formally the equation for the metric can be written as:

Figure 11. Demonstrating Resource allocation metric

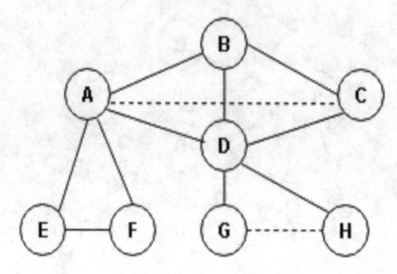

$$S_{xy} = \frac{\Gamma(x) \cap \Gamma(y)}{\sqrt{k(x) \times k(y)}}$$

where k(x) =|Γ(x) |denotes the degree of x. Salton index is also called cosine similarity in the available literature (Srilatha and Manjula 2016).

Preferential Attachment (PA)

According to Jérôme Kunegis et. al. (Kunegis et. al. 2013) the approach claims that the probability of establishing link between nodes depends on how potential a node is. It says that node x having high degree than node y will attract new neighbor nodes faster towards it. Figure demonstrates that since the node degree of node A in the network is 5 and at the same time degree of G is 3, therefore the link prediction probability for AC is more than GH. Mathematically it can be defined as

$$PA_{(x,y)} = \Gamma(x).\Gamma(y)$$

According to the formula discussed above the score for preferential attachment for PA(AC) would be 5* 2 = 10 and PA(GH) = 3 * 2 = 6, hence

Figure 12. Preferential Attachment Demonstration

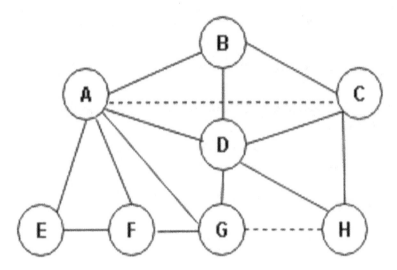

nodes A and C has higher probability to be connected in future rather than nodes G and H.

Sørensen Index

This index is mainly used for ecological community data (Sørensen 1948, Zou et. al. 2009) which is defined as

$$S_{xy} = \frac{2 * \left| \Gamma\left(x\right) \cap \Gamma\left(y\right) \right|}{k\left(x\right) + k\left(y\right)}$$

Hub Promoted Index (HPI)

The metric is introduced to deduce the structural overlapping of substrates pairs in complex networks. The approach defines the ratio of common neighbor nodes between node pairs to the minimum total number of node connected to the node among the node pairs (whichever is minimum x or y). According to Barabasi et. al.(Ravasz et. al.)the metric links connected to the hub node (node with very large degree) will be assigned with higher scores as the denominator with respect to the equation is of low degree only.

$$S_{xy} = \frac{2 * |\Gamma(x) \cap \Gamma(y)|}{\min|k(x), k(y)|}$$

Hub Depressed Index (HDI)

The metric is just analogues to HPI, where denominator is replaced with degree of the node linked with maximum adjacent node. The metric is supposed to produce the opposite effect than nodes having maximum degree. The metric can be defined as

$$S_{xy} = \frac{2 * |\Gamma(x) \cap \Gamma(y)|}{\max|k(x), k(y)|}$$

Leicht–Holme–Newman Index (LHN)

According to Leicht et. al. (Leicht et. al. 2006) the metric proposed as to define a measure exploiting local topological similarity index. The approach is a ratio between common adjacent (neighbor) nodes (x,y) and the multiplication of node x & y degrees. LHN thus written as

$$S_{xy} = \frac{2 * |\Gamma(x) \cap \Gamma(y)|}{k(x) * k(y)|}$$

The value of the metric determined for x-y would be same for y-x as well. It would be noteworthy that value calculated using Salton index/metric differs from LHN as the denominator of both the metrics is different. Salton will always yield a higher value than LHN for the same set of inputs.

Path Based Feature Metrics

These metrics are usually also known as global similarity method that uses all information on network to calculate the similarity matrix between two nodes, the hops between the two nodes to recognize the closeness and similarity will be > 2.

Path Distance

Distance between nodes in a graph is one obvious measure to recognize the closeness of two nodes, also known as geodesic distance. Applying Dijkstra's algorithm for extracting the shortest path would be inefficient between two nodes in a social network rather it can be exploited with a small real world property of the social network by applying expanded ring search. It will compute the (negative) shortest path distance between two nodes. A score calculated is analyzed based on which future link would be predicted between two nodes having shortest path.

Use of negative signed shortest path shows that proximity for GDxy increases with the closeness of nodes x & y. As shown in above figure 7 the path score for AC is -3, score for AE is -2 and score for GH is -4. According to the path distance calculated where AE > AC>GH, thus nodes A and E are more likely to be connected in future compared to other nodes.

Katz(Exponentially Damp Path Counts)

A measurement that takes all paths between two nodes in consideration while rating short paths more heavily. The measurement exponentially reduces the

Figure 13. Path Distance

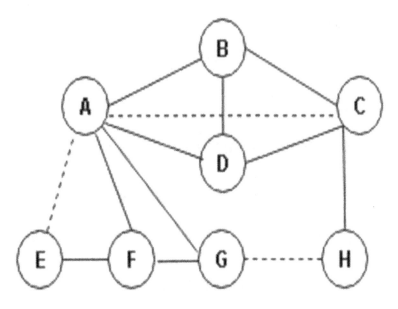

contribution of a path to the metric in order to give less weight to longer paths. Therefore it uses a factor of β_l where l is the path length.

$$\text{Katz}\left(\text{xy}\right) = \sum_{l=0}^{n} \beta^2 < path\left(x, y\right)$$

The β can be used to control how much the length of the paths should be considered. A very small β concludes to an algorithm where paths of length three or more are taken much less into account and therefore the algorithm converge the node neighborhood algorithms. It has roughly has a cubic complexity as it requires matrix inversion (Wang et. al. 2015).

Measurement Index in Weighted Networks

The link prediction methods in weighted networks are: Weighted common neighbor (WCN), Weighted Adamic/Adar (WAA) and Weighted Resource Allocation (WRA).

Weighted Common Neighbor (WCN)

$$S_{xy}^{WCN} = \sum_{z \in O_{xy}} w\left(x, y\right)^{\alpha} + w\left(z, y\right)^{\alpha}$$

Weighted Adamic/Adar (WAA)

$$S_{xy}^{WAA} = \sum_{z \in O_{xy}} \frac{\left(w\left(x, y\right)^{\alpha} + w\left(z, y\right)^{\alpha}\right)}{\log\left(1 + s\left(z\right)\right)}$$

Weighted resource allocation (WRA)

$$S_{xy}^{WRA} = \sum_{z \in O_{xy}} \frac{\left(w\left(x, y\right)^{\alpha} + w\left(z, y\right)^{\alpha}\right)}{s\left(z\right)}$$

Where Oxy is the set of common neighbours of node pair (x,y), w(x,z) is the weight of the link between $S(x) = \sum_{z \in \Gamma(x)} w(x,y)^{\alpha}$ x and z, and. Moreover, when $\alpha = 0$, the s(x) is the degree of node x, and the indices degenerate to the unweighted cases. When $\alpha=1$, the indices are equivalent to the simply weighted indices. Generally, the optimal values of α are smaller than 1in most of the weighted networks.

DISCUSSION

Link prediction metrics or methods in social network are typically used to compute a score known as similarity score based upon common neighborhood friends or nodes. The metric obtained helps in knowing the future links between the nodes within the structure. it is quite noteworthy that the local structure based metrics is computed between the nodes where the path length is maximum of 2. In case of global structure this path length may vary as we traverse the nodes to reach a specific node from a node. The disadvantage of local structure could be that there is possibility of important and potential links could be missed. Exploitation of entire network to compute measures is also time consuming. According to methods based on global structure of the network graph, it has an advantage of exploiting the links missing during local structure based methods. Exploitation of entire network using global structure methods could be time consuming particularly in the case of large and complex social networks as the data and information of such network is of Petabytes.

Thus there is a huge scope of development for scalable local and global structure based metrics or methods which can include all the missing potential links and also consumes less time for crunching of large social networks. There are hybrid methods considering both the methods into consideration also known as quasi-local structure based methods predicting missing or future links appears to be more precise and accurate than each one of these two. Exploring ensemble technique for social network analysis and prediction of missing or future links between nodes accurately and efficiently could be an interesting exercise to work upon.

Figure 14. Summary of similarity based link prediction metrics with their complexities

Metric	Complexity
Common neighborhood	$O(Nk^2)$
Jaccard coefficient	$O(Nk^2)$
Preferential attachment	$O(N^2k^2)$
Katz	$O(N^3)$
Cosine similarity	$O(Nk^3)$
Sorensen Index	$O(Nk^2)$
Hub Promoted Index	$O(Nk^2)$
Hub Depressed Index	$O(Nk^2)$
Leicht Holme Newman Index	$O(Nk^2)$
Adamic Adar	$O(Nk^2)$

All the methods discussed above have been proposed are exploiting the local and global topological structure of the network, community features within the network is not taken in to consideration for computation of similarity score values. There is a strong probability that use of such information will going to improve the accuracy of prediction of links. Hopcraft and soundrajan (Soundarajan & Hopcroft 2012) for RA and CN have shown sustainability in this direction but the metrics is usually not applied over milestone datasets and it will obviously be an interesting challenge to be explored. The summary of discussed metrics along with their complexities is shown in Table (Gao et. al. 2015). Moreover various other datamining and data retrieval techniques (Khamparia & Pandey 2015, 2018) are needed to be explored to retrieve relevant information which may further contribute in prediction of potential links.Rule extraction techniques for information retrieval (Sethi et. al., 2012) can also be explored for links prediction in social network analysis.

CONCLUSION

In this chapter we have put in an effort to simplify the classical metrics based on degree of the nodes used for link prediction in social networks. The pool of metrics is not limited to the discussion made above but there are various other methods have been proposed by authors based on machine learning concepts, these methods are out of the scope of the chapter. The chapter provides a necessary insight to the research newbie's to develop conceptual fundamentals regarding online social networks.

REFERENCES

Adamic, L. A., & Adar, E. (2003). Friends and neighbors on the web. *Social Networks*, *25*(3), 211–230. doi:10.1016/S0378-8733(03)00009-1

Airoldi, E. M., Anderson, A. G., Fienberg, S. E., & Skinner, K. K. (2006, June). Ronald Reagan's radio addresses? *Bayesian Analysis*, *1*(2), 289–320. doi:10.1214/06-BA110

Biggs, N. L., Lloyd, K. E., & Wilson, R. J. (1986). Graph Theory (2nd ed.). New York, NY: The Clarendon Press.

Brin, S., & Page, L. (1998). The anatomy of a large-scale hypertextual Web search engine. *Proceedings of the 7th International Conference on World Wide Web*, 107-117. 10.1016/S0169-7552(98)00110-X

Gao, F., Musial, K., Cooper, C., & Tsoka, S. (2015). Link Prediction Methods and Their Accuracy for Different Social Networks and Network Metrics. Scientific Programming. doi:10.1155/2015/172879

Gao, X., & Guan, J. (2012). Network model of knowledge diffusion. *Scientometrics*, *90*(3), 749–762. doi:10.100711192-011-0554-z

Getoor, L. (2005). Link mining: A new data mining challenge. *SIGKDD Explorations*, *5*(1), 84–89. doi:10.1145/959242.959253

Hage, P., & Harary, F. (1995). Eccentricity and centrality in networks social networks. Elsevier.

Hanneman, R. (2001). *Introduction to Social Network Methods*. Retrieved from http://faculty.ucr.edu/~hanneman/nettext/networks.zip

Hasan, M. A., & Zaki, M. J. (2011). A Survey of Link Prediction in Social Networks. In C. Aggarwal (Ed.), *Social Network Data Analytics*. Boston, MA: Springer. doi:10.1007/978-1-4419-8462-3_9

Hu, K., & Xiang, J. (n.d.). *Link Prediction in Complex Networks by Multi Degree Preferential-Attachment Indices*. Academic Press.

Khamparia, A., & Pandey, B. (2015). Knowledge and intelligent computing methods in e-learning. *Int. J. Technol. Enhanc. Learn.*, *7*(3), 221–242. doi:10.1504/IJTEL.2015.072810

Khamparia, A., & Pandey, B. (2016). Threat driven modeling framework using petri nets for e-learning system. *SpringerPlus*, *5*(1), 446. doi:10.118640064-016-2101-0 PMID:27119050

Khamparia, A., & Pandey, B. (2017). Comprehensive analysis of semantic web reasoners and tools: A survey. *Education and Information Technologies*, *22*(6), 3121–3145. doi:10.100710639-017-9574-5

Khamparia, A., & Pandey, B. (2018). SVM and PCA Based Learning Feature Classification Approaches for E-Learning System. *International Journal of Web-Based Learning and Teaching Technologies*, *13*(2), 32–45. doi:10.4018/IJWLTT.2018040103

Kunegis, J., Blattner, M., & Moser, C. (2013). Preferential attachment in online networks: measurement and explanations. *Proceedings of the 5th Annual ACM Web Science Conference (WebSci '13)*, 205-214. 10.1145/2464464.2464514

Leicht, E. A., Holme, P., & Newman, M. E. J. (2006). Vertex similarit in networks. *Phys. Rev. E*, *73*(2), 026120. doi:10.1103/PhysRevE.73.026120 PMID:16605411

Liben-Nowell, D., & Kleinberg, J. (2003). The link prediction problem for social networks. In *Proceedings of the 12th ACM International Conference on Information and Knowledge Management (CIKM '03)* (pp. 556–559). ACM. 10.1145/956863.956972

Matjaz, K., Jean, S. S., Riste S., & Zelealem, Y., (2018). *Eccentricity of networks with structural constraints*. Academic Press.

Newman, M. E. J. (2001). *Clustering and preferential attachment in growing networks*. Physical Review Letters E. doi:10.1103/PhysRevE.64.025102

Ravasz, E., Somera, A. L., Mongru, D. A., Oltvai, Z. N., & Barabasi, A.-L. (2002). Hierarchical Organization of Modularity in Metabolic Networks. *Science*, *297*(5586), 1553. doi:10.1126cience.1073374 PMID:12202830

Sethi, K. K., Mishra, D. K., & Mishra, B. (2012). KDRuleEx:A Novel Approach for Enhancing User comrehensibility using rule extraction. *Third international conference on intelligent systems modelling and simulation*.

Sørensen, T. (1948). A method of establishing groups of equal amplitude in plant sociology based on similarity of species and its application to analyses of the vegetation on Danish commons. *Biol. Skr.*, *5*, 1–34.

Soundarajan, S., & Hopcroft, J. (2012). Using community information to improve the precision of link prediction methods. *Proceedings of the 21st International Conference on World Wide* 10.1145/2187980.2188150

Srilatha, P., & Manjula, R. (2016). Similarity Index based link prediction algorithms in social networks: A survey. *Journal of Telecommunications and Information Technology.*

Wang, P., Xu, B.W., Wu, Y., & Zhou, X.Y. (2015). Link Prediction in social networks: The state-of-the-art. Information Sciences, 58.

Wasserman, S., & Faust, K. (1994). *Social Network Analysis: Methods and Applications.* Cambridge, UK: Cambridge University Press. doi:10.1017/CBO9780511815478

Wilson, R. J. (1996). *Introduction to Graph Theory* (4th ed.). Prentice Hall Publication.

Zachary, W. W. (1977). An information flow model for conflict and fission in small groups. *Journal of Anthropological Research, 33*(4), 452–473. doi:10.1086/jar.33.4.3629752

Zhou, T., Lü, L., & Zhang, Y. C. (2009). Predicting missing links via local information. *The European Physical Journal B, 71*(4), 623–630. doi:10.1140/epjb/e2009-00335-8

Zou, T., Lu, L., & Zhang, Y. C. (2009). *Predicting Missing Links via Local Information.* EPJ.

Chapter 2
Application and Impact of Social Network in Modern Society

Mamata Rath

(iD) https://orcid.org/0000-0002-2277-1012
Birla Global University, India

ABSTRACT

Social network and its corresponding website permits a client to make a profile, set up an authorized account to create a digital representation of themselves, to select other members of the site as contacts, make connections with them, communicate and engage with these users in different social activities, etc. So, social network includes details of persons, group details, their friends list, contact list, business, affiliations, personal data, personal preferences, and historical information. In this age of smart communication and technology, most of the time people are connected with mobile smart telephones in their work culture, home, office, or any other related places. As they are constantly associated with social systems for long time, they get new posts, messages, and current refreshed news readily available in a flash. This is the constructive part of social networking that individuals consistently remain refreshed with most recent news and innovation. This chapter presents an overview of social network design, various issues, and emerging trends that are evolved simultaneously with modern age. It also presents a detail study on application and impact of social network in modern society as well as exhibits an exhaustive review of security measures in social sites.

DOI: 10.4018/978-1-5225-9096-5.ch002

INTRODUCTION

Different Social Network Sites (SNS) such as facebook, MySpace, YouTube and Bebo etc. got maximum user appreciation and became very prominent during the period and primary decade of the twenty-first century. But it was challenging to know who are their clients, how are they utilized and are social network locales a passing trend or will they be a generally lasting feature of the Internet- all these were difficult to handle. In the meantime, various pro locales have developed many social networking features, including digg.com (news separating), YouTube (video sharing) and Flickr (picture sharing): Are these the future as in social networking will end up installed into different applications as opposed to keeping up a moderately free presence? Social network destinations have pulled in noteworthy media intrigue due to their fast ascent and wide client base, particularly among more youthful individuals, and as a result of different terrifies, for example, the posting of unseemly material by minors and the potential SNS use in personality extortion. There is likewise a justifiable worry from guardians about their kids investing a lot of energy in an obscure online condition (M.Rath et. al, 2018) Be that as it may, there is a little methodical examination into social network destinations to look at the pervasiveness of attractive and bothersome features and to get solid proof of examples of clients and employments. This chapter audits such research and numerous subjective and blended strategy examinations concerning explicit parts of SNS use or into explicit gatherings of clients. One of the issues with social occasion information about SNSs is that they are benefit making endeavours and data about angles, for example, client socioeconomics and use designs are commercial privileged insights. Notwithstanding the usage of security approaches to ensure individuals' data, this makes deliberate investigations troublesome. MySpace is a fractional special case, in any case, and this part exploits to exhibit a few examinations of MySpace clients to supplement the writing surveys(M.Rath et.al, 2018).

Social system information can help with acquiring significant understanding into social practices and uncovering the fundamental advantages. New huge information advances are developing to make it less demanding to find important social data from market examination to counter fear based oppression. Sadly, both various social datasets and huge information advancements raise stringent security concerns. Enemies can dispatch surmising assaults to anticipate delicate idle data, which is reluctant to be distributed by social clients. Along these lines, there is a trad eoff between information advantages and security concerns. It has been examined in some examination work about how to improve the exchange off between idle information protection and modified information utility. We propose an information sanitation system that does not significantly decrease the advantages brought by social system information, while delicate inactive data can in any case be secured. Notwithstanding considering intense foes with ideal deduction assaults, the proposed information sanitation procedure (Z. He et.al, 2018) can at present protect the two information advantages and social structure, while ensuring ideal idle information security.

A social system is a description of the social structure including individuals, for the most part people or affiliations. It speaks to the manners by which they are associated all through different social familiarities extending from easygoing social contact to close natural bonds (J. Jiang et.al, 2018). The casual association is a caught structure made out of social people and associations between them. Huge scale online relational associations like Sina Weibo, Tencent Wechat and Facebook have pulled in a substantial number of customers starting late People should need to use relational associations to pass on or diffuse information. For example, an association develops another thing, they have to advance the thing in a particular casual network. The association has a limited spending so they can simply give free precedent things to couple of customers (Rath et.al, 2018). Four major applications of social networks are as follows.

- Multimedia – Photo-sharing: Flickr – Video-sharing: YouTube – Audio-sharing: imeem
- Entertainment – Virtual Worlds: Second Life – Online Gaming: World of Warcraft
- News/Opinion – Social news: Digg, Reddit – Reviews: Yelp, epinions
- Communication – Microblogs: Twitter, Pownce – Events: Evite – Social Networking Services: Facebook, LinkedIn, MySpace. Figure 1 shows Four important applications of social networks.

They assume that the fundamental customers could influence their buddies to use the things, and their friends could affect theirs colleagues. Through the verbal effect, incalculable finally get the items. Impact help is a basic research issue in relational associations. It picks a course of action of k centers as seeds with a particular ultimate objective to help the inducing of considerations, ends and things.

Figure 1. Four important applications of social networks

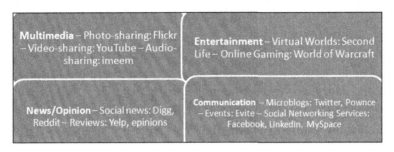

Section one presents the introduction part. Segment 2 shows Exigent features in Social Networking and utility devices utilized in social system for improvement and support, for example, context of big data, delicate registering methods and so on. Segment 3 presents applications and Impact of Social Networking in Modern Society and at last section 4 concludes the chapter.

Exigent Features in Social Networking

Many challenging issues should be tended to execute plan of social system design. Most of them are as per the following:

1. Representation of learning - Although different ontologies catch the rich social ideas, there is no need many "persuasion" ontologies characterizing a similar idea. How might we advance toward having few normal and exhaustive ontologies?
2. Control and administration of learning - Semantic Web is, relative the whole Web, genuinely associated at the RDF diagram level however inadequately associated at the RDF archive level. The open and circulated nature of the Semantic Web likewise presents issues. How would we give productive and powerful components to getting to learning, particularly social systems, on the Semantic Web. There are different types of social network sites that are used by many people now a days in cyber space. They are used for various purposes such as entertainment, education, friendship, lifestyle, business etc. .
3. Analysis, extraction and joining of data from social system Even with all around characterized ontologies for social ideas, separating social systems accurately from the loud and fragmented learning on the (Semantic) Web

is exceptionally troublesome. What are the heuristics for incorporating and intertwining social data and the measurements for the validity and utility of the outcomes?

4. Derivation and honesty in dispersed impedance Provenance partners certainties with social elements which are between associated in social system, and trust among social elements can be gotten from social systems. How to oversee and lessen the multifaceted nature of circulated induction by using provenance of learning with regards to a given trust show?.

Applications and Impact of Social Networking in Modern Society

Inoculation and Security in Social Network

W. Yang et.al (2015) recommend how to keep the engendering of social network worms through the immunization of key nodes. Not at all like existing control models for worm proliferation, a novel immunization methodology is proposed dependent on network vertex impact. The procedure chooses the basic vertices in the entire network. At that point the immunization is connected on the chosen vertices to accomplish the maximal impact of worm control with insignificant expense. Diverse calculations are executed to choose vertices. Reenactment tests are introduced to break down and assess the execution of various calculations.

Social Set Identification and Analysis

In view of the human science of affiliations and the arithmetic of set hypothesis, R. Bhatrapu et. al, (2016) presents another way to deal with huge information investigation called social set analysis. Social set analysis comprises of a generative system for the methods of insight of computational social science, hypothesis of social information, applied and formal models of social information, and a systematic structure for consolidating huge social informational indexes with authoritative and societal informational indexes. Figure 2 shows example of some social media available in internet.

Figure 2. Example of some social media

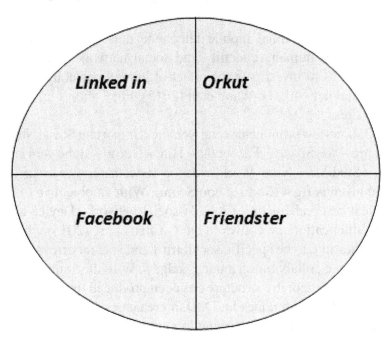

Table 1. Represents various impact and issues of social network on society

Sl. No	Literature	Year	Impact of Social Network
1.	M.Davidekova et.al	2017	Emergency social network approach that uses emergency posting through Application Program Interface.
2.	C.Marche et.al	2017	Object navigation in social network as per distance from one node to other
3.	Merini et.al	2017	Image tracing in social network using CNN approach
4.	P.Santi et.al	2012	Analysis of mobile social network based on mobility model for the purpose of next generation network
5.	L.Nie et.al	2016	Learning and Teaching from Multiple Social Networks
6.	E. Hargitai et.al	2016	Investigation on Social network analysis based on big data, big problems and Internet Log Data
7.	Z.Zhao et.al	2018	Recommendation of movie for social awareness through multi modal network learning
8.	A.Mitra et.al	2016	Analytical study of dynamic models in social network
9.	Rachael P. et.al	2017	Focus on positive aspects of social security measures
10.	Md.S. Kamal et.al	2016	An automated system for Monitoring of facebook data

Longitudinal Mobile Telephone Dataset:

An enormous, longitudinal mobile telephone dataset has been explored that comprises of human versatility and social network data at the same time, enabling us to investigate the effect of human portability designs on the basic social network. D. Wang et.al (2015). Fig.3 shows few prominent social web sites.

Figure 3 shows few prominent social web sites. Important Social Networking Websites are – MySpace – Facebook – Hi5 – Orkut – Bebo – Friendster – LinkedIn – StudiVZ – Xing. Worldwide top 10 websites as per August 2008 survey are given is fig.4 (Source: comScore). With an objective to build up a methodical comprehension of mobile social networks Device to Device (D2D) communication are conveyed by X. Chen et. al, (2015) who use two key social question, to be specific social trust and social correspondence, to advance effective collaboration among gadgets. With this understanding, an alliance diversion theoretic structure has been produced to devise social-tie-based collaboration techniques for D2D interchanges. Table 2 shows details of various issues in social networking in modern society.

Figure 3. Few prominent social web sites

Table 2. Details of various issues in social networking in modern society

Sl. No	Literature	Year	Social Network Issues/ Challenges
1	W.Yang et.al	2016	Immunization Strategy for Social Network
2	R. Vatrapu et.al	2016	Social set analysis with big data analysis
3	D.Wang et.al	2015	Impact of human mobility on social network
4	X. Chen et.al	2015	Mobile social networking – D2D communication
5	M. Trier et.al	2009	Exploring and searching social architecture
6	L. Meng et.al	2016	Interplay between individuals evolving interaction patterns
7	S. Ghani et.al	2013	Visual analysis for multi-modal social network analysis
8	W. Chen et.al	2015	Global Service network for web service discovery
9	Y. Song et.al	2015	Friendship influence on mobile behaviour of location based social network users
10	Y. Wang et.al	2015	Epidemic spreading model based on social active degree in social network
11	H. Zhao et.al	2015	Social discovery and exploring the correlation among 3D serial relationship
12	Y. Wu et.al	2018	Challenges of Mobile social device cashing
13	Y. Zhu et.al	2013	A survey of social based routing in delay tolerant network
14	T. Silawan et.al	2017	Sybilvote: Formulas to quantify the success probability
15	L. Zhang et.al	2018	Social networks public opinion propagation influence models
16	B.Schneier	2010	Taxonomy of social networking data
17	C.Yu et.al	2014	Collective learning for the social norms
18	V.K.Singh et.al	2014	Online and physical network with social implications
19	Z. Yan et.al	2015	Trustworthy pervasive social networking
20	Z. Wang et.al	2013	Peer-assisted social media streaming with social receprocity
21	A.M. Vegni et.al	2015	Social network with vehicular communication
22	F. Xia	2014	Exploiting social relationship to enable ad-hoc social network
23	M. Yuan et.al	2013	Security in social network with sensitive labels protection scheme
24	C. Timmerer	2014	Social multimedia in social network

Social network analysis (SNA) is becoming increasingly concerned not only with actors and their relations, but also with distinguishing between different types of such entities. For example, social scientists may want to investigate asymmetric relations in organizations with strict chains of command, or incorporate non-actors such as conferences and projects when analyzing coauthorship patterns. Multimodal social networks are those where actors and relations belong to different types, or modes, and multimodal social network analysis (mSNA) is accordingly SNA for such networks. S. Ghani et.al (2013) present a design study that we conducted with several social scientist collaborators on how to support mSNA using visual analytics tools. Based on an openended, formative design process, a visual representation called parallel node-link bands (PNLBs) has been devised that splits modes into separate bands and renders connections between adjacent ones, similar to the list view in Jigsaw. We then used the tool in a qualitative evaluation involving five social scientists whose feedback informed a second design phase that incorporated additional network metrics. Finally, a second qualitative evaluation has been conducted with social scientist collaborators that provided further insights on the utility of the PNLBs representation and the potential of visual analytics for mSNA.

Impact of Social Network on Education

A most noticeable resources for Universities are the information and must be shielded from security break. Security dangers and prevention (C. Joshi et.al, 2017) particularly develop in University's network, and with thought of these issues, proposed data security structure for University network condition. The proposed structure decreases the danger of security rupture by supporting three stage exercises; the primary stage surveys the dangers and vulnerabilities with a specific end goal to distinguish the frail point in instructive condition[8], the second stage concentrates on the most noteworthy hazard and make significant remediation design, the third period of hazard appraisal display perceives the helplessness administration consistence necessity so as to enhance University's security position. The proposed structure is connected on Vikram University Ujjain India's, processing condition and the assessment result demonstrated the proposed system upgrades the security level of University grounds network. This model can be utilized by chance investigator and security administrator of University to perform dependable and repeatable hazard examination in practical and reasonable way. W. Chen et. al (2015) propose associating the secluded administration islands into a global social administration system to improve the administrations' friendliness on a global scale. In the first place, connected social administration particular standards are proposed dependent on connected information standards for distributing administrations on the open Web as connected social administrations. At that point, another system has been proposed for building the global social administration organize following connected social administration particular standards dependent on complex system speculations. Table 3 describes Social networking design and focused challenges in society.

Table 3. Social networking design and focused challenges

Sl. No	Literature	Year	Highlighted Topics
1	R. M. Bond *et.al*	2017	Effect of social networks on academic outcomes
2	S.Rathore *et.al*	2017	Survey of security and privacy threats of social network users
3	J.Zhu *et.al*	2017	Influence maximization in social networks
4	F.Meng *et.al*	2017	Data communication between vehicle social network
5	W.Wang *et.al*	2017	Crowd sourcing complex tasks by team formation in social network
6	V.Amelkin *et.al*	2017	Polar opinion dynamics in social network
7	R. Schlegel *et.al*	2017	Privacy preservation location sharing
8	C.Joshi *et.al*	2017	Security threats in Educational Social network
9	J.Kim *et.al*	2018	Social network in disaster management
10	A.Ahmad *et.al*	2017	Authentication of delegation of resource use in social networking
11	B.Tarbush *et.al*	2017	Dynamic model of social network formation
12	R.Rau *et.al*	2017	Financial outcome of social networks
13	D.Quick *et.al*	2017	Pervasive social networking forensic
14	S.Janabi *et.al*	2017	Privacy as a concern among social network users
15	L.C.Hua *et.al*	2017	Cooperation among members of social network in VANET

In mobile figuring research zone, it is very alluring to comprehend the attributes of client development with the goal that the easy to understand area mindful administrations could be rendered successfully. Area based social systems (LBSNs) have thrived as of late and are of incredible potential for development conduct investigation and information driven application plan. While there have been a few endeavors on client registration development conduct in LBSNs, they need exhaustive examination of social effect on them. To this end, the social-spatial impact and social-fleeting impact are broke down artificially by Y. Song et. al (2015) in light of the related data uncovered in LBSNs. The registration development practices of clients are observed to be influenced by their social fellowships both from spatial and fleeting measurements. Besides, a probabilistic model of client mobile conduct is proposed, joining the thorough social impact display with degree individual inclination show. The trial results approve that the proposed model can enhance expectation precision contrasted with the best in class social recorded model thinking about fleeting data (SHM+T), which for the most part ponders the transient cyclic examples and utilizations them to show client versatility, while being with reasonable unpredictability.

An enhanced Susceptible-Infected-Susceptible (SIS) plague spreading model is proposed (Y. Wang et.al, 2015) with the end goal to give a hypothetical technique to examine and foresee the spreading of illnesses. As a moving station in a city, a vehicle has its own dataset of directions. On every direction, remote connections can be worked between various clients and the vehicle Since every vehicle is related with a particular territory that covers certain potential client gatherings, such portable vehicles have turned into the premise of a Vehicle Social Network (VSN) for prescribing items to potential clients in present day society .However, little research has concentrated on publicizing through a VSN . For VSN-based publicizing, the advertiser normally situated in a remote Central Office (CO)chooses certain vehicles to go about as recommenders as indicated by their scope territories. Data about the vehicles' scope zones will be sent from the VSN to the advertiser working at the CO i.e., information backhauling. Moreover, the advertiser will sent the outcomes in regards to the picked recommenders to all vehicles in the VSN, i.e., information front hauling. Naturally, a compelling correspondence framework is desperately required to help information transmission.

CONCLUSION

From the study above, it can be summarised that there are many positive impact of social networking systems on current society. Communicating with people and making friendship is a very natural method of connecting people, moreover who are of different age groups and different backgrounds. It was never been less demanding to make companions than it is at the present time. Furthermore, that is primarily on account of social networking locales. Only a couple of decades back it was really hard to associate with individuals, except if you were the excessively cordial sort ready to make discussion with anybody at a gathering. The increasing use of mobile smart phones among people helped change this, associating individuals recently. It's completely conceivable to have groups, friendship and communication among several companions on Facebook. They may not be companions you know on an individual dimension and invest energy with in reality on a week after week premise. Be that as it may, they're companions regardless. There are a few people I consider companions who I have never met — actually, I may never meet them — yet that doesn't decrease the association we have because of social networks. They for the most part do mind, and will let you know so. They will tune in to what you need to state, and help you manage any issues you might confront. In the event that this isn't the situation, you might need to discover new companions. The fact of the matter is that on social networking destinations, we're ready to sympathize with one another. A companion may have experienced a comparative difficulty that you are right now experiencing, and they will have the capacity to enable you to get past it. Social networks support sparing of quality time because of quick correspondence among friends and group members. Our time is being extended more trim and lesser by work and family duties. In any case, social networking sites offer an opportunity to impart in a rapid and productive way. Composing a relaxed comment for twitter takes only few seconds, and one can finalise a business deal, an appointment, an interview, a conference, a business meeting through these social sites very easily. So, there are many positive impact of social networks on people.

REFERENCES

Ahmad, A., Whitworth, B., Zeshan, F., Bertino, E., & Friedman, R. (2017). Extending social networks with delegation. In *Computers & Security* (Vol. 70, pp. 546–564). Elsevier.

Al-Janabi, Al-Shourbaji, Shojafar, & Shamshirband. (2017). Survey of main challenges (security and privacy) in wireless body area networks for healthcare applications. *Egyptian Informatics Journal, 18*(2), 113-122.

Amelkin, V., Bullo, F., & Singh, A. K. (2017). Polar Opinion Dynamics in Social Networks. *IEEE Transactions on Automatic Control, 62*(11), 5650–5665. doi:10.1109/TAC.2017.2694341

Bond, Chykina, & Jones. (2017). Social network effects on academic achievement. *The Social Science Journal, 54*(4), 438-449. doi:10.1016/j.soscij.2017.06.001

Chen, W., Paik, I., & Hung, P. C. K. (2015). Constructing a Global Social Service Network for Better Quality of Web Service Discovery. *IEEE Transactions on Services Computing, 8*(2), 284–298. doi:10.1109/TSC.2013.20

Chen, X., Proulx, B., Gong, X., & Zhang, J. (2015). Exploiting Social Ties for Cooperative D2D Communications: A Mobile Social Networking Case. *IEEE/ACM Transactions on Networking, 23*(5), 1471–1484. doi:10.1109/TNET.2014.2329956

Dávideková, M., & Greguš, M. (2017). Social Network Types: An Emergency Social Network Approach - A Concept of Possible Inclusion of Emergency Posts in Social Networks through an API. *2017 IEEE International Conference on Cognitive Computing (ICCC)*, 40-47. 10.1109/IEEE.ICCC.2017.13

Ghani, S., Kwon, B. C., Lee, S., Yi, J. S., & Elmqvist, N. (2013). Visual Analytics for Multimodal Social Network Analysis: A Design Study with Social Scientists. *IEEE Transactions on Visualization and Computer Graphics, 19*(12), 2032–2041. doi:10.1109/TVCG.2013.223 PMID:24051769

Hargittai, E., & Sandvig, C. (2016). *Big Data, Big Problems, Big Opportunities: Using Internet Log Data to Conduct Social Network Analysis Research. In Digital Research Confidential: The Secrets of Studying Behavior Online* (p. 288). MIT Press.

He, Z., Cai, Z., & Yu, J. (2018). Latent-Data Privacy Preserving With Customized Data Utility for Social Network Data. *IEEE Transactions on Vehicular Technology, 67*(1), 665–673. doi:10.1109/TVT.2017.2738018

Hua, L. C., Anisi, M. H., Yee, P. L., & Alam, M. (2017). Social networking-based cooperation mechanisms in vehicular ad-hoc network—a survey. In *Vehicular Communications*. Elsevier. doi:10.1016/j.vehcom.2017.11.001

Jiang, J., Wen, S., Yu, S., Xiang, Y., & Zhou, W. (2018). Rumor Source Identification in Social Networks with Time-Varying Topology. IEEE Transactions on Dependable and Secure Computing, 15(1), 166-179. doi:10.1109/TDSC.2016.2522436

Joshi, C., & Singh, U. K. (2017). Information security risks management framework – A step towards mitigating security risks in university network. *Journal of Information Security and Applications, 35*, 128-137.

Kim, J., & Hastak, M. (2018). Social network analysis: Characteristics of online social networks after a disaster. *International Journal of Information Management, 38*(1), 86-96.

Mady & Blumstein. (2017). Social security: are socially connected individuals less vigilant? *Animal Behaviour, 134*, 79-85.

Marche, Atzori, Iera, Militano, & Nitti. (n.d.). Navigability in Social Networks of Objects: The Importance of Friendship Type and Nodes' Distance. *IEEE Globecom Workshops (GC Workshops)*, 1-6.

Meng, F., Gong, X., Guo, L., Cai, X., & Zhang, Q. (2017). Software-Reconfigurable System Supporting Point-to-Point Data Communication Between Vehicle Social Networks and Marketers. *IEEE Access: Practical Innovations, Open Solutions, 5*, 22796–22803. doi:10.1109/ACCESS.2017.2764098

Meng, L., Hulovatyy, Y., Striegel, A., & Milenković, T. (2016). On the Interplay Between Individuals' Evolving Interaction Patterns and Traits in Dynamic Multiplex Social Networks. IEEE Transactions on Network Science and Engineering, 3(1), 32-43. doi:10.1109/TNSE.2016.2523798

Merini, T. U., & Caldelli, R. (2017). Tracing images back to their social network of origin: A CNN-based approach. *IEEE Workshop on Information Forensics and Security (WIFS)*, 1-6.doi: 10.1109/WIFS.2017.8267660

Mitra, A., Paul, S., Panda, S., & Padhi, P. (2016). A Study on the Representation of the Various Models for Dynamic Social Networks. *Procedia Computer Science, 79*, 624-631.

Nie, L., Song, X., & Chua, T.-S. (2016). *Learning from Multiple Social Networks. In Learning from Multiple Social Networks*. Morgan & Claypool.

Quick, D., & Choo, K.-K. R. (2017). Pervasive social networking forensics: Intelligence and evidence from mobile device extracts. *Journal of Network and Computer Applications, 86*, 24-33. doi:10.1016/j.jnca.2016.11.018

Rath, Pati, & Pattanayak. (2018). An Overview on Social Networking: Design, Issues, Emerging Trends, and Security. *Social Network Analytics: Computational Research Methods and Techniques*, 21-47.

Rath, M. (2017). Resource provision and QoS support with added security for client side applications in cloud computing. *International Journal of Information Technology, 9*(3), 1–8.

Rath, M., & Panda, M. R. (2017). MAQ system development in mobile ad-hoc networks using mobile agents. *IEEE 2nd International Conference on Contemporary Computing and Informatics (IC3I)*, 794-798.

Rath, M., & Pati, B. (2017). *Load balanced routing scheme for MANETs with power and delay optimization. International Journal of Communication Network and Distributed Systems, 19.*

Rath, M., Pati, B., Panigrahi, C. R., & Sarkar, J. L. (2019). QTM: A QoS Task Monitoring System for Mobile Ad hoc Networks. In P. Sa, S. Bakshi, I. Hatzilygeroudis, & M. Sahoo (Eds.), *Recent Findings in Intelligent Computing Techniques. Advances in Intelligent Systems and Computing* (Vol. 707). Singapore: Springer. doi:10.1007/978-981-10-8639-7_57

Rath, M., Pati, B., Panigrahi, C. R., & Sarkar, J. L. (2019). QTM: A QoS Task Monitoring System for Mobile Ad hoc Networks. In P. Sa, S. Bakshi, I. Hatzilygeroudis, & M. Sahoo (Eds.), *Recent Findings in Intelligent Computing Techniques. Advances in Intelligent Systems and Computing* (Vol. 707). Singapore: Springer. doi:10.1007/978-981-10-8639-7_57

Rath, M., Pati, B., & Pattanayak, B. K. (2016). Inter-Layer Communication Based QoS Platform for Real Time Multimedia Applications in MANET. Wireless Communications, Signal Processing and Networking (IEEE WiSPNET), 613-617. doi:10.1109/WiSPNET.2016.7566203

Rath, M., Pati, B., & Pattanayak, B. K. (2017). Cross layer based QoS platform for multimedia transmission in MANET. *11th International Conference on Intelligent Systems and Control (ISCO)*, 402-407. 10.1109/ISCO.2017.7856026

Rath, M., & Pattanayak, B. (2017). MAQ: A Mobile Agent Based QoS Platform for MANETs. *International Journal of Business Data Communications and Networking, IGI Global, 13*(1), 1–8. doi:10.4018/IJBDCN.2017010101

Rath, M., & Pattanayak, B. (2018). Technological improvement in modern health care applications using Internet of Things (IoT) and proposal of novel health care approach. *International Journal of Human Rights in Healthcare*. doi:10.1108/IJHRH-01-2018-0007

Rath, M., & Pattanayak, B. (2018). Technological improvement in modern health care applications using Internet of Things (IoT) and proposal of novel health care approach. *International Journal of Human Rights in Healthcare*. doi:10.1108/IJHRH-01-2018-0007

Rath, M., & Pattanayak, B. K. (2014). A methodical survey on real time applications in MANETS: Focussing On Key Issues. *International Conference on, High Performance Computing and Applications (IEEE ICHPCA),* 1-5, 22-24. 10.1109/ICHPCA.2014.7045301

Rath, M., & Pattanayak, B. K. (2018). Monitoring of QoS in MANET Based Real Time Applications. Smart Innovation, Systems and Technologies, 84, 579-586. doi:10.1007/978-3-319-63645-0_64

Rath, M., & Pattanayak, B. K. (2018). SCICS: A Soft Computing Based Intelligent Communication System in VANET. Smart Secure Systems – IoT and Analytics Perspective. *Communications in Computer and Information Science, 808,* 255–261. doi:10.1007/978-981-10-7635-0_19

Rath, M., Pattanayak, B. K., & Pati, B. (2017). *Energetic Routing Protocol Design for Real-time Transmission in Mobile Ad hoc Network. In Computing and Network Sustainability, Lecture Notes in Networks and Systems* (Vol. 12). Singapore: Springer.

Rathore, S., Sharma, P. K., Loia, V., Jeong, Y.-S., & Park, J. H. (2017). Social network security: Issues, challenges, threats, and solutions. *Information Sciences, 421*, 43-69. doi:10.1016/j.ins.08.063

Rau, R. (2017). Social networks and financial outcomes. *Current Opinion in Behavioral Sciences, 18*, 75-78.

Rtah, M. (2018). Big Data and IoT-Allied Challenges Associated With Healthcare Applications in Smart and Automated Systems. *International Journal of Strategic Information Technology and Applications*, *9*(2). doi:10.4018/IJSITA.201804010

Sajadi, S. H., Fazli, M., & Habibi, J. (2018). The Affective Evolution of Social Norms in Social Networks. IEEE Transactions on Computational Social Systems, 5(3), 727-735. doi:10.1109/TCSS.2018.2855417

Santi. (2012). Mobile Social Network Analysis. In *Mobility Models for Next Generation Wireless Networks: Ad Hoc, Vehicular and Mesh Networks*. Wiley Telecom. doi:10.1002/9781118344774.ch19

Sarwar Kamal, M. (2017). De-Bruijn graph with MapReduce framework towards metagenomic data classification. *International Journal of Information Technology*, *9*(1), 59–75. doi:10.100741870-017-0005-z

Schlegel, R., Chow, C. Y., Huang, Q., & Wong, D. S. (2017). Privacy-Preserving Location Sharing Services for Social Networks. *IEEE Transactions on Services Computing*, *10*(5), 811–825. doi:10.1109/TSC.2016.2514338

Schneier, B. (2010). A Taxonomy of Social Networking Data. *IEEE Security and Privacy*, *8*(4), 88–88. doi:10.1109/MSP.2010.118

Silawan, T., & Aswakul, C. (2017). SybilVote: Formulas to Quantify the Success Probability of Sybil Attack in Online Social Network Voting. IEEE Communications Letters, 21(7), 1553-1556.

Singh, V. K., Mani, A., & Pentland, A. (2014). Social Persuasion in Online and Physical Networks. *Proceedings of the IEEE, 102*(12), 1903–1910. doi:10.1109/JPROC.2014.2363986

Song, Y., Hu, Z., Leng, X., Tian, H., Yang, K., & Ke, X. (2015). Friendship influence on mobile behavior of location based social network users. *Journal of Communications and Networks (Seoul), 17*(2), 126–132. doi:10.1109/JCN.2015.000026

Tarbush, B., & Teytelboym, A. (2017). Social groups and social network formation. *Games and Economic Behavior, 103*, 286-312.

Timmerer, C., & Rainer, B. (2014). The Social Multimedia Experience. Computer, 47(3), 67-69.

Trier, M., & Bobrik, A. (2009). Social Search: Exploring and Searching Social Architectures in Digital Networks. *IEEE Internet Computing, 13*(2), 51–59. doi:10.1109/MIC.2009.44

Vatrapu, R., Mukkamala, R. R., Hussain, A., & Flesch, B. (2016). Social Set Analysis: A Set Theoretical Approach to Big Data Analytics. *IEEE Access: Practical Innovations, Open Solutions, 4*, 2542–2571. doi:10.1109/ACCESS.2016.2559584

Vegni, A. M., & Loscrí, V. (2015). A Survey on Vehicular Social Networks. *IEEE Communications Surveys and Tutorials, 17*(4), 2397–2419. doi:10.1109/COMST.2015.2453481

Wang, D., & Song, C. (2015). Impact of human mobility on social networks. Journal of Communications and Networks, 17(2), 100-109.

Wang, W., Jiang, J., An, B., Jiang, Y., & Chen, B. (2017). Toward Efficient Team Formation for Crowdsourcing in Noncooperative Social Networks. IEEE Transactions on Cybernetics, 47(12), 4208-4222.

Wang, Y., & Cai, W. (2015). Epidemic spreading model based on social active degree in social networks. *China Communications, 12*(12), 101–108. doi:10.1109/CC.2015.7385518

Wang, Z., Wu, C., Sun, L., & Yang, S. (2013). Peer-Assisted Social Media Streaming with Social Reciprocity. *IEEE eTransactions on Network and Service Management, 10*(1), 84–94. doi:10.1109/TNSM.2012.12.120244

Wu, Y. (2016). Challenges of Mobile Social Device Caching. IEEE Access, 4, 8938-8947.

Xia, F., Ahmed, A. M., Yang, L. T., Ma, J., & Rodrigues, J. J. P. C. (2014). Exploiting Social Relationship to Enable Efficient Replica Allocation in Ad-hoc Social Networks. *IEEE Transactions on Parallel and Distributed Systems*, 25(12), 3167–3176. doi:10.1109/TPDS.2013.2295805

Yan, Z., Feng, W., & Wang, P. (2015). Anonymous Authentication for Trustworthy Pervasive Social Networking. IEEE Transactions on Computational Social Systems, 2(3), 88-98. doi:10.1109/TCSS.2016.2519463

Yang, W., Wang, H., & Yao, Y. (2015). An immunization strategy for social network worms based on network vertex influence. *China Communications*, 12(7), 154–166. doi:10.1109/CC.2015.7188533

Yu, C., Zhang, M., & Ren, F. (2014). Collective Learning for the Emergence of Social Norms in Networked Multiagent Systems. *IEEE Transactions on Cybernetics*, 44(12), 2342–2355. doi:10.1109/TCYB.2014.2306919 PMID:25415942

Yuan, M., Chen, L., Yu, P. S., & Yu, T. (2013). Protecting Sensitive Labels in Social Network Data Anonymization. *IEEE Transactions on Knowledge and Data Engineering*, 25(3), 633–647. doi:10.1109/TKDE.2011.259

Zhang, L., Wang, T., Jin, Z., Su, N., Zhao, C., & He, Y. (2018). The research on social networks public opinion propagation influence models and its controllability. *China Communications*, 15(7), 98–110. doi:10.1109/CC.2018.8424607

Zhao, H., Zhou, H., Yuan, C., Huang, Y., & Chen, J. (2015). Social Discovery: Exploring the Correlation Among Three-Dimensional Social Relationships. IEEE Transactions on Computational Social Systems, 2(3), 77-87.

Zhao, Z., Yang, Q., Lu, H., Weninger, T., Cai, D., He, X., & Zhuang, Y. (2018). Social-Aware Movie Recommendation via Multimodal Network Learning. *IEEE Transactions on Multimedia*, 20(2), 430–440. doi:10.1109/TMM.2017.2740022

Zhu, J., Liu, Y., & Yin, X. (2017). A New Structure-Hole-Based Algorithm For Influence Maximization in Large Online Social Networks. IEEE Access, 5, 23405-23412. doi:10.1109/ACCESS.2017.2758353

Zhu, Y., Xu, B., Shi, X., & Wang, Y. (2013). A Survey of Social-Based Routing in Delay Tolerant Networks: Positive and Negative Social Effects. IEEE Communications Surveys & Tutorials, 15(1), 387-401.

Chapter 3
Online Social Network Analysis

Praveen Kumar Bhanodia
Lovely Professional University, India

Aditya Khamparia
 https://orcid.org/0000-0001-9019-8230
Lovely Professional University, India

Babita Pandey
Babasaheb Bhimrao Ambedkar University, India

Shaligram Prajapat
IIPS DAV, India

ABSTRACT

Expansion of online social networks is rapid and furious. Millions of users are appending to it and enriching the nature and behavior, and the information generated has various dimensional properties providing new opportunities and perspective for computation of network properties. The structure of social networks is comprised of nodes and edges whereas users are entities represented by node and relationships designated by edges. Processing of online social networks structural features yields fair knowledge which can be used in many of recommendation and prediction systems. This is referred to as social network analysis, and the features exploited usually are local and global both plays significant role in processing and computation. Local features include properties of nodes like degree of the node (in-degree, out-degree) while global feature process the path between nodes in the entire network. The chapter is an effort in the direction of online social network analysis that explores the basic methods that can be process and analyze the network with a suitable approach to yield knowledge.

DOI: 10.4018/978-1-5225-9096-5.ch003

INTRODUCTION

Advent of internet and internet facilities has provided a conducive environment which has nurtured and cultivated social networks quite rapidly and profoundly since its inception around us. Devices equipped with internet and compatible with its applications like mobile phones, computers, laptops and other smart gadgets are within the reach of common men. Facebook, linkedln, twitter, flickr, etc. are the most popular web applications of online social networks evolved over the years and are still in development mode by understanding the behavior of its users. Tremendous generation of wide variety of data through these social networking sites as per evolution of their context such as Flickr is designed basically for various kinds of content sharing amongst users whereas Facebook is designed explicitly for social interactions amongst the users and linkdln is designed specifically for professional interaction. Generally directly or indirectly the social networking sites are being developed for social interactions. In other words social network can be referred as network of relationships where nodes are the users or individuals and edges or links connecting nodes represents some kind of relationship (friends, brothers, sisters, father-son, coauthors, classmates, etc.) between them. It was obvious that social networks are not evolved for specifically internet based networks like Facebook; these social networks have been studied from the point of sociology for generic interaction amongst the groups of nodes(user/actors) and biomedical science for understanding the biomedical structures like protein-protein network. There are various types of networks prevailing around us which are categorized below as to understand their nature and behavior.

- **Social networks:** It is an online social network where in network users are represented as nodes and the relationship or interaction between them is represented through edges.
- **Networks With Ground-Truth Communities:** Social and information networks having sub networks or communities evolved with their actual local ground truth attributes. For example a YouTube networks having different communities developed such as fans of real Madrid, a group subscribed to lady Gagas vedios and another group is a follower of Volvo. All these communities are having their own inherent properties even though all these three networks are integrated part of YouTube network.

- **Web Graphs:** Such type of online networks having nodes represented through webpages and the edges are through hyperlinks between pages.
- **Amazon Networks:** Network wherein nodes are products and the edges between is the link of products commonly co-purchased.
- **Internet Networks:** Networks of machines connected in LAN, MAN and WAN. Computers are nodes and communications are edges.
- **Signed Networks:** Social and information networks can be of signed and unsigned nature, in signed the network has positive(friends/trust) and negative edges(enemy/foe/distrust).
- **Location-Based Online Social Networks:** The network where in users is having their geographical check-in data.
- **Metadata, Articles and Wikipedia:** Voting, Interaction, and article data available on Wikipedia. Using such data we can predict positive and negative links between nodes
- **Temporal Social Network:** The social or information networks wherein the edges are having timestamps or information related to time such as at what time it is built or how long it is built.
- **Twitter and Meme Tracker:** Another kind of social network where users follow other user's tweets with likes and dislikes. The network data has phrases, Tweets and links.
- **Online Communities:** Various online social networks are being in to existence which is evolved in to a form of online community such as Reddit and Flikr. The data from such online communities can be processed for further prediction.
- **Freindship Network:** A network where in nodes are people and the links and edges between them represents some kind of relationships showing that the nodes are friends with each other or may be friend in near future. Ex: Facbook, linkedln, Twitter whatsapp network. This type of network is an undirected one.
- **Road Transport Network:** According to this network nodes are represented by cities and the road connecting the cities represents the edges or links. This is also an undirected network.
- **Email Network or Communication Networks:** Here the nodes will be people and there will be a directed link between the person who sends an email to the peer persons or other persons on the email network. Therefore by its nature categorized as directed network.
- **Citation Network:** A research paper citing some kind of information from another research paper and cite it in the paper. Accordingly

several citations are being cited. Such type of information is captured under citation network; it is categorized in directed network as well.

- **Collaboration/Coauthorship Network:** Research scientist collaborate with each other to carry out some kind of research assignment and the relevant information is captured in the form of collaboration network.

Power of Social Network Connectivity

In a class of 60 students no two students are friends with each other initially. If we say after certain time instance at random any three students are chosen to be friend with a student and get connected with each other. In this way according to the policy if we see the status of the network of the class we find that the entire network of the class will become connected. It is not limited to the connected ness of three students even if two students at random in the entire classroom are friends then there is a strong possibility of connectedness within the network. Because it is improbable and unlikely that all of the students in the class will never become friends with each other as a little probability to have friendship between two will make it possible.

To understand the concept of connectedness let us divide the class into two clusters of 30 students each, the 30 students of the class are friends with each other by having a few friends per student at random. But at the same time both the clusters are way apart and there are no two students existing across the two clusters connected with each other. There is a probability of 30*30 = 900 that two nodes will become friendship across the clusters but out of these 900 choices there is none exists which is quite unlikely. And this is even unprobable if we consider social networks of n nodes (millions of users) because a single probability of having a friendship across between two nodes out of 900 will make these two clusters (networks) connected and the entire network will become one and this is what emergence of connectedness.

The study of social networks drives in for the classification of the entire network in its contributing components which are basically three group categories: *the single nodes*, *the major component* and *the middle region* (Kumar et. al. 2006). The single nodes (singletons) are the nodes which are not connected with any other node within and across the network, for example the user has joined Facebook but has never created any connection with other users of the network also termed as isolated nodes having degree zero. The major component of the network is referred to the large group of the network where nodes are densely connected with each other with some kind of relationship

Figure 1. Two separate clusters

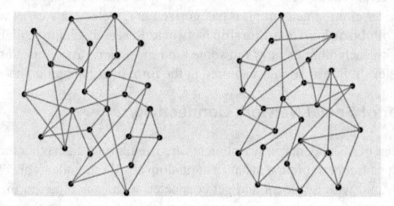

via links. nodes of this category are of potentially connected directly or indirectly to a major portion of the entire social network. Maximum nodes the section would perhaps be of high degree relatively. Another category of the social network is the middle region consisting of various relatively small communities with in the network wherein users (nodes) of the community interact with one another within the community but not with network at large. Community detection techniques have been evolved to identify and detect such partially isolated communities and groups in order to see how such communities would grow and merge.

BACKGROUND

Social network is not a new terminology it was initially coined by J.A. Bames in the year 1954 to illustrate the human relationships (Travers & Milgram, 1969, Tang et. al. 2011). Social networks are presumed to be portrayed as a structure containing different nodes and links between nodes. Online Social network sites usually capture huge gigabytes of data with respect to time which has been recorded periodically for future references. This data is of utmost importance as crunching of various parameters and measure could create legitimate and useful information that can be further used for deriving knowledge. The exploitation of social network typically emphasize upon the structure of the nodes and links between the nodes (persons, organizations, cities etc.). Any online system created for set of entities and links between entities can be easily conceptualized as social network and studied purposefully. Friendship of school students within the school, relations amongst the people of a social community specific, network of businessmen, structure of road, rail, train and air network across country and abroad. Even hyperlinks between different website can also create a kind of structural network that can be well analyzed and studied. Social network analysis does not include only crunching of data and its attributes but it includes other relevant information pertaining to the network as well. For example if researcher wants to know the total number of nodes in the network, number of edges or links in the network, node with highest degree, node with minimum degree, etc. he can yield the desirable information as an when required. Other machine learning algorithms can also be applied to exploit the topological attributes of the social network to yield contributory information for prediction and recommendation of policies.

The process and definition can be referred to (Serrat O. 2017) where the author has enlisted beautifully enlisted the benefits of social network analysis as well. The history and development of social network analysis is illustrated in (Scott, J. 1988).

SOCIAL NETWORK ANALYSIS

Majority of the studies done so far is giving an inclination that social network analysis is directly or indirectly a kind of graph analysis or we can say these networks are represented as graphs and they are studied extensively from topological perspective. The properties of graph which have been studied includes the size of the graph, density of the graph, degree distribution across the graph, path distance between nodes of the graph (average path distance), clustering coefficient, common neiborhood, communities, potential nodes, potential links, etc. As illustrated in (Faloutsos, et. al. 1999) the degree distribution over the internet generally follows power law which has also found its presence in the graphs defined for WWW(Kumar et. al. 1999), (Barabasi & Albert, 1999). In the same fashion friendship networks and emails were been studied to analyze the friendships and association amongst the nodes (Kumar et. al., 2004). All the analysis carried out to these studies just mentions are performed over static large graphs, but now a days these static graphs are transformed into dynamic as social networks over the internet are growing exponentially. Readers may refer latest review work carried out by various distinguished researchers (Sapountzi & Psannis, 2018)(Peng et. al.,2018)(Leppink & Fuster,2018). To analyze the real world data of such social networks like Facebook, twitter, snapshots of such networks at periodic time instances are captured and studied. Topological properties of different networks snapshots has been studied by Fetterly et. al and Cho et al (Fetterly et. al, 2004)(Cho et al., 2004).

Real World Social Network Datasets for Analysis

It has been clearly understood that earlier we were having lots of data stored from various large social networks and at that time we were (perhaps 30 to 40 years back) not having compatible softwares and appropriate technologies to crunch large datasets. But today with the advent of internet facility, high end computing and advanced storage technology we are capable to crunch the whole lot such datasets. Techlogies like python and networkx and other APIs are really helpful in exploitation of network datasets. The entire social network has certain features which when exploited the result generated may be used to recommend a potential node and a potential link between the nodes.

Network Dataset Formats

There are various formats available on the internet that can be downloaded for further exploitation and processing. The most commonly used formats are briefed below. These files are available on various dataset repositories such as https://snap.stanford.edu/data/.

1.   CSV
2.   GML
3.   Pajek Net
4.   GraphML
5.   GEXF

1.   CSV: Comma Separated Values

The file containing topological information about the network (source node number, destination node number and weight of the link between the nodes) and is available with *.txt or *.csv extensions, usually contains edgelist or adjacency list (Adjlist) where in mapping between nodes is given for further analysis.

Figure 2. Edge list Format

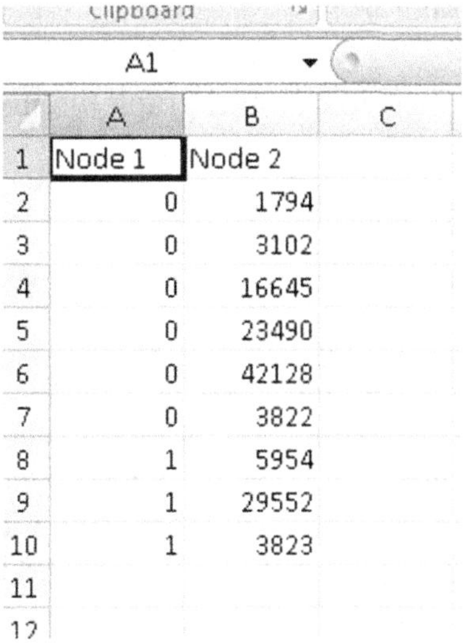

	A	B	C
	Clipboard		
	A1	▼	
1	Node 1	Node 2	
2	0	1794	
3	0	3102	
4	0	16645	
5	0	23490	
6	0	42128	
7	0	3822	
8	1	5954	
9	1	29552	
10	1	3823	
11			
12			

2.GML: Graph modeling Language

It is quite different with CSV where in the information about the nodes and links is available in text mode. Using python and netwokx following piece of code could be used for writing up and reading any GML dataset file. Manipulation in this format is possible like if we want to add node labels or attribute within the dataset we can do that as well.

```
g = nx.path_graph(10)
nx.write_gml(g, 'test.gml')
r = nx.read_gml('test.gml')
```

3. Pajek Net Format

This type of format uses .NET extension, addition of node aatributes with in the dataset is possible the advantage of this dataset file is that it has a valid information about the total number of nodes with in the network. For reading a graph in Pajeck format parameter required to be passed is path srting which will return a graph G and the return type would be multigraph or a multidigraph.

```
g = nx.path_graph(10)
```

nx.write_pajek(g, "test.net")
g = nx.read_pajek("test.net")

For creating a graph instead of multi graph the instruction would be

G1= nx.Graph(G)

4.   GraphML Format

Its implementation not supports mixed type of graphs which includes directed and undirected edges together. It is quite easy to use file format for graph analysis. it used a language for desicription of topological graph structure properties with flexibility to allow additon of application specific data. It generally supports Directed, Undirected and hybrid graph, Hypergraphs, hierarchical graphs, graphical representations, references to external data, aplication-specific attribute data and light-weight parsers

Reading GraphML format too needs path string to be passed as parameter and it returns Graph or Digraph

5.   GEXF: Graph Exchange XML Format

Graph EXF is typically a language that used to describe structures of complex networks, its associated data and dynamics. this format is created by Gephi people at Gephi project by different actors who were intensely working on graph exchange isuues. The XML features makes it quite possible to support the mathematical description as well as the inoformation about the various application of graph based data structures. Path string would be passed in the function as parameter which returns a grpah (Networkx graph), if there are no parallel edges found then a Graph or DiGraph would be returnd esle MultiGraph or MultiDigraph would be returned.

g=nx.path_graph(10)
nx.write_gexf(g, "test.gexf")

Summary of Dataset Formats

Various graph modules availabe to handle social network graph analysis but in order to do it some kind of functions has to be imported/exported to facilitate the package as to compatible with external program utilities.

Figure 3. GEXF Format

```
<?xml version="1.0" encoding="UTF-8"?>
<gexf xmlns="http://www.gexf.net/1.2draft" version="1.2">
    <meta lastmodifieddate="2009-03-20">
        <creator>Gexf.net</creator>
        <description>A hello world! file</description>
    </meta>
    <graph mode="static" defaultedgetype="directed">
        <nodes>
            <node id="0" label="Hello" />
            <node id="1" label="Word" />
        </nodes>
        <edges>
            <edge id="0" source="0" target="1" />
        </edges>
    </graph>
</gexf>
```

Figure 4. Graph Formats
Reference: http://igraph.org/python/doc/tutorial/tutorial.html

Dataset File Format	Short name	Reading Procedure	Writing Procedure
Adjacency list	Lgl	Graph.Read_Lgl()	Graph.write_lgl()
Adjacency matrix	Adjacency	Graph.Read_Adjacency()	Graph.write_adjacency()
DIMACS	Dimacs	Graph.Read_DIMACS()	Graph.write_dimacs()
Edge list	edgelist, edges, edge	Graph.Read_Edgelist()	Graph.write_edgelist()
GraphViz	graphviz, dot	not supported yet	Graph.write_dot()
GML	Gml	Graph.Read_GML()	Graph.write_gml()
GraphML	Graphml	Graph.Read_GraphML()	Graph.write_graphml()
Gzipped GraphML	Graphmlz	Graph.Read_GraphMLz()	Graph.write_graphmlz()
Labeled edgelist	Ncol	Graph.Read_Ncol()	Graph.write_ncol()
Pajek format	pajek, net	Graph.Read_Pajek()	Graph.write_pajek()
Pickled graph	Pickle	Graph.Read_Pickle()	Graph.write_pickle()

Reference: http://igraph.org/python/doc/tutorial/tutorial.html

similarly igraph do also need same excercise to read the common graph formats which are summarized in below figure.[http://igraph.org/python/doc/tutorial/tutorial.html]

Analyzing Network

The network datasets for different kinds of social networks like Facebook, linkedln etc can be downloaded from various sources in any of the above mentioned format. these datasets can be crunched using python and networkx package. Basic functions to analyse and visualize facebook network are described in given peice of code.

```
import networkx as nx
import matplotlib.pyplot as plt
G = nx.read_edgelist('c:\desktop\facebook_combined.txt')
print nx.info(G)
print nx.is_directed(G)
```

The output of the above code display basic information about the network:

Type: Graph
Number of nodes: 4039
Number of edges: 88234
Average degree: 43.690
False

If we want to know only about the nodes or edges or degree even that also possible we can use functions accordingly. This is how we can read an edgelist format of social network.

Similarly pajek format datasets can also be read the only function need to be changed is read function rest of the code would be same as written above.

```
import networkx as nx
import matplotlib.pyplot as plt
G = nx.read_pajek('c:\desktop\football.net')
print nx.info(G)
print nx.is_directed(G)
```

The output of the code is:

Type: MultiDigraph
Number of nodes: 35
Number of edges: 118
Average in degree: 3.3714
Average out degree: 3.3714
True

Unlike Facebook social network which was undirected this graph is directed one. In the same fashion other formats of social network datasets for further analysis can be used for network analysis. For detail study NPTEL online course for social networks can be referred.

G = nx.read_graphml('c:\dataset\wikipedia.graphml')
G = nx.read_gexf('c:\dataset\EuroSiS_Generale_Pays.gexf')

CONCLUSION

Processing real online social network data for analysis to suggest favorable and significant recommendation for further use can be and is possible with analytical tools such as python and gephi, we did not illustrated the use of Gephi in this particular chapter, but basic python functions are illustrated as to analyze any online social network graph. There are various social network's datasets are available for crunching and further processing and even we can crawl it from respective social network sites. It has been studied that these datasets are found in various distinct formats which is application dependent. The chapter is an effort to give an experimental introduction of basic methods involved in analysis of online social network or graph using python.

REFERENCES

Barabasi, A., & Albert, R. (1999). Emrgance of scaling in random networks. *Science, 286*(5439), 509–512. doi:10.1126cience.286.5439.509 PMID:10521342

Faloutsos, M., Faloutsos, P., & Faloutsos, C. (1999). On power-law relationships of the Internet topology. In *Proceedings of the conference on Applications, technologies, architectures, and protocols for computer communication (SIGCOMM '99)*. ACM. 10.1145/316188.316229

Fetterly, M., Manasse, M., Najork, M., & Wiener, J. L. (2004). A large-scale study of the evolution of web pages. *Software, Practice & Experience, 34*(2), 213–237. doi:10.1002pe.577

Kumar, R., Novak, J., Raghavan, P., & Tomkins, A. (2004, December). Structure and evolution of blogspace. *Communications of the ACM, 47*(12), 35–39. doi:10.1145/1035134.1035162

Kumar, R., Novak, J., & Tomkin, A. (2006). Structure and Evolution of Online Social Networks. In *KDD '06*. ACM.

Kumar, R., Raghavan, P., Rajagopalan, S., & Tomkins, A. (1999). Trawling the Web for emerging cyber-communities. In *Proceedings of the eighth international conference on World Wide Web (WWW '99)*. Elsevier North-Holland, Inc.

Leppink, J., & Fuster, P. (2018). *Social Networks as an Approach to Systematic review*. Health Professions Education. doi:10.1016/j.hpe.2018.09.002

Ntoulas, C. J., & Olston, C. (2004). What's new on the web? The evolution of the web from a search engine perspective. *13th WWW*, 1–12.

Peng, S., Zhou, Y., Cao, L., Yu, S., Niu, J., & Jia, W. (2018). Influence analysis in social networks: A survey. *Journal of Network and Computer Applications, 106*, 17-32. doi:10.1016/j.jnca.2018.01.005

Sapountzi, A., & Psannis, K. E. (2018). Social networking data analysis tools & challenges. *Future Generation Computer Systems, 86*, 893-913. doi:10.1016/j.future.2016.10.019

Scott, J. (1988). Social Network Analysis. *Sociology*, *22*(1), 109–127. doi:10.1177/0038038588022001007

Serrat, O. (2017). Social Network Analysis. In *Knowledge solutions*. Singapore: Springer. doi:10.1007/978-981-10-0983-9_9

Tang, F., Mao, C., Yu, J., & Chen, J. (2011). The implementation of information service based on social network systems. *Information Science and Service Science (NISS), 2011 5th International Conference on New Trends,* 46 – 49.

Travers, J., & Milgram, S. (1969). An experimental study of the small world problem. *American Sociological Association.* Retrieved from http://www.jstor.org/stable/2786545

Chapter 4
Position Independent Mobile User Authentication Using Keystroke Dynamics

Baljit Singh Saini
ⓘD https://orcid.org/0000-0001-5649-4255
Lovely Professional University, India & Sri Guru Granth Sahib World University, India

Navdeep Kaur
Sri Guru Granth Sahib World University, India

Kamaljit Singh Bhatia
IKGPTU, India

ABSTRACT

In this chapter, a novel technique to authenticate a mobile phone user irrespective of his/her typing position is presented. The user is never always in sitting position while using mobile phone. Thus, it becomes very important to check the accuracy of keystroke dynamics technique while taking input in all positions but authenticating the user irrespective of these positions. Three user positions were considered for input – sitting, walking, and relaxed. The input was taken in uncontrolled environment to get realistic results. Hold time, latency, and motion features using accelerometer data were extracted, and the analysis was done using random forest and KNN classifiers. The accelerometer data provides additional features like mean of all X, Y, and Z axis values. The inclusion of these features improved the results drastically and played a very significant role in determining the user typing behavior. An EER of 4.3% was achieved with a best FAR of 0.9% and an FRR of 15.2%.

DOI: 10.4018/978-1-5225-9096-5.ch004

INTRODUCTION

User authentication is a key operation in the use of mobile devices. Authentication ensures that the device is being used by a legitimate user. Authentication methods can be broadly divided into three categories (Wood, 1997):

1. **Knowledge Based:** Process in which a user is authenticated based on PIN or Password.
2. **Token Based:** Process in which a user is authenticated with the help of smart cards or ID cards etc.
3. **Biometric:** Process in which a user is authenticated based on his physical (finger scan, retina scan etc.) or behavioural attributes (keystroke dynamics, signature etc.).

Keystroke dynamics is the science of building up a user biometric based on his/her typing pattern. It is one of the upcoming methods for authentication (Khamparia and Pandey, 2015). Just like any other biometric system the authentication process in keystroke dynamics can be divided into enrollment and authentication phases. In the enrollment phase, the user input is taken and the system is trained by building and saving the user profile. In the authentication phase, a new profile is built and matched with the existing profile in the database. Error metrics like false acceptance rate (FAR), false rejection rate (FRR) and equal error rate (EER) are used to evaluate the performance of the system.

The most significant advantage of using keystroke dynamics over other biometrics is that it can be used for static as well as continuous authentication. Static authentication involves authenticating the user once during login whereas continuous authentication means authenticating the user for the entire session. Since a user types many times during a session hence his/her typing pattern can be analyzed continuously for the entire session.

Mobile phones do not limit the way we type as compared to typing on a hard keyboard used with personal computers or laptops. A mobile phone user may type when he is sitting, walking or in a relaxed position like lying on a bed or sofa. The research done so far in the field of keystroke dynamics related to mobile phones has considered the user in a specific position only. In most of the cases the position is sitting position, but some researchers have also considered a user in walking or in a moving car also. Even in these situations, the user profile has been developed separately for each situation.

This research proposes a novel idea of considering the input from a user independent of the position in which he/she types. The user input is taken in three different situations – sitting, walking and relaxed but the authentication process is done without considering any specific typing situation so as develop a system which can authenticate a user in all positions.

The rest of the chapter is organized as follows, Introduction includes the concept of keystroke dynamics and the motivation behind the research, Background the work related to the field of keystroke dynamics that has been done so far. Then the Main Idea behind the chapter is discussed followed by the Methodology and Results. Finally, the conclusion of the study is presented along with Future scope.

Background

The most crucial aspect of keystroke dynamics is the features extracted from data for analysis. Hold time and latency are the most frequently used features. Hold time is the time for which a key is pressed, and latency is the time difference between the press and release time of two consecutive keys. Latency can be press-press latency, press-release latency, release-press latency and release-release latency (Balagani, Phoha, Ray and Phoha, 2011). Figure 1 shows these features. Trojahn and Ortmeier (2013) observed that press-press latency (also known as digraph) gave better results as compared to other latencies. In addition to these other features like pressure (of key press), n-graphs, hand movement, and typing speed. Saevanee and Bhattararakosol (2009) used pressure with which a key is pressed as a feature and used Probabilistic Neural Network to obtain an EER of 1%. Use of mobile phone also provides additional features like accelerometer features. Use of accelerometer as a feature helped researchers (Giuffrida, Majdanik, Conti and Bos, 2014) to achieve FAR of 0.08%.

The environment in which the input is taken also plays a key role in the practical aspect of the research (Khamparia and Pandey, 2016). Experimenting in a controlled environment limits the instincts of a user whereas taking input from user in uncontrolled manner provides the result close to a real-life situation. Researchers have also used different text as input varying from PIN

Figure 1. Commonly used features

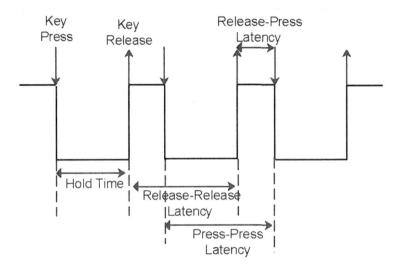

to complex passwords. Researchers have used fixed as well as user-chosen input for analysis. Sitova et al. (2016) used hand movement, orientation and grasp features and achieved an EER of 7.16% for walking position and 10.05% in sitting position. Other features related to touch like single and multi-touch were used by Meng, Wong and Schlegel (2013). They used Radial Basis Network Function in combination with Particle Swarm optimization to achieve a best FAR o7.08% and FRR of 8.34%.

Motion-based and tap-based features in sitting and walking positions were used in (Sitova et al., 2016 and Bo et al., 2013) to get error rate values of 7.16%(EER) and 0%(FAR) respectively. Takahashi, Ogura, Bista and Takata (2016) experimented by incorporating flick input along with keystroke and motion features. The inputs were taken for different user positions like sitting, walking and sitting in a car. Table 1 summarizes some of the previous research done in this field.

The classifier selected also plays an important role in the outcome. The most commonly used classifiers are State Vector Machine (SVM) (Khamparia and Pandey, 2018), Random Forest (RF), K-Nearest Neighbour (KNN) etc. Every classifier does not work with the same accuracy for all datasets as the data collection conditions and the features differ from dataset to dataset.

Table 1. Summary of Previous Research Work

Study	Features	EER (%)	FAR (%)	FRR (%)
Chang, Tsai and Lin (2012)	Pressure	14.6	14.54	14.6
Campisi, Maiorana, Bosco and Neri (2009)	Latency	13	--	--
Tasia, Chang, Cheng and Lin (2014)	Time, pressure	8.4	8.32	8.4
Trojahn and Ortmeier (2013)	Digraph, pressure, size	--	2.03	2.67
Meng, Wong and Schlegel (2013)	Touch inputs	--	7.08	8.34
Jeanjaitrong and Bhattarakosol (2013)	Hold time, latency	--	.02	.178
Giuffrida, Majdanik, Conti and Bos (2014)	Accelerometer	.08	--	--

MAIN FOCUS OF THE CHAPTER

Research in the field of keystroke dynamics is now more focused on mobile devices. Since the mobile devices do not restrict the way they are being used, i.e. they can be used in sitting position, walking, standing, in a car, while lying down, etc. it becomes essential to analyze the feasibility of authenticating the user in different positions. A few studies (Sitova et al., 2016; Crawford and Ahmadzadeh, 2017) in sitting and walking position. The authors in this study have extended this base idea by analyzing user typing position in sitting, walking and lying positions. Further, the mobile orientation has also been considered as it also plays an important role in typing position due to a change in keyboard size in different orientations. No previous study has considered mobile orientation for analysis.

Methodology

The methodology adopted for this research is shown in Figure 2. Dataset developed by Saini, Kaur and Bhatia (2018) was used. The dataset consists of data from 40 users who have typed the input ".tie5Roanl" in sitting, walking and relaxing positions. The data was collected in an uncontrolled manner by installing a data collection app on each user's mobile phone.

From the data, three different features were extracted – hold time, latency and motion (using accelerometer data). A total of 10 hold times, 36 latency and 3 motion features (mean of X-axis readings, mean of Y-axis readings, mean of Z-axis readings) were extracted. Before doing the classification, the data was also subjected to pre-processing for removal of outlier values. Removing outlier values improves the results. Since the data was collected

Figure 2. Research Methodology

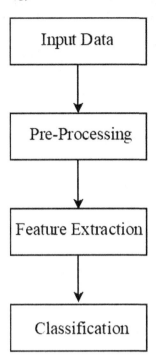

in an uncontrolled manner, the user sometimes gets distracted (conversation, waking, etc.) while giving the input. So, outlier removal is important. The data was also subjected to normalization. Normalization brings the distributed values to a fixed range, generally 0-1. Z-score normalization method was used for normalization. Two classifiers Random Forest and K-Nearest Neighbour (KNN) were used for classification. WEKA tool was used for analysis as all the above-mentioned techniques are implemented in it.

Results and Discussion

Table 2 shows the error rate values when hold time was used as a feature. Results with and without outlier removal are depicted in the table. Random Forest classifier performed better as compared to KNN. The average FRR value achieved was 40.8% which means that almost half the time the correct user is rejected. The high FRR value is not desirable as it can frustrate the authentic user. The average value for FAR is 2.5% which means that only 3 out of 100 imposter attempts are successful which is a very good sign. This means that imposters cannot impersonate as being someone else. The average

EER value is 15.33%. The results before and after outlier removal do not deviate much in case of Random Forest but there is a slight improvement in results in case of KNN classifier.

Figure 3 shows the scatter plot for hold time features (for keys 't' and 'a'). For simplicity and clarity 10 inputs from 5 users have been considered. It is clear from the plot that the input of one user is not totally separate from

Figure 3. Scatter plot for hold time features

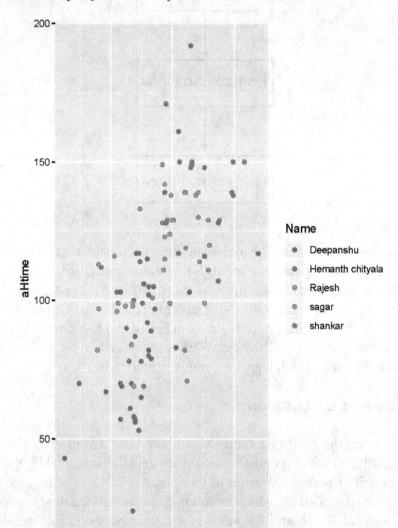

For a more accurate representation see the electronic version.

Table 2. Error rates using hold time only

	Random Forest			KNN		
	FRR (%)	FAR (%)	EER (%)	FRR (%)	FAR (%)	EER (%)
Without Outlier Removal	40.8	2.5	15.33	59.8	3.6	21.54
With Outlier Removal	40.6	2.5	15.32	56.9	3.4	20.9

input of another user. There is overlapping of inputs of different users which justifies the high error rates from the analysis.

The Box and Whisker plot as shown in Figure 4 also shows the overlapping of values for the hold time of '.' key. The values of users "Deepanshu" and "Rajesh" although have different mean values, but there are a lot of values between the minimum and the maximum range that overlap. This overlapping of values results in high error rates.

Table 3 shows the error rates when hold time, press-press latency, press-release latency, release-press latency, and release-release latency features were considered together. The FAR achieved was 1.7%, the FRR value achieved was 27.1% and the EER values achieved was 9.2%. Random Forest classifier gave better results than KNN. Removing outlier values improved the results significantly for KNN but did not have much impact on the error rates obtained by using Random Forest classifier.

Figure 4. Box and Whisker plot for '.' key

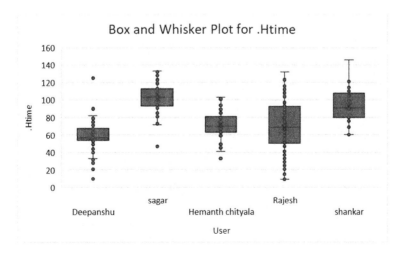

Table 3. Error rates using hold time and latency features combined

	Random Forest			KNN		
	FRR (%)	FAR (%)	EER (%)	FRR (%)	FAR (%)	EER (%)
Without Outlier Removal	28.3	1.7	9.3	54.6	3.3	19.3
With Outlier Removal	27.1	1.7	9.2	35.3	2.1	14.1

Figure 5. Variable Importance Plot for hold time and latency features

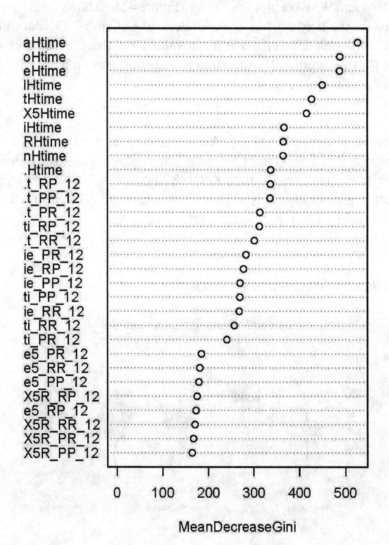

To select the common features that best identifies a user in all position CfsSubsetEval filter and Variable importance plot were used with hold time and all latency feature set. Using CfsSubsetEval 12 features were selected out of a total of 46 features. The 12 features consist of all the hold time features, one release-press and one press-press feature. Using the Variable Importance Plot (as shown in Figure 5) different subset of features was selected. A total of 30 features were selected out of a total of 46. The results of classification are as shown in Table 4.

In the last part of this analysis, we analyzed the user typing pattern by taking into consideration hold time, press-press time, press-release time, release-press time, release-release time and motion feature, i.e., mean(X), mean(Y) and mean(Z) axis.

Table 5 shows the result with and without outlier removal using both the classifiers. Here again, the performance of Random Forest is far better than the KNN classifier. The results did not improve much after outlier removal with Random Forest but there was a slight improvement in the results after outlier removal in case of KNN classifier.

The error rates achieved using the combination of all the features were the lowest with the best EER of 0.9% which means that only 1 out of 100 imposters attempts are successful. The FRR value achieved was 15%, i.e., 15 out of 100 genuine attempts are rejected. The EER achieved was 4.3% which is the best result achieved so far.

Table 4. Error rates after applying filters on hold time and latency features

Filter	Random Forest			KNN		
	FRR (%)	FAR (%)	EER (%)	FRR (%)	FAR (%)	EER (%)
CfsSubsetEval	31.3	1.9	9.4	45.	2.7	18.6
Variable Importance Plot	27	1.7	9.1	35.6	2.1	14.1

Table 5. Error rates using hold time, latency and motion features

	Random Forest			KNN		
	FRR (%)	FAR (%)	EER (%)	FRR (%)	FAR (%)	EER (%)
Without Outlier Removal	15.9	1	4.5	26	1.6	13.5
With Outlier Removal	15	0.9	4.3	23.8	1.4	13

Figure 6. Variable Importance Plot for hold time, latency and motion features

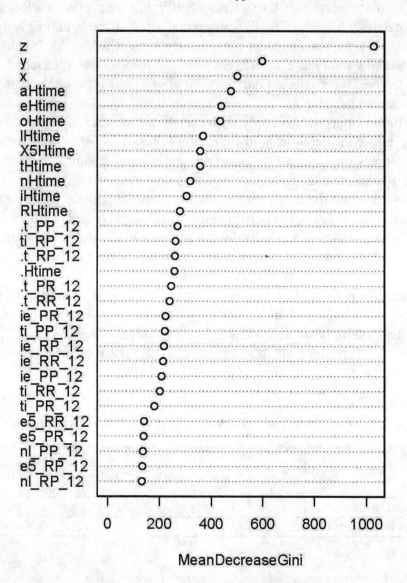

Although, the error rates decreased but combining all these features results in a total of 49 features which is very large. Since the computation is to be done on a mobile device having a lower number of features is desired. To achieve this CfsSubsetEval filter and Variable importance plot were used with hold time and latency as a feature set. Using CfsSubsetEval 15 features

Table 6. Error rates after applying filters on hold time, latency and motion features

Filter	Random Forest			KNN		
	FRR (%)	FAR (%)	EER (%)	FRR (%)	FAR (%)	EER (%)
CfsSubsetEval	17.4	.9	4.3	26.8	1.7	13.6
Variable Importance Plot	15.2	1	4.5	24.2	1.5	13.3

were selected out of a total of 49 features. The 15 features consist of all the hold times, all motion features, press-press time for the keys '.' and 't' and keys 'i' and 'e'. Figure 6 shows the Variable Importance Plot.

The plot shows the significance of the top 30 features out of 49. The motion features are the most useful in determining the user typing pattern followed by the hold times, latency features of keys '.' and 't' and so on. There is a significant difference in the impact made by the top feature, i.e., mean(Z) axis and the bottom-most feature, i.e. release-press time for keys 'n' and 'l'. A manual selection was done to choose a set of features out of these 30 which gives the same or better performance. Analyzing different sets finally a set of 25 features was selected.

The above analysis shows that the error rates improved when more features were added. The FRR value improved from 40.6% to 15%, the FAR value improved from 2.5% to 0.9% and the EER value improved from 15.32% to 4.3%.

CONCLUSION

This research explored the novel idea of authenticating a user irrespective of his/her typing position. The research concludes that it is in fact possible to with quite a high degree of accuracy to authenticate a user irrespective of his typing position. The FRR value was high with 15.2% which means a genuine user might get a bit frustrated, but the FAR value of 0.9% is encouraging as it ensures the rejection of imposters. It was found that the Random Forest classifier is the most suitable for authenticating users. The input data for the research did not consider the emotions of a user while giving the input. As a future scope, it is planned to consider the emotion of the user also as an input. Also, since the system is being developed for mobile phones we plan to lower the number of features and improve the error rates.

REFERENCES

Balagani, K. S., Phoha, V. V., Ray, A., & Phoha, S. (2011). On the discriminability of keystroke feature vectors used in fixed text keystroke authentication. *Pattern Recognition Letters*, *32*(7), 1070–1080. doi:10.1016/j.patrec.2011.02.014

Bo, C., Zhang, L., Li, X. Y., Huang, Q., & Wang, Y. (2013, September). Silentsense: silent user identification via touch and movement behavioral biometrics. In *Proceedings of the 19th annual international conference on Mobile computing & networking* (pp. 187-190). ACM.

Campisi, P., Maiorana, E., Bosco, M. L., & Neri, A. (2009). User authentication using keystroke dynamics for cellular phones. *IET Signal Processing*, *3*(4), 333–341. doi:10.1049/iet-spr.2008.0171

Chang, T. Y., Tsai, C. J., & Lin, J. H. (2012). A graphical-based password keystroke dynamic authentication system for touch screen handheld mobile devices. *Journal of Systems and Software*, *85*(5), 1157–1165. doi:10.1016/j.jss.2011.12.044

Crawford, H., & Ahmadzadeh, E. (2017, July). Authentication on the go: assessing the effect of movement on mobile device keystroke dynamics. In *Thirteenth Symposium on Usable Privacy and Security* (pp. 163-173). Academic Press.

Giuffrida, C., Majdanik, K., Conti, M., & Bos, H. (2014, July). I sensed it was you: authenticating mobile users with sensor-enhanced keystroke dynamics. In *International Conference on Detection of Intrusions and Malware, and Vulnerability Assessment* (pp. 92-111). Springer. 10.1007/978-3-319-08509-8_6

Jeanjaitrong, N., & Bhattarakosol, P. (2013, September). Feasibility study on authentication based keystroke dynamic over touch-screen devices. In *13th International Symposium on Communications and Information Technologies (ISCIT)*, (pp. 238-242). IEEE. 10.1109/ISCIT.2013.6645856

Khamparia, A., & Pandey, B. (2015). Knowledge and intelligent computing methods in e-learning. *International Journal of Technology Enhanced Learning*, *7*(3), 221–242. doi:10.1504/IJTEL.2015.072810

Khamparia, A., & Pandey, B. (2016). Threat driven modeling framework using petri nets for e-learing. *SpringerPlus*, *5*(1), 446. doi:10.118640064-016-2101-0 PMID:27119050

Khamparia, A., & Pandey, B. (2018). SVM and PCA Based Learning Feature Classification Approaches for E-Learning System. *International Journal of Web-Based Learning and Teaching Technologies*, *13*(2), 32–45. doi:10.4018/IJWLTT.2018040103

Meng, Y., Wong, D. S., & Schlegel, R. (2012, November). Touch gestures based biometric authentication scheme for touchscreen mobile phones. In *International Conference on Information Security and Cryptology* (pp. 331-350). Springer.

Saevanee, H., & Bhattarakosol, P. (2009, January). Authenticating user using keystroke dynamics and finger pressure. *In Consumer Communications and Networking Conference* (pp. 1-2). IEEE. 10.1109/CCNC.2009.4784783

Saini, B. S., Kaur, N., & Bhatia, K. S. (2018). Authenticating Mobile Phone Users Based on Their Typing Position Using Keystroke Dynamics. In *Proceedings of 2nd International Conference on Communication, Computing and Networking* (pp. 25-33). Springer.

Sitová, Z., Šeděnka, J., Yang, Q., Peng, G., Zhou, G., Gasti, P., & Balagani, K. S. (2016). HMOG: New behavioral biometric features for continuous authentication of smartphone users. *IEEE Transactions on Information Forensics and Security*, *11*(5), 877–892. doi:10.1109/TIFS.2015.2506542

Takahashi, H., Ogura, K., Bista, B. B., & Takata, T. (2016, October). A user authentication scheme using keystrokes for smartphones while moving. In *International Symposium on Information Theory and Its Applications (ISITA)*, (pp. 310-314). IEEE.

Tasia, C. J., Chang, T. Y., Cheng, P. C., & Lin, J. H. (2014). Two novel biometric features in keystroke dynamics authentication systems for touch screen devices. *Security and Communication Networks*, *7*(4), 750–758. doi:10.1002ec.776

Trojahn, M., & Ortmeier, F. (2013, March). Toward mobile authentication with keystroke dynamics on mobile phones and tablets. In *27th International Conference on Advanced Information Networking and Applications Workshops (WAINA)*, (pp. 697-702). IEEE. 10.1109/WAINA.2013.36

Wood, H. M. (1977). *The use of passwords for controlled access to computer resources*. US Department of Commerce, National Bureau of Standards.

ADDITIONAL READING

De Ru, W. G., & Eloff, J. H. (1997). Enhanced password authentication through fuzzy logic. *IEEE Expert*, *12*(6), 38–45. doi:10.1109/64.642960

Wang, X., Guo, F., & Ma, J. F. (2012). User authentication via keystroke dynamics based on difference subspace and slope correlation degree. *Digital Signal Processing*, *22*(5), 707–712. doi:10.1016/j.dsp.2012.04.012

KEY TERMS AND DEFINITIONS

ERR: Equal error rate is the value at which FAR becomes equal to FRR.

FAR: False acceptance rate is the percentage of imposter users identified as genuine users.

FRR: False rejection rate is the percentage of genuine users identified as imposter users.

Chapter 5
Drug Prediction in Healthcare Using Big Data and Machine Learning

Mamoon Rashid
Lovely Professional University, India & Punjabi University, India

Vishal Goyal
Punjabi University, India

Shabir Ahmad Parah
University of Kashmir, India

Harjeet Singh
ⓘ https://orcid.org/0000-0003-3575-4673
Mata Gujri College, India

ABSTRACT

The healthcare system is literally losing patients due to improper diagnosis, accidents, and infections in hospitals alone. To address these challenges, the authors are proposing the drug prediction model that will act as informative guide for patients and help them for taking right medicines for the cure of particular disease. In this chapter, the authors are proposing use of Hadoop distributed file system for the storage of medical datasets related to medicinal drugs. MLLib Library of Apache Spark is to be used for initial data analysis for drug suggestions related to symptoms gathered from particular user. The model will analyze the previous history of patients for any side effects of the drug to be recommended. This proposal will consider weather and maps

DOI: 10.4018/978-1-5225-9096-5.ch005

API from Google as well so that the patients can easily locate the nearby stores where the medicines will be available. It is believed that this proposal of research will surely eradicate the issues by prescribing the optimal drug and its availability by giving the location of the retailer of that drug near the customer.

INTRODUCTION

This section of chapter provides a brief outline of introduction to machine learning and health care, use of big data pipeline in health care systems and role of machine learning and big data in drug prediction. The authors have tried to provide the utility of drug discovery in terms of machine learning and big data pipeline.

Introduction to Machine Learning and Health Care

Machine Learning is presently playing major role in Health Care Systems by using various forms of data accumulated over years to derive meaningful insights. Health Care Systems are actively making use of machine learning along with Big Data Analytics to provide proper diagnosis and solutions for diseases by predicting right kinds of drugs. Whenever patient's complaint for any kind of disease, all symptoms are recorded and forwarded to computer with machine learning intelligence. Physicians usually recommend patients to undergo various tests and the inferences are carried out to resolve patient problems by using machine learning approach. For example, once the patient visits any consulting physician, the next step is to take scans in terms of X-rays and MRI's. These scans are later provided as input to machine learning models to diagnose patient problems and health condition with better results.

Use of Big Data Pipeline in Health Care Systems

The inclusion of Big Data Analytics has brought new opportunities for treating patients in the domain of drug development and precision medicines. The use of Big Data Analytics along with Machine Learning has transformed health care systems to the next level. However still Health Care systems are fighting for the right understanding of diseases and drugs. According to (Schork, N.

J. 2015), only 25% patients are benefitted from the top 10% drugs which are prescribed in United States Health Care Systems. This percentage is only 2% for patients who are prescribed for cholesterol drugs. The implementation of Big Data helps in tasks for maintaining data in terms of Electronic Health Records and brings data in perfect shape for data monitoring. Big Data is playing its vital role for bringing global medical system together and allowing places and countries to get best treatments and consultation. Social media is the medium where Big Data Analytics has contributed in Health Care Systems. People speak about diseases on social networking sites like Facebook and Twitter. This kind of real data is to be analyzed for insights for various kinds of health care information's by various Big Data Techniques and help in awareness among masses at global level (Bachrach, Y. et al. 2012). The valuable insights can be drawn out of clinical data by the use of smart healthcare technology in terms of big data analytics. This process achieves success in presenting patients risk forecast. This approach will certainly replace the expensive procedures used for maintaining records for patients in Health Care Systems. Big Data Technology has allowed to store huge amounts of patient data in terms of quantity and thus to continuously analyze it for improving quality of life. Big Data Market in terms of Health Care Systems is estimated to grow its market place from 10 billion dollars in year 2016 to 27.6 billion dollars by year 2021 (Kalyan Banga, 2016). The year wise increase in Big Data markets is shown in Figure 1.

Figure 1. Year Wise Big Data Health Care Estimation from 2016 to 2021

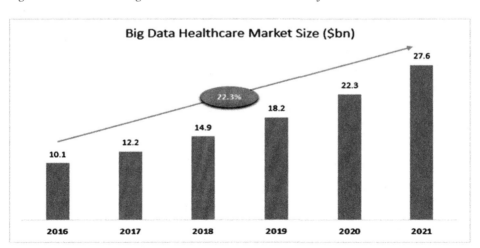

Role of Machine Learning and Big Data in Drug Prediction

The algorithms in machine learning are becoming quite useful in the discovery of drugs and their development. In drug development methodology, machine learning plays vital role in several steps. The prediction of various kinds of compounds, the biological activity of molecules, predictions of table structures are some of the areas where the machine learning algorithms contribute in better ways (Lima, A. N. et al 2016). Machine learning procedures help in transformation of discovering of new drugs in the same way as it is used in classifying the unknown people on social networking sites. Machine learning classifies images with different experimental compounds. The compounds with same lighting speed are grouped together by the application of algorithms. Machine learning approach in terms of usage of algorithms turns to be faster and viable method that traditional approaches for getting biological insights. Drug interaction with different target molecules in body speak about its effect. The target variables and drug are bound by different intermolecular forces to leave effect on disease. However when drug interacts with non-target molecules, it can cause various complications for that body in action. Thus efforts are made to point out these kind of detections which are not favored to body and must be avoided.

The biomedical data is a huge collection of structured and unstructured data which needs to be processed and analyzed for the discovery of drugs. Usually this huge data comprises data related to molecules, drug and protein interaction and Electronic Health Records data. To get insights out of this data, various algorithms are needed which are scalable and efficient as well. These algorithms identify patterns in data for predicting various side-effects included in drugs. Big Data Pipelines are formed for running these algorithms for making entire process scalable. The correlation between machine learning and big data pipelines for health care datasets is shown in Figure 2.

BACKGROUND

(Vangsted, A. J et. al 2018) developed drug response prediction model for gene expression profiling from tumor samples. The authors in this work identified the patients with myeloma having high sensitivity for drugs for various suffering toxicity. A machine learning approach along with feature

Figure 2. Big data and machine learning approach for health care datasets

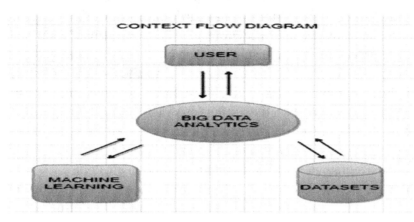

selection technique is performed for the analysis of peptides. This work has given SMO based classifier which predicted the presence of lantibiotics with an accuracy of 88.5% (Poorin mohammad, N.et al., 2018). The application of artificial intelligence in health care systems was discussed in (Jiang, F. et al., 2017) for past, present and future. The work is outlined to use Artificial Intelligence for cardiology, neurology and cancer. This work has provided the detailed review for the detection and treatment of these diseases in health care systems. The real time processing of health care data has been projected in (Basco, J. A. 2017) where data from different medical related applications and mobile applications stored in Electronic Medical Records is brought in to hadoop and MongoDB environments. This work approach minimized the processing time in patient records to greater extent. (Dimitri, G. M. & Lió, P., 2017) have devised machine learning algorithm, DrugClust, which predicts the side effects in drugs. In this research, the devised machine learning algorithm first clusters the drugs on the basis of their features and then later Bayesian scores is used to predict the various side effects of drugs. The results achieved in this research are promising when evaluated by using 5-folds cross validation procedure. The computational method was proposed in (Ferdousi, R., Safdari, R., & Omidi, Y. 2017) for the prediction of drug-drug interactions. This model claims predictions of 250,000 unknown drug-drug interactions. Predictions in this model are based on similarities in drugs which are functional in nature. (Harnie, D. et al., 2017) used apache spark based pipeline for scaling target predictions in drugs using machine learning approach. The authors in this research claim a speedup factor up to 8 nodes linear in nature and thus enhancing the processing performance in drug discovery. This work basically partitioned the work among various compounds and provided intermediate results. The network bandwidth and time is saved by processing the intermediate data on the same nodes that produce it. (Khamparia, A. et al. 2015) have given a detailed study on knowledge and intelligent computing methods. This research work outlined various rule based learning and case based learnings as well. (Sukhpal Kaur et al. 2016) worked on Big Data News Clusters and managed Web News Big Data and categorizing it on the basis of text and content using different classifiers to provide the accurate news with less running time in clusters.

(Lo, Y. C. et al., 2018) have provided machine learning approach for mining chemical information from chemical databases for drug discovery. This research has provided a means of extracting and processing data related to chemical structures for identifying drugs with important biological properties. The work is tested for various machine learning models and utility of each model is discussed as well. (Chen, R., et al. 2018) have provided a detailed review of machine learning for drug target interaction prediction. This research has highlighted the various databases which are used for drug discovery. The various classification schemes are outlined as well with methods for each category. This research further discusses all the challenges of machine learning for drug target predictions. (Panteleev, J.et al. 2018) discussed the recent advancements in machine learning for drug discovery. This research outlined approaches in deep learning for synthesis and design of compounds, binding predictions and other important properties. This research concludes that machine learning aims to reduce cost, labor demands and cycle time in early levels of drug discovery. (Kolachalama, V. B., 2018) have provided the perspective of machine learning to that of medical education. The authors put emphasis on machine learning inclusion among medical students, residents and fellows. This research directs educational systems especially medical side to include machine learning in curricular time and draw valuable insights. (Lavecchia, A. 2015) has discussed the various methods and applications based on machine learning for discovery of drugs. The major focus given in this research is given to machine learning techniques for ligand based virtual screening. The limitations have been discussed in detail with opportunities and successes kept under consideration as well. (Zhang, L., 2017) summarized various deep learning approaches of machine learning along with applications for discovery of rational drugs. This research suggests that big data pipeline along with machine intelligence can be helpful guide for design and discovery of drugs. (Chen, H., 2018) discusses the remarkable achievements of drug discovery with the use of deep learning procedures. This research concludes that deep learning is having more flexibility for its architecture in comparison to machine learning and there is ease for creating neural network architectures in deep learning. However this research outlines the limitation of deep learning for its need of large training sets. (Khamparia, A. et al 2018) have proposed PCA and SVM based approach for classifying student based E-learning system. This research have used eight attributes of National Centre of Biotechnical Information in terms of Motivation, Personality, Anxiety, Style of Learning, Previous Grades, Prior Student Knowledge, Study Level and Cognitive Style for classification purposes. (M Rashid, R Chawla, 2013) discusses the measures to bring security in data storage on public clouds by providing the extended model of Role Based Access Control where the authenticated users can only access the data in terms of roles with assigned permissions and restricts the unknown users from accessing data by adding variable constraints.

(Colwell, L. J. 2018) has discussed machine learning and statistical techniques and approaches for the prediction of protein-ligand interactions in discovery of drugs. This research outlined the major difficulties and challenges for the prediction of ligands and highlighted challenges for using datasets which are unbiased for models. (Brown, N., 2018) have given overview of using big data in drug discovery. This research concludes that artificial intelligence with NLP pipelines can draw successes in the field of drug discovery. Moreover the authors have given outline to prepare models in Big Data for handling various issues in discovery of drugs. (Khamparia, A. et al. 2016) presented a model driven framework for identifying threats in E-Learning System. This research also provided case study based on petri net models for improving consistency and reliability in e-learning systems.

NOVEL APPROACH FOR DRUG PREDICTION USING BIG DATA AND MACHINE LEARNING

Nowadays medicine consuming has become day to day activities for the people who are suffering from diseases. Most of the people are not also aware of the medication prescribed by doctors or pharmacies. Sometimes patients get other kind of complications as well by taking the medicines prescribed by medical practitioners. According to Forbes, there are many reasons associated with it and some problems associated with it are given.

1. Overuse and unnecessary care accounts for high amount of money and is more common than you might imagine. Unnecessary tests and drugs explains Why Health Care Costs So Much.
2. Traditionally, health plans, Medicare and Medicaid pay providers for whatever services they deliver, regardless of whether services truly benefit the patient or not.
3. Transparency galvanizes change like nothing else. Transparency is a vital component to build an effective and efficient health care system and the lack of transparency in Indian healthcare threatens to erode public trust.
4. Awareness of the people: A lot of primary health problems can be solved if we provide effective training and the knowledge to the local population. The lack of awareness among the patients provides doctors to take benefit of "supplier induced demand" to extract money.
5. Accessibility: The rural-urban divide is enormous; therefore, proper supply chain management is indispensable. The usage technology is good for accessibility, the use of telemedicine is very helpful.

For addressing the above challenges, the authors tried to eradicate these issues somehow by prescribing the optimal drug, its usage and its availability by giving the location of the retailer of that drug near the customer. The proposal of big data pipeline along with machine learning approach for the prediction and suggestion of right drugs is shown in Figure 3.

Figure 3. Drug prediction model using big data and machine learning

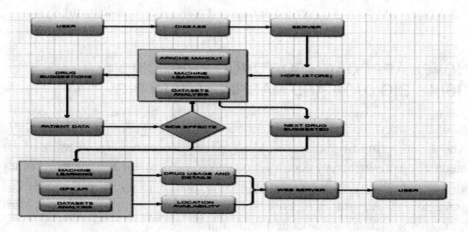

The idea is to prepare Big Data Pipeline and store Health Care Data in terms of patient's previous summary and medicines in Hadoop Distributed File System. Later when the patient will come with any kind of symptoms, machine learning algorithms are applied in terms of Mllib library of Apache Spark to provide drug suggestions keeping side effects of patient under consideration on the basis of previous log data. The machine learning approach is to be used iteratively until the best suited medicine is to be suggested for patient. Later concept of GPS API is to be added in idea which will provide the availability of location where the medicine is to be available. The various functions performed by this big data pipeline is explained in steps:

1.   Drug Analysis and Prediction

Providing the transparency to the people who do not know that which medicine is good for the disease and which is not will save patients from the wrong diagnosis by the doctors. Based on the historical datasets and machine learning algorithms, optimal drug is prescribed according to the disease input by the user.

2.   Side Effects Analysis

This module is for analyzing patient's data that can lead to side effects by that prescribed drug. A medicine may have a side-effect of skin-irritation. But if the patient is already having some other skin problem then taking this medicine can worsen the condition of patient.

3.   Next Optimal Drug Suggestion

This module follows the side effect analysis module. If the prescribed drug leads to side effects based on the drug records and patient records, then the drug dataset is analyzed again and next optimal drug is suggested.

4.   GPS API

Geo location refers to the identification of the geographic location of a user or computing device via a variety of data collection mechanisms. Typically, most geo location services use network routing addresses or internal GPS devices to determine this location. By adding the GPS API, we will be able to fetch the location of the user.

5.   Drug Location Availability

Based on the user's location, drug retailers and medicinal shops near the user's location are shown to the customers.

6.   Speech Recognition

Speech recognition will be implemented for the blind and the physically disabled so that they can speak the disease name and they would be suggested for the medicines which can be an antidote to their disease, especially useful for users with disability.

The drug details and usage will also be given to patient for effective use of drugs. The step procedure of drug prediction model using big data pipeline is shown in Figure 4.

The patient is required to enter disease name or symptoms to the web interface from where the data is to be fetched and stored in Hadoop Distributed File System (HDFS). Patient query is checked from the log data present on HDFS and machine learning approach is to be applied to check side effects of drug suggested. Alternate medicines are suggested in case the recommended drug is having side effects for patient.

Figure 4. Step procedure of drug prediction model using big data pipeline

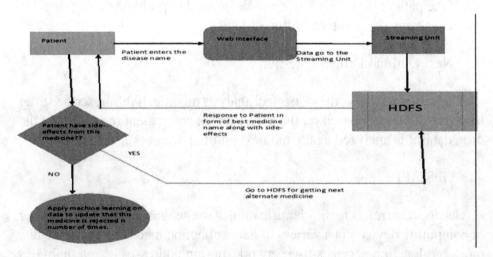

EXPECTED OUTCOME OF WORK

Save Time and Money

Going to hospital costs a great deal of time and money. You have to make an appointment in advance but sometimes still wait for hours to see doctors, and then stand in line to get your medicines. By utilizing data analytics in this model, last health records can be used to reduce diagnostic process and avoid cost-intensive treatments that they did not work in history.

Better Care

This idea will help the patients to get confirmation that they are being diagnosed for the correct disease by entering the symptoms and then getting the disease name. Now, the second problem may be that doctor have identified the diseases correctly, but medicine is not proper for it or it has some side-effects. This problem will also get solved by getting the list of medicines from HDFS for that disease. Third thing is that sometimes patients find it difficult for getting a particular medicine because it may not be available on local stores. So authors are proposing the availability of locations of various medical stores where that medicine can be found.

CONCLUSION

This chapter of research will surely eradicate the issues somehow by prescribing the optimal drug, its usage and its availability by giving the location of the retailer of that drug near the customer. This research chapter takes a step-in order to reduce various errors in medical system. It will reduce the unnecessary costs and overuse of drug which is more common in today's world. It will also bring the transparency, along with awareness regarding the details of medicines and its usage which is a vital component to build an effective and efficient health care system.

REFERENCES

Bachrach, Y., Kosinski, M., Graepel, T., Kohli, P., & Stillwell, D. (2012, June). Personality and patterns of Facebook usage. In *Proceedings of the 4th annual ACM web science conference* (pp. 24-32). ACM. 10.1145/2380718.2380722

Banga, K. (2016, October). Big Data Healthcare Market to reach $27.6bn by 2021. *Future Analytics World.* Retrieved from http://fusionanalyticsworld.com/big-data-healthcare-market-reach-27-6bn-2021/

Basco, J. A. (2017, November). Real-time analysis of healthcare using big data analytics. *IOP Conference Series. Materials Science and Engineering, 263*(4), 042056. doi:10.1088/1757-899X/263/4/042056

Brown, N., Cambruzzi, J., Cox, P. J., Davies, M., Dunbar, J., Plumbley, D., & Sheppard, D. W. (2018). Big Data in Drug Discovery. *Progress in Medicinal Chemistry, 57,* 277–356. doi:10.1016/bs.pmch.2017.12.003 PMID:29680150

Chen, H., Engkvist, O., Wang, Y., Olivecrona, M., & Blaschke, T. (2018). The rise of deep learning in drug discovery. *Drug Discovery Today, 23*(6), 1241–1250. doi:10.1016/j.drudis.2018.01.039 PMID:29366762

Chen, R., Liu, X., Jin, S., Lin, J., & Liu, J. (2018). Machine Learning for Drug-Target Interaction Prediction. *Molecules (Basel, Switzerland), 23*(9), 2208. doi:10.3390/molecules23092208 PMID:30200333

Colwell, L. J. (2018). Statistical and machine learning approaches to predicting protein-ligand interactions. *Current Opinion in Structural Biology, 49,* 123–128. doi:10.1016/j.sbi.2018.01.006 PMID:29452923

Dimitri, G. M., & Lió, P. (2017). DrugClust: A machine learning approach for drugs side effects prediction. *Computational Biology and Chemistry, 68,* 204–210. doi:10.1016/j.compbiolchem.2017.03.008 PMID:28391063

Ferdousi, R., Safdari, R., & Omidi, Y. (2017). Computational prediction of drug-drug interactions based on drugs functional similarities. *Journal of Biomedical Informatics, 70,* 54–64. doi:10.1016/j.jbi.2017.04.021 PMID:28465082

Harnie, D., Saey, M., Vapirev, A. E., Wegner, J. K., Gedich, A., Steijaert, M., & De Meuter, W. (2017). Scaling machine learning for target prediction in drug discovery using apache spark. *Future Generation Computer Systems, 67*, 409–417. doi:10.1016/j.future.2016.04.023

Jiang, F., Jiang, Y., Zhi, H., Dong, Y., Li, H., Ma, S. & Wang, Y. (2017). Artificial intelligence in healthcare: past, present and future. *Stroke and Vascular Neurology, 2*(4), 230-243.

Kaur, S., & Rashid, M. (2016). Web News Mining using Back Propagation Neural Network and Clustering using K-Means Algorithm in Big Data. *Indian Journal of Science and Technology, 9*(41). doi:10.17485/ijst/2016/v9i41/95598

Khamparia, A., & Pandey, B. (2015). Knowledge and intelligent computing methods in e-learning. *International Journal of Technology Enhanced Learning, 7*(3), 221–242. doi:10.1504/IJTEL.2015.072810

Khamparia, A., & Pandey, B. (2016). Threat driven modeling framework using petri nets for e-learning system. *SpringerPlus, 5*(1), 446. doi:10.118640064-016-2101-0 PMID:27119050

Khamparia, A., & Pandey, B. (2018). SVM and PCA Based Learning Feature Classification Approaches for E-Learning System. *International Journal of Web-Based Learning and Teaching Technologies, 13*(2), 32–45. doi:10.4018/IJWLTT.2018040103

Kolachalama, V. B., & Garg, P. S. (2018). Machine learning and medical education. *NPJ Digital Medicine, 1*(1), 54.

Lavecchia, A. (2015). Machine-learning approaches in drug discovery: Methods and applications. *Drug Discovery Today, 20*(3), 318–331. doi:10.1016/j.drudis.2014.10.012 PMID:25448759

Lima, A. N., Philot, E. A., Trossini, G. H. G., Scott, L. P. B., Maltarollo, V. G., & Honorio, K. M. (2016). Use of machine learning approaches for novel drug discovery. *Expert Opinion on Drug Discovery, 11*(3), 225–239. doi:10.1517/17460441.2016.1146250 PMID:26814169

Lo, Y. C., Rensi, S. E., Torng, W., & Altman, R. B. (2018). Machine learning in chemoinformatics and drug discovery. *Drug Discovery Today*, *23*(8), 1538–1546. doi:10.1016/j.drudis.2018.05.010 PMID:29750902

Panteleev, J., Gao, H., & Jia, L. (2018). Recent applications of machine learning in medicinal chemistry. *Bioorganic & Medicinal Chemistry Letters*, *28*(17), 2807–2815. doi:10.1016/j.bmcl.2018.06.046 PMID:30122222

Poorin Mohammad, N., Hamedi, J., & Moghaddam, M. H. A. M. (2018). Sequence-based analysis and prediction of lantibiotics: a machine learning approach. *Computational Biology and Chemistry*.

Rashid, M., & Chawla, R. (2013). Securing Data Storage by Extending Role Based Access Control. *International Journal of Cloud Applications and Computing*, *3*(4), 28–37. doi:10.4018/ijcac.2013100103

Schork, N. J. (2015). Personalized medicine: Time for one-person trials. *Nature*, *520*(7549), 609–611. doi:10.1038/520609a PMID:25925459

Vangsted, A. J., Helm-Petersen, S., Cowland, J. B., Jensen, P. B., Gimsing, P., Barlogie, B., & Knudsen, S. (2018). Drug response prediction in high-risk multiple myeloma. *Gene*, *644*, 80–86. doi:10.1016/j.gene.2017.10.071 PMID:29122646

Zhang, L., Tan, J., Han, D., & Zhu, H. (2017). From machine learning to deep learning: Progress in machine intelligence for rational drug discovery. *Drug Discovery Today*, *22*(11), 1680–1685. doi:10.1016/j.drudis.2017.08.010 PMID:28881183

Chapter 6
Analysis of Access Delay in Ad Hoc Wireless Networks for Multimedia Applications

Arundhati Arjaria
https://orcid.org/0000-0001-5107-1544
Rajiv Gandhi Proudyogiki Vishwavidyalaya, India

ABSTRACT

Mobile ad hoc networks are infrastructure-less wireless networks; all nodes can quickly share information without using any fixed infrastructure like base station or access point. Wireless ad hoc networks are characterized by frequent topology changes, unreliable wireless channel, network congestion, and resource contention. Multimedia applications usually are bandwidth hungry with stringent delay, jitter, and loss requirements. Designing ad hoc networks which support multimedia applications, hence, is considered a hard task. The hidden and exposed terminal problems are the main which consequently reduces the network capacity. Hidden and exposed nodes reduce the performance of the wireless ad hoc networks. Access delay is the major parameter that is to be taken under consideration. Due to hidden and exposed terminal problems, the network suffers from a serious unfairness problem.

DOI: 10.4018/978-1-5225-9096-5.ch006

INTRODUCTION

In wireless ad hoc networks, the well-known hidden terminal and exposed terminal problems may degrade the performance of the network in terms of lesser throughput and unfairness problems. Medium Access Control (MAC) protocol is a contention based protocol which has been simulated and implemented widely for various reasons. MAC has a critical role in the performance computation in Wireless Ad hoc Networks. The main aim to design this protocol is to increase the channel utilization. Where multiple contending terminals are there to access the same medium, MAC protocol is used for association of the all the nodes for channel utilization.

To achieve this goal MAC scheme has to minimize the chances of collisions and at the same time maximize the Spatial reuse Ad hoc networks are continuously becoming popular because of their characteristics such as lesser cost, easy to install and no need of any fixed and pre-installed infrastructure. An ad hoc network is known because of its self-organized behavior. Ad hoc network plays very important role in various applications includes a fety operations, catastrophic recovery, ad hoc formation of networks in conferences, connecting wirelessly in rustic places where any stable infrastructure is not available. Such a network is expected to work in the lack of any infrastructure by independently creating multi-hop paths for carriage of the packets. Multimedia has a significant function in the development of wireless networks supporting high bandwidth applications with QoS.

An ad hoc network is a set of wireless mobile nodes where there is no need of interference of incorporated access points or base stations that form a dynamic autonomous network. Ad hoc networks are different from traditional wireless networks, which do not need any fixed network infrastructure and can be deployed as multi-hop packet networks rapidly and with relatively low price. Such networks can be very useful in the environment where natural condition or time restraints makes it impossible to have infrastructure pre-deployed or in emergency cases. Ad hoc networks are useful in military, emergency services, meetings, and home or official instruments.

Ad hoc wireless networks are becoming popular because of their advantages such as less costly, easy to deploy and no need of any stable and pre-deployed infrastructure. An ad hoc network is characterized by its self-organized behavior.

To achieve high utilization of a channel in a medium, Medium Access Control protocol also needs to enhance the spatial reuse level. To achieve this goal exposed terminal problem should get resolved. Exposed terminal problem is a factor that affects the spatial reuse. An exposed terminal senses the transmission at the transmitter end & does not interfere with the reception at the receiver end.

The introduction towards hidden and exposed terminal problem is as follows:

Consider the scenario with three mobile nodes. The transmission area of node A can sense node B, but not node C (the detection range does not reach C either). The transmission range of node C can sense node B, but not node A. Finally, the transmission range of node B can sense node A and node C, i.e., node A cannot detect node C and vice versa. A starts sending to B, C does not receive this transmission. C also wants to send something to B and senses the medium. The medium appears to be free, the carrier sense fails. C also starts sending causing a collision at B. But A cannot detect this collision at B and continues with its transmission. A is hidden for C and vice versa. While hidden terminals may cause collisions, the next effect only causes unnecessary delay. Now consider the situation that B sends something to A and C wants to transmit data to some other mobile phone outside the interference ranges of A and B. C senses the carrier and detects that the carrier is busy (B's signal). C postpones its transmission until it detects the medium as being idle again. But as A is outside the interference range of C, waiting is not necessary. Causing a 'collision' at B does not matter because the collision is too weak to propagate to A. In this situation, C is exposed to B.

BACKGROUND

In order to address hidden and exposed terminal problems many MAC based schemes are proposed in the literature but none of them completely resolves the hidden and exposed terminal problems except DBTMA scheme using RTS/CTS mechanism. However the RTS/CTS method is not more effective to avoid collisions in the region where large number of hidden terminals are there. Some busy tone based approaches are also used to resolve the hidden and exposed terminal problems. Busy Tone multiple access (BTMA) scheme is used (Gupta and Kumar, 2000) where there is a base station which broadcast

Figure 1. Hidden and exposed node problem

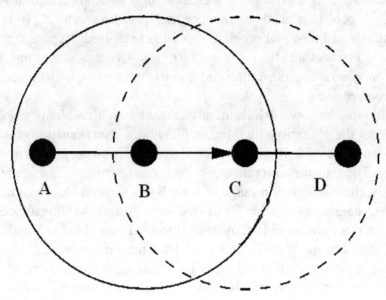

a busy tone signal to let the potential hidden terminals that channel is busy by sensing the channel.

Dual Busy Tone Multiple Access (DBTMA) is an extension of BTMA in which a distributed approach is used of sending the busy tones. In this method, two out-of-band busy tones are used, transmit busy tone (BTt) and receive busy tone (BTr), to protect the RTS packets and data packets respectively. This csheme can solve te hidden terminal problem but cannot resolve the exposed terminal problem.

Xu (He, Cai, Shen, & Ho, 2006) proposed that the interference range can be taken as a function of the distances between the sender and receiver nodes. They also researched that RTS/CTS handshake is more effective in terms of reducing interference.

He (Cesana, Maniezzo, Bergamo, & Gerla, 2003) introduced the consummation of IEEE 802.11 DCF MAC protocol in multihopAdhoc networks. Here taking variable interference range into account has shown significant results.

Choudhury (Karn, 1990, pp. 134-140) proposes ToneDMAC protocol where the transmitter's node id encoded the busy tone to remove the deafness problem.

Karn (Bharghavan, Demers, Shenker, & Zhang, 1994) proposed a MACA protocol in which Request-To-Send (RTS) and Clear-To-Send (CTS) packets mechanism for the collision avoidance is used. A ready node or sender transmits an RTS packet to request the channel to the receiver. The Receiver replies to the sender by sending a CTS packet. MACA reduces the data packet collision which causes by hidden terminals by using RTS/CTS packets.

Talucci (Wang, Jiang, & Zhuang, 2008) introduced MACA-BI. In this protocol it is defined that in a network with periodic data traffic, the receiver can predict its future reception times.

MACAW protocol has suggested by Bharghavan ("Wireless Multiple Networks", 1997) in which RTS-CTS-DS-DATA-ACK message exchange for a data packet transmission is used. The Data sending (DS) packet was used in this protocol to notify all nodes in the transmitter range that it is using the channel. The ACK packet was used for the acknowledgment.

There was some unfairness problems were there in MACA protocol; in MACAW some new back-off algorithm is introduced to solve the unfairness problems known as MILD algorithm.

SYSTEM MODEL

Consider a scenario of ad hoc wireless network where data and voice traffic are transmitted. There is a communication channel, via which every node send their data frames in the network. Any overlay of transmissions at a receiver end can cause a collision, and because of this none of the overlaid frame can be received correctly. The successful simultaneous transmissions are possible due to spatial reuse. In this paper, one hop transmissions are taken into consideration.

In this paper we had taken the IEEE 802.11 MAC protocol to delineate the problems. These problems not only affiliated with the IEEE 802.11 MAC but many Medium Acees Control schemes which uses backoff mechanism also suffers from these problems. Along with all this we had also taken multiple data rate support of the wireless ad hoc network into consideration. Multiple Data Rates depend upon the bit error ratio of the communication channel.

PROPOSED SYSTEM

In our scheme, a single medium is divided into two sub-mediums: a data channel and a control channel. Two busy tones, busy tone transmit (BTt) and busy tone receiver (BTr), are allocated two separate single frequencies in the control channel. Here Busy Tone Receiver (BTr) associated with the receiver and Busy Tone Transmitter (BTr) associated with the transmitter. A terminal that uses the transmission medium to transmit data turns on BTt/ BTr, which can be heard by all terminals within its transmission area. The difference of proposed scheme from DBTMA is that, by acclimatize the sensitivity of receiver's end, we set the channels' carrier sensing range in a way that the BTtmedium's carrier sensing range covers the two-hop domain of the concern terminal, while the BTr channel's carrier sense range covers the one-hop domain of the concern terminal.

In this paper, we have proposed a busy tone based MAC scheme in which a busy tone transmitter and busy tone receiver is used. Busy tone transmitter is associated at the receiver side and busy tone receiver associates with the transmitter side. Due to busy tone transmitter and receiver, the hidden nodes differs there transmission and exposed nodes senses the channel and can continue its ongoing transmission without doing any delay.

Solution to the Hidden Node Problem

When the receiver node wants to send the data frame, it first senses the carrier f it sense the carrier free, it sends the data or RTS frame to the receiver and simultaneously sends a busy tone to the busy tone transmitter, by sending the busy tone the carrier sensing range of the network increases and due to increased carrier sense all the hidden nodes corresponding to the receiver end postpones there transmission or differs there transmission until the ongoing transmission get finished.

Solution to the Exposed Node Problem

To resolve the exposed node problem, a busy tone receiver is associated with the transmitter end, when receiver node gets the data or RTS frame; it sends a busy tone to the busy tone receiver which is associated at the transmitter end. This busy tone works as acknowledgement or CTS.

After sending DATA frame, the sender senses the BTr medium. The status of a busy channel indicates that the DATA frame has been successfully received by the receiver; otherwise, a collision has occurred.

After simulating the network we have analyzed the throughput of the network and we have found that our scheme resolves the hidden and exposed terminal problems completely and the aggregate throughput of our scheme is higher than all the other schemes.

OPERATION PROCEDURE

The protocol operates as follows:

When a sender gets ready to transmit data, it first hears the medium for BTr to make firm that the intended recipient is not getting data from another "hidden" node currently. If intending receiver is not receiving from any other source, the sender sends a RTS frame to the intended receiver. Upon receiving this RTS frame, the receiver senses for BTt to make sure that the data it is expected to receive will not collide with another ongoing data transmission nearby. If BTt is not present, it replies with a CTS frame and turns on BTr until data is completely received. Upon receiving the CTS frame from the intended receiver, the sender begins data transmission and turns on BTt until data transmission is completed.

PERFORMANCE EVALUATION

Simulation Environment

The simulations are done in NCTUns 5.0 simulator. The NCTUns network simulator and emulator (NCTUns) is a high-fidelity and extensible network simulator having the capability of simulating various devices and protocols used in both wired and wireless networks.

TABLE 1. Corresponding Table 1 reperesents the parameters and there values which we have taken under consideration while simulating our results

Parameters	Value
Data Transmission Range	250 m
Data Interference Range	550m
RTS Threshold Value	300 Bytes
Data Packet Size	1400
Link Bandwidth	5.5 Mbps
Duration	70
Basic Rate(RTS/CTS) Transmission	2 Mbps

It uses a distributed architecture to support remote simulations and concurrent simulations. It uses open system architecture to enable protocol modules to be easily added to the simulator.

SIMULATION PARAMETERS

Results and Discussion

We evaluate the performance of the network under various topologies. The performance of the system is evaluated under certain topologies firstly then arbitrary topologies are simulated for more extensive evaluation. Figure 2 describes the hidden terminal problem in which node 1 and node 3 are sending data to node 2. In our scheme, node 3 waits until node completes its transmission. Figure 3 represents the exposed terminal problem, in our proposed system; nodes can send their data frames without waiting for the completion of the ongoing transmission.

Access delay has been calculated in our scheme by providing access delay measurement factor to various nodes in NCTUns simulator.

Figure 4 shows the access delay measurement. We have calculated the access delay at 5.5 Mbps of data rate. In our proposed system the access delay is calculated and it has shown that the access delay in our proposed scheme is lesser than the previous schemes.

Figure 2. The hidden terminal problem

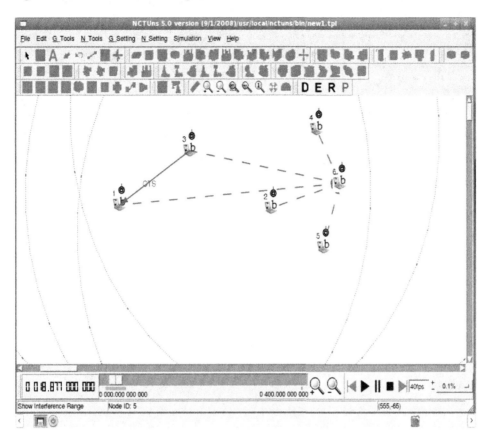

Figure 5 represents the time vs. access delay measurement for exposed nodes. We have calculated the access delay of the network after simulating the network and we found in our proposed scheme that the measurement of access delay in our scheme provides the better results.

Figure 6 represents the total throughput ratio of our proposed scheme and previous scheme.

CONCLUSION

In this paper, we identified the hidden and exposed terminal problems that are the main reason of performance degradation of the IEEE 802.11 MAC in

Figure 3. The Exposed Node Problem

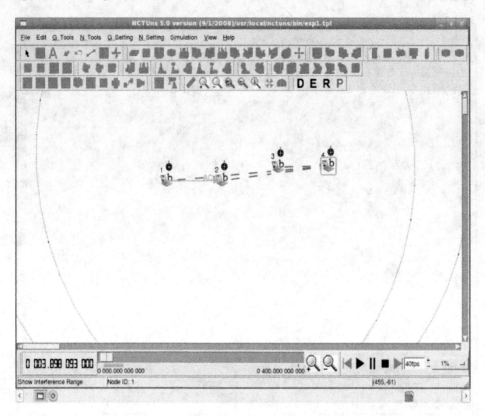

Figure 4. Time vs. Access Delay

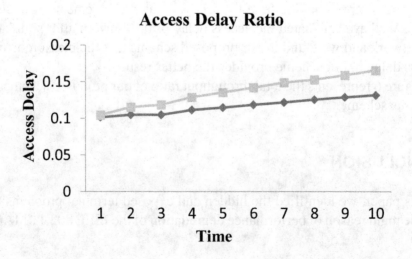

Figure 5. Time vs. Access Delay

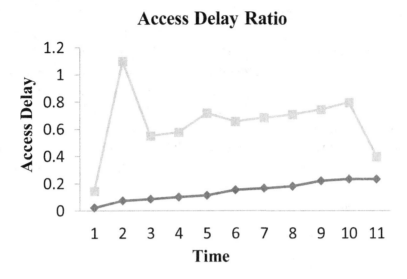

Figure 6. Time vs. Throughput

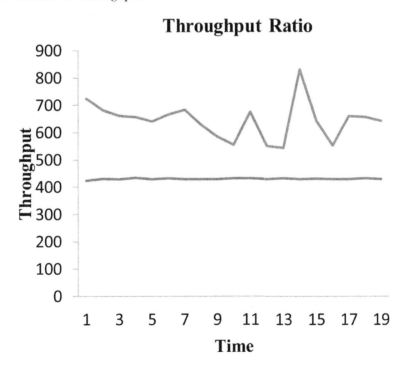

ad hoc networks, namely, the hidden terminal problem, the exposed terminal problem, To avoid these problems, we proposed a new MAC protocol which uses two channels, a busy tone signal is used to solve the hidden terminal problem. Our scheme resolves the hidden as well as exposed terminal problem. We have also considered the access delay parameter under consideration and we have shown that the total access delay of our proposed scheme is lesser than the all previous schemes. Here, we have used a dual busy tone based MAC protocol scheme to completely alleviate the hidden and exposed terminal problem and along with that we have calculated access delay of the network. We have done the access delay measurement in 1 Mbps and 2 Mbps data rate as well as 5.5 Mbps data rate and we found that our scheme provides better results as compare to other previous methods.

REFERENCES

Bharghavan, V., Demers, A., Shenker, S., & Zhang, L. (1994). MACAW: A Media Access Protocol for Wireless LAN. *Proceedings of ACM SIGCOM '94*, 212-225. 10.1145/190314.190334

Cesana, M., Maniezzo, D., Bergamo, P., & Gerla, M. (2003). Interference Aware (IA) MAC: an Enhancement to IEEE802.11b DCF. *Proceedings of IEEE Vehicular Technology Conference*. 10.1109/VETECF.2003.1286110

Cesana, M., Maniezzo, D., Bergamo, P., & Gerla, M. (2003). Interference Aware (IA) MAC: an Enhancement to IEEE802.11b DCF. *Proceedings of IEEE Vehicular Technology Conference*. 10.1109/VETECF.2003.1286110

Cesana, M., Maniezzo, D., Bergamo, P., & Gerla, M. (2003). Interference Aware (IA) MAC: an Enhancement to IEEE802.11b DCF. *Proceedings of IEEE Vehicular Technology Conference*. 10.1109/VETECF.2003.1286110

Choudhury, R. R., & Vaidya, N. (2004). Deafness: A MAC Problem in Ad Hoc Networks when using Directional Antennas. Proc. of IEEE ICNP. doi:10.1109/ICNP.2004.1348118

Chow & Leung. (1999). *Performance of IEEE 802.11 medium access control protocol over a wireless local area network with distributed radio bridges*. WCNC 1999, New Orleans, LA.

Gupta, P., & Kumar, P. R. (2000, March). The Capacity of Wireless Networks. *IEEE Transactions on Information Theory*, *46*(2), 388–404. doi:10.1109/18.825799

Haas, Z. J., & Deng, J. (2002). Dual Busy Tone Multiple Access (DBTMA): A Multiple Access Control Scheme for Ad Hoc Networks. *IEEE Transactions on Communications*, *50*(6), 975–985. doi:10.1109/TCOMM.2002.1010617

He, J., Kaleshi, D., Munro, A., Wang, Y., Doufexi, A., & McGeehan, J. (2005). Performance Investigation of IEEE 802.11 MAC in Multihop Wireless Networks. *Proceedings of the 8th ACM international symposium on Modeling, analysis and simulation of wireless and mobile systems*. 10.1145/1089444.1089487

He, Q., Cai, L., Shen, X., & Ho, P.-H. (2006). Improving TCP Performance over Wireless Ad Hoc Networks with Busy Tone Assisted Scheme. *EURASIP J. Wireless Comm. and Networking, Article ID, 51610,* 11.

IEEE 802.11 WG, Part 11: Wireless LAN Medium Access Control (MAC) and Physical Layer (PHY) Specification, Standard, IEEE, Aug. 1999.

IEEE Standards Department. (1999). *ANSI//IEEE Standard 802.11.* IEEE Press.

Jurdak, R., Lopes, C. V., & Baldi, P. (2004). A Survey, Classification and. Comparative Analysis of Medium Access Control Protocols for Ad. Hoc Networks. *IEEE Communications Surveys and Tutorials,* 6(1), 2–16. doi:10.1109/COMST.2004.5342231

Karn, P. (1990). MACA - A New Channel Access Method for Packet Radio. *ARRL/CRRL Amateur Radio 9th Computer Networking Conference,* 134-140.

Khamparia, A., & Pandey, B. (2015). Knowledge and intelligent computing methods in e-learning. *Int. J. Technol. Enhanc. Learn.,* 7(3), 221–242. doi:10.1504/IJTEL.2015.072810

Khamparia, A., & Pandey, B. (2016). Threat driven modeling framework using petri nets for e-learning system. *SpringerPlus,* 5(1), 446. doi:10.118640064-016-2101-0 PMID:27119050

Khamparia, A., & Pandey, B. (2017). A novel method of case representation and retrieval in CBR for e-learning. *Education and Information Technologies,* 22(1), 337–354. doi:10.100710639-015-9447-8

Khamparia, A., & Pandey, B. (2017). Effects of visual mapping placed game-based learning on students learning performance in defence-based courses. *Int. J. TechnologyEnhanced Learning,* 9(1), 37–50.

Khamparia, A., & Pandey, B. (2017). Comprehensive analysis of semantic web reasoners and tools: A survey. *Education and Information Technologies,* 22(6), 3121–3145. doi:10.100710639-017-9574-5

Khamparia, A., & Pandey, B. (2018). SVM and PCA Based Learning Feature Classification Approaches for E-Learning System. *International Journal of Web-Based Learning and Teaching Technologies,* 13(2), 32–45. doi:10.4018/IJWLTT.2018040103

Khamparia, A., & Pandey, B. (2018). Effects of visual map embedded approach on students learning performance using BriggsMyers learning style in word puzzle gaming course. *Computers & Electrical Engineering, 66*(C), 531–540. doi:10.1016/j.compeleceng.2017.12.041

Li, J., Blake, C., De Couto, D. S. J., Lee, H. I., & Morris, R. (2001). Capacity of Ad Hoc Wireless Networks. *7th ACM International Conference on Mobile Computing and Networking*, Rome, Italy.

Tobagi, F. A., & Kleinrock, L. (1975). Packet Switching inRadio Channels: Part II — The Hidden Terminal Problem inCarrier Sense Multiple-Access and the Busy-Tone Solution. *IEEE Transactions on Communications, 23*(12), 1417–1433. doi:10.1109/TCOM.1975.1092767

Wang, P., Jiang, H., & Zhuang, W. (2008). A New MAC Scheme supporting Multimedia Applications in Wireless Ad hoc networks. *IEEE Transactions on Mobile Computing, 7*(12).

Xu, Gerla, & Bae. (2003). Effectiveness of RTS/CTS handshake in IEEE 802.11 based ad hoc networks. *Journal of Ad Hoc Networks*, 107–123.

Ye, F., Yi, S., & Sikdar, B. (2003). Improving Spatial Reuse of IEEE 802.11. Based Ad Hoc Networks. *Proc. GLOBECOM 2003*.

Ye, F., Yi, S., & Sikdar, B. (2003). Improving Spatial Reuse of IEEE 802.11. Based Ad Hoc Networks. *Proc. GLOBECOM 2003*.

Chapter 7
Deep Learning:
An Overview and Innovative Approach in Machine Learning

Amit Sinha
ABES Engineering College, India

Suneet Kumar Gupta
Bennett University, India

Anurag Tiwari
Indian Institute of Technology (BHU), India

Amrita Chaturvedi
Indian Institute of Technology (BHU), India

ABSTRACT

Deep learning approaches have been found to be suitable for the agricultural field with successful applications to vegetable infection through plant disease. In this chapter, the authors discuss some widely used deep learning architecture and their practical applications. Nowadays, in many typical applications of machine vision, there is a tendency to replace classical techniques with deep learning algorithms. The benefits are valuable; on one hand, it avoids the need of specialized handcrafted features extractors, and on the other hand, results are not damaged. Moreover, they typically get improved.

DOI: 10.4018/978-1-5225-9096-5.ch007

INTRODUCTION

Deep Learning is a representation of learning with several features at different layers. These features are self-evolutionary and are produced after each iteration. The features re observed at each layer and are inter dependent on previous layer. Each feature may be an input for the next layer. It is an emerging technique and a procedure that incorporates ANN. Deep learning is one of the machine learning techniques that enables computers with lots of data and intermediate results that machine can analyze and provide justification for any answer.

Deep learning algorithm are used to apply on large amount of unsupervised data and provide different views of relationship or view of complex representation. Deep learning algorithms use the basic theory and concept of Artificial Intelligence and therefore these algorithms are able to emulate the human brain's ability to analyze, learn and able to make decision even in the case of complex problems.

It has a wide variety of applications in different field of learning and experiment. A model empaneled with deep learning methodology can perform classification tasks over images, texts, video or a combination of these. The models are trained by large amount of unsupervised data, follow the NN architecture and hence deep learning models are able to achieve accuracy at significant level that consider different aspects of result and accepted by larger end users.

Since it works on huge amount of data, a substantial computing power is required such as high performance GPU which may perform parallel computing. The parallel computing is one of major requirement for deep learning. As the data set is huge and the applications may be combined with clusters or cloud computing, the high performance computing tools reduce the training time for a deep learning network. The architecture of deep learning can generalize the learning patterns and trends beyond immediate neighbors in non-local and global ways.

The deep learning can be applied in several applications such as voice control in phones, blue tooth speakers, intelligent TVs and in agriculture sectors. One of the most recent applications of this learning is driver-less cars where car itself recognize stop-signs or distinguish a pedestrian from a lamppost.

This chapter provides an overall development and concepts of deep learning along with the use of this technology in agriculture especially the identification of crop disease.

Chapter Objectives

The main objective of Deep Learning is known as a process to learn a structure of attributes at different levels. This process can be entirely unsupervised and tries to learn from the attributes of the previous levels to obtain and rebuild the original data.

The chapter is written for understanding the DL approaches. The objectives of this chapter are focusing on following two points

1.   Concepts and features of DL
2.   Applications of DL in different sectors such as Agriculture.

The readers will definitely be benefited through its unique content towards different sections such as Recurring Themes of DL. The recurring themes involves dynamic Programming for supervised and unsupervised learning.

The understanding of Convolutional Neural Network (CNN) is one of the important aspects in DL and have various features. Thus, the objective of the chapter is very clear and is written in structured format.

Author Contribution

Amit Sinha (AS) and Suneet Kr. Gupta (SKG) conceived of the presented idea. AS developed the theory and performed the computations. Dr. Amrita Chaturvedi (AC) encouraged AS and Anurag Tiwari (AT) to investigate and supervised the findings of this work followed by a verification of the analytical methods. All authors discussed the results and contributed to the final manuscript.

AC, AT and SKG carried out the experiment and wrote the manuscript with support from AS. SKG and AS developed the theoretical formalism, performed the analytic calculations and the numerical simulations. Both AS and AT contributed to the final version of the manuscript. All authors provided critical feedback and helped the research, analysis and writing the manuscript.

Chapter Organization

The chapter is divided in six sections viz; Introduction, Deep Learning: A word of Technology, Recurring Themes of DL, DL in Agriculture Sector, Conclusion and References. Each section is divided in sub sections. The section 1 comprises of overall structure of the chapter such as chapter objectives, author contribution and chapter organization. Section 2 explains about the concepts, frameworks and challenges & opportunities in DL. This section creates a foundation for the readers. The section 3 contains the technical aspects of DL regarding Recurring Themes, Dynamic programming, Supervised & Unsupervised Learning and Convolution Neural Network Architecture. Section 4 tells about the application areas of DL. The use of DL in agriculture has been discussed with a concept over crop disease, its data sets and CNN for plant classification. The sections 5 and 6 are the conclusion and references. We have consulted the recent papers published in good journals.

DEEP LEARNING: A WORD ON TECHNOLOGY

The DL is a machine learning technique that learns features directly from data. The data can be images, text or sound. DL is often referred to as end-to-end learning, e.g. set of images is given and we have to recognize which category of objects they belong to- car, trucks or boats. DL algorithm learns how to classify input data and put these into different level of data.

Machine Learning Basics

Deep learning is a class of methods and techniques that extends functionalities of neural networks in context of increasing computing layers as well as different categories of activation functions. Deep learning is a kind of representation learning in which there are multiple levels of features. These features are automatically discovered and they are composed together in various levels to produce the output. Each level represents abstract features that are discovered from the features represented in the previous level. It is machine learning technique that teaches computers to do what comes naturally to human i.e., learn by example.

Deep learning algorithms use a huge amount of unsupervised data to automatically extract complex representation. These algorithms are largely motivated by the field of Artificial Intelligence, which has the general goal of emulating the human brain's ability to observe, analyze, learn, and make decisions, especially for extremely complex problems.

The deep Learning can be used in almost all areas. Few of the areas where several research activities are going on, are:

- Self-Driving Car
- Deep Learning in Health Care
- Voice Search & Voice Activated Assistants
- Automatic Image Caption Generation
- Deep Learning for Brain Cancer Detection
- Deep Learning in Finance
- Automatic Game Playing

Deep Learning Frame Work

Harnessing the work of the students and teachers and using it as the foundation for deeply supported collective capacity- building — accelerated by technology and enabled by systems — can exponentially expand our impact. The implementation framework shows how the pieces of this plan fit together (Figure 1).

Figure 1. Deep learning framework

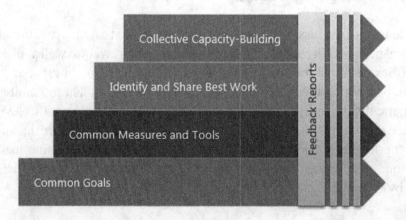

The framework is premised upon purposeful learning by doing, beginning with a small number of ambitious goals (as defined in this whitepaper). The next steps are to design a set of common measures and tools to be used across school clusters; to identify and share the best cases of new pedagogies and deep learning work; and for teachers to analyze, share and reflect on the best exemplars for both student work and learning activities as a key part of collective capacity-building efforts. Capacity-building will also be supported by ongoing measures of learning conditions and assessment outcomes, shared back with schools and teachers through frequent feedback reporting. Feedback reports and analysis will allow both schools and the global partnership to focus on developing the learning conditions that produce stronger learning activities and student work.

Literature Review

As deep learning algorithm works on huge and complex amount of data, high performance units such as GPUs are required to process it. This is again an important ingredient in case of clusters or cloud computing where the researchers demand for less training time with acceptable accuracy. Its architecture has both the patters and relationships at the local level and global level and it is beyond immediate neighbors. In recent years, this technology gives us a wide variety of research area that can be used in various applications such as voice control in consumer devices, TVs and hands free speakers, vegetables and crops. Deep learning is a key technology behind one of the most recent technology trends- driverless cars (Kamilaris, & Prenafeta-Boldú, 2018; Pawara, Okafor, Surinta, Schomaker, & Wiering, 2017; Picon, et al., 2018).

Challenges and Opportunities

Deep Learning approaches are significantly applicable over those computing problems which require high level of information abstraction from very large input data. Some common applications such as: Speech acoustics, Signal processing, big data analytics, Image Processing and NLP are based on subsequent applications of Deep Learning. Several deep Learning algorithms are inspired from human behavior and its ability to synchronize with surroundings for learning purpose. These algorithms progressively learn from behavior or type of input data and response according to past experience. Apart from all aforesaid rapid efficacy in learning, there are significant challenges in Deep Learning systems which we have to look out for.

- **Dealing With Huge Learning Data:** Conventionally, deep learning algorithms are developed for recognizing the behavior of huge input data. The tendency towards huge data application is based on coving maximum learning clauses to increase efficacy of algorithm so that it can precisely response in the case of new situations for which learning is not done. In this case, it is not easy to handle such large amount of input data because of certain limitations. For ex. Deep learning algorithms such as CNN and RNN are fascinated with wide range of input parameters and their tuning approaches. Obviously, it is a time consuming process to find best performing parameters sequence from a bundle of millions of images or temporal patterns.

  Copious amount of data is needed to make sure that the delivered machine response will minimize different empirical and expected risks caused by difference between actual ground truth and obtained results. If we want to train and learn a single language, the researchers need huge amount of data for the algorithm. It requires much time and high data processing capabilities. The speech recognition algorithm requires conversation, dialogue between two persons at different time. Therefore, solving a task through Deep Learning depends on the availability of large corpus of data on which the training can be done.

- **Performance on Unseen Data:** One of the challenges with deep learning is to improve the prediction over unseen data. The researchers found a difference between error encountered among training data and error observed in an unseen data set. They found this generally happened in the case of too many attributes corresponding to an application. The success of a deep learning algorithm depends on the ability to perform on an unseen data set with the similar performance on the training data set.

- **High Configured Hardware:** The requirement of high configured hardware is another challenge for the implementation of deep learning algorithm. This is due to large and complex amount of data with a variety of data sets. It generally applies for solving real world problem therefore it requires adequate processing speed (Series, Series, Peches, Statistiques, & Coleccion, 1980; Hall, McCool, Dayoub, Sunderhauf, & Upcroft, 2015; Rydahl, Jensen, Dyrmann, Nielsen, & Jørgensen, 2017). The GPUs and similar processing units may be one of the solution and necessary requirement for the implementation of deep learning algorithm.

- **Hyper Parameter Optimization:** Hyper parameters are the parameters which are apriori approximated before application of learning approaches (Tyagi, 2016; Kamilaris, Gao, Prenafeta-Boldú, & Ali, 2016; Mohanty, Hughes, & Salathé, 2016). Different learning algorithms comprise various range of hyper parameters such as ordinary least square requires no hypermeter while some complex learning algorithm LSTM and CNN requires more no. of parameters. These parameters are very sensitive for small update in input data which influences performance of proposed model rapidly.

- **Openness and Multitasking:** Deep Learning models can provide an efficient and accurate solution to a problem. It requires neural network architecture to make a platform for performing an experiment to solve a problem (LeCun & Bengio, 1995; Khamparia & Pandey, 2017; Xue, Zhang, & Dana, 2018). The researchers have provided several facts and results with respect to deep learning models so that it can perform multitask without the need of reworking on the whole architecture.

"There is no neural network in the world, and no method right now that can be trained to identify objects and images, play Space Invaders, and listen to music." This model work on this theme.

In recent era, some of AI developers are working over generalization as well as Multi-tasking learning problem of deep network. They are intending towards Progressive Neural Networks which requires minimum retraining and reassessment of working environment (Weaver & Marr, 2013; Johannes et al., 2017; Nagasubramanian et al., 2018).

Recently Google's Brain functioning AI developer team and University of Toronto presented a theoretical model of multi -Model as extension of neural network that is capable to deal vision, language and audio networks and simultaneously solve various related problems. They are concentrating over enhancement and covering more and more areas within same extension without compromising accuracy level.

RECURRING THEMES OF DEEP LEARNING

Artificial Intelligence is a discipline of Computer science, where machines are demonstrated with intelligence development schemes by deploying intelligent agents. Often these schemes are termed as blueprint of knowledge bases of application. Machine learning is a subset of Artificial Intelligence; which includes application of diverse set of statistical techniques for learning from patterns of data. It is also known as Experience learning. DL is a subset of Machine learning; which is based on natural training of algorithm and complex representation of data using multi layered neural network. Deep learning is more capable to process a long range of parameters present in an application as compared to machine learning. This is the reason why high training time is required to train procedures.

One major difference between Machine learning and DL is cascading of feature abstraction step and transformation schemes in implementation of data processing algorithm (Kitzes et al., 2008; Liaghat & Balasundram, 2010; Mohanty, Hughes, & Salathé, 2016; Reyes, Caicedo, & Camargo, 2015; Dyrmann, Jørgensen, & Midtiby, 2017). In Machine learning, algorithms learn from data patterns and then apply this learning over upcoming queries for estimation of precise decision where as Deep learning data patterns are recognized by using specific architecture network and provide capabilities to take decisions like human beings.

Dynamic Programming for Supervised Learning/ Reinforcement Learning

Now a days, a wide range of machine learning algorithms rely upon known status of ground truth of observations. Such type of learning algorithms come under supervised learning where a mapping function measures available patterns between ground truth and observation in a way such that

$$Y = f(X)$$

The goal is to approximate the mapping function so well that when you have new input data (x) that you can predict the output variables (Y) for that data. One main characteristic of supervised learning is that each input type has its own ground truth or response. Mathematically it can be represented as f(set of input parameters)=Response

Another class of learning algorithms specially designed for real time conditions where responses are initiated between object and its environment. Such type of learning is called as Reinforcement learning (RL) which allows interaction between a machine and its environment through a software agent. Agent collect responses from environment, decipher it and develop a roadmap for selecting appropriate action which is supported by environment (reward maximization).

To resolve a given interactive problem, a software agent invokes an action A(t) at discrete time stamp (t) against its environment and environment responses to software agent by giving reward R(t). This scenario is identified as S(t). In next iteration, software agent modifies its action and tries to get more optimal reward and this scenario continuous till best reward is gained.

Figure 2. Specification of mapping function in deep learning

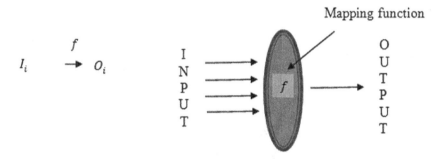

Figure 3. An interactive action-reward model between software agent and environment

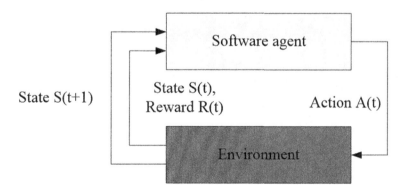

In order to boost performance of an application, RL is mostly determined in a specific context. The key characteristic of reinforcement learning is its reward dependent learning that tries to converge for a global optimum. The central idea behind vast application of RL in different research domains such as decision making, robotics, game theory and related fields is its strong knowledge abstraction mechanism corresponding to learning algorithms (Liaghat & Balasundram, 2010; Teke, Deveci, Haliloğlu, Gürbüz, & Sakarya, 2013; Ramcharan, 2017). In functionality, RL is different from supervised and unsupervised learning because it does not have ground truth available. It only focuses on performance gain in a given application. In subsequent sections, we will see reinforcement learning in details.

Back Propagation to Train Multilayer Architecture

A typical multilayer perceptron architecture is a class of artificial neural network where connections between layer distributed computing units forms a acyclic network. Such types of network are often termed as feed-forward

Figure 4. Multilayer perceptron architecture and its application to develop mapping function between i/p and o/p

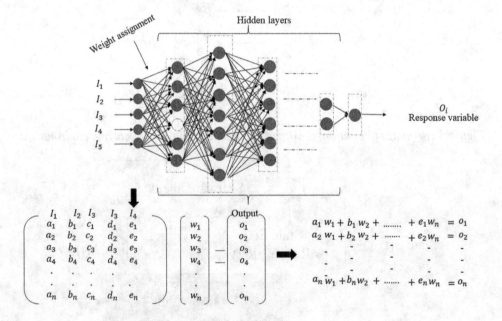

network. It consists of one input layer which intakes a set of input parameters, a set of hidden layers which process input parameters by applying weight vector and an output layer which shows output after processing.

Multilayer perceptron is a mathematical framework to solve complex computing problems such as regression and classification. The precision of the output obtained highly depends on learning of the network. There are a number of algorithms that are used for learning purpose. Let's discuss a popular learning algorithm known as "Back-propagation".

Back propagation is a specific learning algorithms which is commonly used in deep neural network where size of hidden layers is usually greater than three. The gist of back-propagation algorithm is based on relative change in error or cost function with respect to weight vector or bias. The definition of cost or error function is given as:

$$\text{Error function (C)} = \frac{1}{n} \sqrt[2]{\sum_{i=1}^{n} \left(o_i - e_i\right)^2} = \Delta w_{ji} = -\varepsilon \left[\frac{\delta E}{\delta w_{ji}}\right]$$

Back-Prop learning rule follow a chain learning mechanism to rewrite the error gradient for each pattern as the product of two partial derivatives. The first partial derivative shows the variations in error as a function of the net input while the second partial derivative shows the influence of a weight recasting on a small change in input variable. Thus, the error gradient can be formulated as:

$$\frac{\delta E_p}{\delta w_{ji}} = [{\delta E_p}\big/{\delta net_{pj}}][{\delta net_{pj}}\big/{\delta w_{ji}}]$$

As we know what the equation for the net input to a unit is, we can calculate the second partial derivative also

$${\delta net_{pj}}\big/{\delta w_{ji}} = \frac{\delta \sum_k w_{jk} o_{pk}}{\delta w_{ji}} = O_{pi}$$

We will call the negative of the first partial derivative the error signal:

$$d_{pj} = \frac{-\delta E_p}{\delta net_{pj}}$$

Thus, the appropriate change in the weight w_{ji} with respect to the error $\mathbf{E_p}$ can be written as

$$\Delta_p w_{ji} = \varepsilon d_{pj} o_{pj} \text{ where } \varepsilon \text{ is learning rate}$$

The last task in the derivation of the Back propagation learning rule is to find approximate value of d_{pj} for each unit in the network. However, to compute d_{pj} we need to again apply the chain rule. The error derivative d_{pj} can be rewritten as the product of two partial derivatives:

$$d_{pj} = -\left(\frac{\delta E_p}{\delta o_{pj}}\right)\left(\frac{\delta o_{pj}}{\delta net_{pj}}\right)$$

Consider the calculation of the second factor first. Since

$$o_{pj} = f\left(net_{pj}\right)$$

$$\frac{\delta o_{pj}}{\delta net_{pj}} = f\left(net_{pj}\right)$$

Convolution Neural Network Architecture (CNN)

Convolution neural network (CNN) is a specific class of deep feed forward neural network which is commonly applied in image processing. Similar to conventional neural network, CNN consists of one input layer, a set of hidden layers and one output layer to process input image (Kamilaris, Kartakoullis, & Prenafeta-Boldú, 2017; Dyrmann, Jørgensen, & Midtiby, 2017; Johannes, 2017; Zhang, Huang, & Zhang, 2018). Main difference between CNN and conventional neural network is architecture of hidden layer. In CNN, hidden layer is not only a channel of neuron layers but also distributed in four components: (1) convolution layers, (2) pooling layers, (3) fully connected layers and (4) normalized layers.

Figure 5. Architecture of convolution neural network

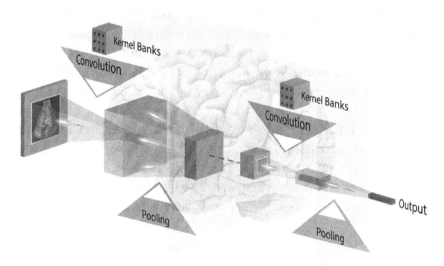

- **Convolution Layers:** Term convolution refers a mathematical operation which maps two input functions f and g and forms a new function h which may differ in functionality from its original input functions. Although definition of convolution operation is application specific but traditionally convolution operation is defined as:

$$(f(x) * g(\text{x})) \rightarrow \int\limits_{-\infty}^{\infty} f(\tau) g(x - \tau) d\tau$$

In convolution layer, convolution operation performs feature extraction from input image.

- **Pooling Layers:** The objective of pooling layer is to reduce dimension of input data which reduces computing time too. These two advantages do not modify generic characteristics of input data. The Pooling Layer performs its operations independently on every depth slice of the input data and resizes it according to application using the MAX operation (Rahnemoonfar & Sheppard, 2017; Khamparia & Pandey, 2017). Conventionally, pooling layer is applied with filters of size 2x2 with a stride of 2. It down samples every depth slice in the input by 2 along both width and height, discarding 75% of the activations. Every

MAX operation would in this case be taking a max over 4 numbers (small 2 x 2 regions in some depth slice). The depth dimension remains unchanged.

- **Fully Connected Layer:** The concept of fully connected layer is inherited from multi-layer perceptron based neural architecture. It states that every neuron in one layer is connected with every neuron in other layer.
- **Normalized Layers:** Normalization refers conversion of processed data into standard format such that it can improve performance of network and make network more stable because neural network is considered as an unstable network. The idea being that, instead of just normalizing the inputs to the network, we normalize the inputs to layers

Figure 6. Pooling procedure details in CNN

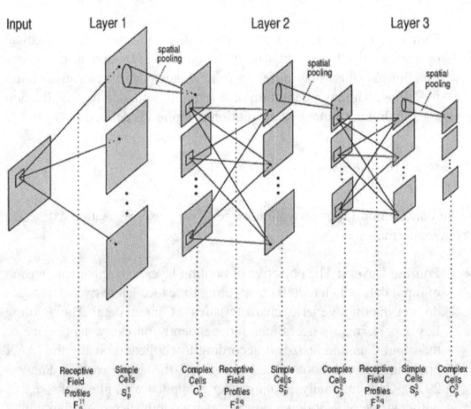

within the network. It's called "batch" normalization because during training, we normalize the activations of the previous layer for each batch, i.e. apply a transformation that maintains the mean activation close to 0 and the activation standard deviation close to 1 (Khamparia & Pandey, 2017; Khamparia & Pandey, 2018; Johannes et al., 2017). Some prominent advantages of this step are faster learning suitable initialization of weight vectors and make a scope of regularization if noise is added during normalization.

Image Understanding With Deep Convolution Network

Deep learning is rich in image handling approaches. Mostly deep learning uses fully connected neural network having greater than 3 layers for image processing. The traditional image processing steps are shown in Figure 7.

- **Deep Learning Applications in Image Processing:** Image processing term includes those approaches that enhance characteristics of input images by applying complex mathematical analysis through suitable image processing frameworks such as deep neural network and convolution neural network. To enhance characteristics, it surpasses existing noise in image and highlights processing specific features. Some deep learning-oriented steps in image processing include the factors shown in Table 1.

Figure 7. Prominent application of deep learning in image processing

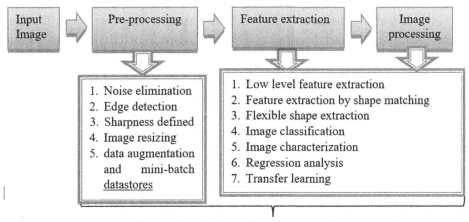

Prominent application of deep learning in image processing

Table 1. Prominent area and techniques to analyze the agricultural dataset

Objective	Prominent approaches
Image resizing	Scaling by factor, Scaling by aspect- ratio
Data augmentation	Bayesian Data Augmentation
Low level feature extraction	Robert cross, Smoothing and curve fitting etc
Feature extraction using shape extract	Image threshold, Image subtraction, Intensity template, Binary templates, Hough transform etc.
Regression analysis	Linear regression, Polynomial regression Support vector regression, Deep neural network

DEEP LEARNING IN AGRICULTURE

Due to availability of strong hardware i.e. GPUs, deep learning is so popular in today's scenario. There are various domains such as image processing, data analysis, prediction using time series data in agriculture where deep learning is successful.

Smart farming is the need of the world, as population has been increasing continuously day by day (Kitzes et al., 2008). Moreover, the smart farming is also so important to face the challenges related with farming such as environmental impact, productivity, food security and sustainability (Tyagi, 2016). As population has been increasing continuously then quantity of food must also increase (Series et al., 1980) with desired nutrition's across the globe with maintaining the natural eco-system. To face the challenges related with agriculture, it is desired that we should understand the farming eco-system by monitoring, gaging and examining continuously various physical aspects and phenomena related with agriculture. To handle the challenges related with farming, it is desired that an analysis of big agricultural data must be taken place (Kamilaris, Kartakoullis, & Prenafeta-Boldú, 2017) for short-scale crop/farm management as well as for larger-scale ecosystems' observation, enhancing the existing tasks of management and decision/policy making by context, situation and location awareness. The larger-scale observation is eased by means of airplanes, unmanned aerial vehicles and satellites by providing the images of the farming environments. This mechanism is better than to collect the information of large geographical area manually (Liaghat & Balasundram, 2010; Ozdogan, Yang, Allez, & Cervantes, 2010). Moreover, with the help of discussed methods, we get the data in the form of images or video and this data could address the variety of challenges (Liaghat & Balasundram, 2010; Ozdogan, Yang, Allez, & Cervantes, 2010). Hence, image and video analysis are one of important research area in the agriculture domain and intelligent data analysis techniques may use for identification/classification and anomaly detection in various farming applications (Teke, Deveci, Haliloğlu, Gürbüz, & Sakarya, 2013; Hall, McCool, Dayoub, Sunderhauf, & Upcroft, 2015; Sa, Ge, Dayoub, Upcroft, Perez, & McCool, 2016). With reference to agriculture domain, there is a discussion about prominent area and potential methods mentioned in Table 2.

Here, most of the popular methods have been discussed. Moreover, there is a discussion about various methods to collect the data. The most popular data collection techniques are satellite image data using satellite, thermal camera for thermal images and optical camera to collect the normal images. On these kinds of the data generally classification and regression analysis can be performed.

Table 2. Prominent area and techniques to analyze the agricultural dataset

Domain in Agriculture	Form of dataset	Techniques for data analysis
Expansion of agriculture	Satellite images	Filters using various transformation
Global warming	Thermal images using thermal camera	IR thermography, logistic/linear regression, classification
Irrigation	Hyper spectral imagine	Linear regression
Nitrogen content detection and solution in soil and leaf	Thermal and hyper spectral imaging	Regression techniques
Crop management	Images from satellite	Feature extraction, polarization, regression analysis, stepwise discriminate analysis
Drought conditions	Thermal imaging, satellite remote sensing, radar images	Linear regression, Frun holder Line Depth
Water management	Thermal imaging, satellite remote sensing, radar images	Linear regression, Frun holder Line Depth
Recognition of seed and spices	Thermal imaging, hyper spectral and multispectral imaging	Regression
Health monitoring of the crop	Images of leaf using regular camera	Classification
Weed detection	Photo detector, optical camera	Clustering, feature extraction, regression

Besides the machine learning techniques discussed in above table, a new paradigm is gaining the momentum known as DL (LeCun & Bengio, 1995). DL belongs to the machine learning domain and very similar to artificial neural network. To analyze the image-based data convolutional neural network (CNN) is used, which is the part of Deep learning. In CNN a convolution matrix is operated on the image data to learn the model.

Crop Disease and its Data Sets

To apply the Deep learning, it is desired that the size of the data of images should be very large. In some of the cases dataset consist the thousands of real images (Mohanty, Hughes, & Salathé, 2016; Reyes, Caicedo, & Camargo, 2015; Dyrmann, Jørgensen, & Midtiby, 2017). Moreover, some of the researchers also developed the synthetic data (Dyrmann, Jørgensen, & Midtiby, 2017; Rahnemoonfar & Sheppard, 2017). Beside it there are some other datasets are also available, which is originated from well-known and publicly-available datasets. The details of some of these datasets are presented in Table 3.

In following section, disease detection using deep learning in potato crop has been discussed. For the experimental purpose, the images of potato leaves have been downloaded for Plant Village ("Crops", n.d.).

Table 3. Agriculture relevance datasets

Data set	Description of dataset	Source
Plant village	The dataset consists images of various crop species such as Blueberry, Potato, Grape, Corn and Orange etc. In the dataset, there are 54,309 images and there are 38 classes. The dataset consists images of 4 bacterial diseases, 17 fungal diseases with 1 disease triggered by a mite.	https://www.plantvillage.org/en/crops. Accessed on 22 Sep. 2018
Leaf snap Dataset	This dataset consists the images of 185 tree species from North-eastern United States. The dataset consists two types of images: 23147 high quality augmented images and 7719 field images.	http://leafsnap.com/dataset/, accessed on 23-09-2018.
Image-Net Dataset	Image-Net dataset is developed by researchers of Princeton University. In this dataset, there are 1000 classes and consist images as per the word net hierarchy.	http://image-net.org/explore?wnid=n07707451
Flavia leaf dataset	This dataset consists 2520 images of 32 different plants.	http://flavia.sourceforge.net/ accessed on 23-09-2018
Crop/Weed Field Image Dataset	This dataset comprises field images, vegetation segmentation masks and crop/weed plant type annotations. The paper provides details, e.g. on the field setting, acquisition conditions, image and ground truth data format.	https://github.com/cwfid/dataset accessed on 23-09-2018

Disease Detection Using Deep Learning in Potato Crop

In this section, we represent how we use the deep learning to detect the disease in the potato crop by analysing the leaf of potato.

In terms of crop production, the potato is the third largest crop in the world after rice and wheat. There are 195 countries in the world and out of 195 125 countries cropping the potato. Moreover, there are more than 4000 native species over 180 wild spices of potato crop. The potato is important in our life as it is full with nutrition's including vitamin C, Potassium and deity fibre (Weaver & Marr, 2013). Generally, in potato crop, there are two different diseases 1) early blight and 2) late blight. The first disease is very common and occurring on the foliage at any stage of the growth. Due to this disease there are small black lesions on the leaf. Late blight disease damages the leaves, stem and tubers. The leaves are blistered and dry due to this disease.

Dataset for the Experiment

To detect the disease in the potato crop, a deep learning-based model has been proposed. Moreover, for the experimental purpose we have used data from plant village ("Crops", n.d.). There are more than 50000 images of 14 crops such as tomato, potato, soya been etc. For the experiment, we have used images related with potato. For the potato crop, images are available under three category 1) healthy 2) early blight and late blight. The sample images are depicted in figure 8.

Figure 8. The image of the potato crop

(a) (b) (c)

CNN for Plant Disease Classification

Due to high computational power (i.e. GPU), research community has explored the area of artificial intelligence (AI) in last decade. Moreover, the sub paradigm of AI named as deep learning is highly explored to develop the expert system. For the potato crop disease detection, a convolution neural network has been used. The architecture of this network is shown in Figure 9.

From figure 9, it is observed that there are 3 convolution and max-polling layers. The network takes input as image of size 128 * 128 with 3 channels i.e. Red, Green and Blue. In first hidden layer there are 32 convolution filters with size 3 * 3. The role of these filters to extract the key features of the image. After then max-polling layer is there and result of this layer is collection of images with size 64 * 64, as we have used 2 * 2 polling size. Similarly, we performed another two convolutions and max pooling operation (Xue, Zhang, & Dana, 2018; Zhang, Huang, & Zhang, 2018; Too, Yujian, Njuki, & Yingchun, 2018; Wang et al., 2018; Wang et al., 2018). After performing the flatten operation nodes relate to other 128 units. As there are 3 output classes so these 128 hidden nodes relate to 3 output nodes.

CONCLUSION

The deep learning techniques have various wings in each area. It has been demanded by researchers for their work. The prediction and analysis report

Figure 9. The architecture of the convolution neural network

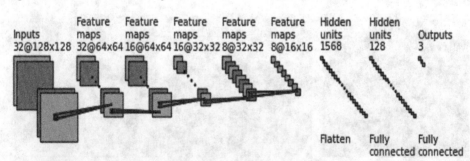

can be generated through CNN using Deep Learning approaches. Deep learning approaches have also been found to be suitable for agriculture field with successful applications to vegetables infection through plant disease. In this chapter, we discuss some widely-used deep learning architecture and their practical applications. Nowadays, in many typical applications of machine vision there is a tendency to replace classical techniques with deep learning algorithms. The benefits are valuable on one hand it avoids the need of specialized handcrafted features extractors and on the other hand, results are not damaged, moreover they typically get improved.

Deep learning is an example of representation learning where an object is characterized in terms of multiple levels of features set. These features set are automatically discovered from applications of different mathematical transformations and composed together in the various levels to produce the output. These levels are hierarchal distributed and each lower level derives corresponding features from the higher level derivable feature set. As an input stream, deep learning algorithms exploit corpus amount of unsupervised data to automatically abstract complex representation of available patterns. The prominent applications of these learning algorithms are frequently applied in artificial intelligence, which has the general goal of emulating the human brain's ability to observe, analyze, learn, and make decisions, especially for extremely complex problems. In deep learning, a computing model learns to perform classification tasks directly from images, text, or sound. The efficiency of proposed deep learning approach in a given application highly depends over spatial-temporal properties of input data. These properties are distributed among a set of complex layers and computing functions in a classification task. Models are trained by using a pair of suitable learning algorithm and extracted feature set. It requires substantial computing power, time other advance CPU supportable hardware's such as graphic processing unit (GPU), Field-Programmable Gate Arrays (FPGA) and Neural Processing Units (NPU).

These hardware's are commonly used as parallel architecture that is efficiently exploited for decomposing a complex problem into smaller segments. These segments are executed over described hardware's which enable development teams to gradually reduce learning time for a given deep learning network. It's predicted that many deep learning applications will affect our life in the near future. In contemporary researches, Internet of Things (IOT) is one of the noticeable field which is influencing our life in different ways from inside home to outside office environment. Within the next five to 10 years, deep learning development tools, libraries, and languages will become standard components of every software development toolkit. There is a lot of excitement around Artificial Intelligence along with its branch: Deep Learning at the moment.

REFERENCES

Amara, J., Bouaziz, B., & Algergawy, A. (2017). A Deep Learning-based Approach for Banana Leaf Diseases Classification. In BTW (Workshops) (pp. 79-88). Academic Press.

Barbedo, J. G. A. (2018). Impact of dataset size and variety on the effectiveness of deep learning and transfer learning for plant disease classification. *Computers and Electronics in Agriculture*, *153*, 46–53. doi:10.1016/j.compag.2018.08.013

Crops. (n.d.). Retrieved from https://www.plantvillage.org/en/crops

Dyrmann, M., Jørgensen, R. N., & Midtiby, H. S. (2017). RoboWeedSupport-Detection of weed locations in leaf occluded cereal crops using a fully convolutional neural network. *Advances in Animal Biosciences*, *8*(2), 842–847. doi:10.1017/S2040470017000206

Ferentinos, K. P. (2018). Deep learning models for plant disease detection and diagnosis. *Computers and Electronics in Agriculture*, *145*, 311–318. doi:10.1016/j.compag.2018.01.009

Hall, D., McCool, C., Dayoub, F., Sunderhauf, N., & Upcroft, B. (2015, January). Evaluation of features for leaf classification in challenging conditions. In *Applications of Computer Vision (WACV), 2015 IEEE Winter Conference on* (pp. 797-804). IEEE. 10.1109/WACV.2015.111

Itzhaky, Y., Farjon, G., Khoroshevsky, F., Shpigler, A., & Hillel, A. B. (2018). *Leaf counting: Multiple scale regression and detection using deep cnns*. Academic Press.

Johannes, A., Picon, A., Alvarez-Gila, A., Echazarra, J., Rodriguez-Vaamonde, S., Navajas, A. D., & Ortiz-Barredo, A. (2017). Automatic plant disease diagnosis using mobile capture devices, applied on a wheat use case. *Computers and Electronics in Agriculture*, *138*, 200–209. doi:10.1016/j.compag.2017.04.013

Kamilaris, A., Gao, F., Prenafeta-Boldú, F. X., & Ali, M. I. (2016, December). Agri-IoT: A semantic framework for Internet of Things-enabled smart farming applications. In *Internet of Things (WF-IoT), 2016 IEEE 3rd World Forum on* (pp. 442-447). IEEE. 10.1109/WF-IoT.2016.7845467

Kamilaris, A., Kartakoullis, A., & Prenafeta-Boldú, F. X. (2017). A review on the practice of big data analysis in agriculture. *Computers and Electronics in Agriculture*, *143*, 23–37. doi:10.1016/j.compag.2017.09.037

Kamilaris, A., & Prenafeta-Boldú, F. X. (2018). Deep learning in agriculture: A survey. *Computers and Electronics in Agriculture*, *147*, 70–90. doi:10.1016/j. compag.2018.02.016

Kanehisa, M., Goto, S., Furumichi, M., Tanabe, M., & Hirakawa, M. (2009). KEGG for representation and analysis of molecular networks involving diseases and drugs. *Nucleic Acids Research, 38*(suppl_1), D355-D360.

Khamparia, A., & Pandey, B. (2017, January). A novel method of case representation and retrieval in CBR for e-learning. *Education and Information Technologies, Vol, 22*(1), 337–354. doi:10.100710639-015-9447-8

Khamparia, A., & Pandey, B. (2018). SVM and PCA Based Learning Feature Classification Approaches for E-Learning System. *International Journal of Web-Based Learning and Teaching Technologies*, *13*(2), 32–45. doi:10.4018/ IJWLTT.2018040103

Kitzes, J., Wackernagel, M., Loh, J., Peller, A., Goldfinger, S., Cheng, D., & Tea, K. (2008). Shrink and share: Humanity's present and future Ecological Footprint. *Philosophical Transactions of the Royal Society of London. Series B, Biological Sciences*, *363*(1491), 467–475. doi:10.1098/rstb.2007.2164 PMID:17652075

LeCun, Y., & Bengio, Y. (1995). Convolutional networks for images, speech, and time series. The Handbook of Brain Theory and Neural Networks, 3361(10), 1995.

Liaghat, S., & Balasundram, S. K. (2010). A review: The role of remote sensing in precision agriculture. *American Journal of Agricultural and Biological Sciences*, *5*(1), 50–55. doi:10.3844/ajabssp.2010.50.55

Mohanty, S. P., Hughes, D. P., & Salathé, M. (2016). Using deep learning for image-based plant disease detection. *Frontiers in Plant Science*, *7*, 1419. doi:10.3389/fpls.2016.01419 PMID:27713752

Nagasubramanian, K., Jones, S., Singh, A. K., Singh, A., Ganapathysubramanian, B., & Sarkar, S. (2018). *Explaining hyperspectral imaging based plant disease identification: 3D CNN and saliency maps.* arXiv preprint arXiv:1804.08831

Ozdogan, M., Yang, Y., Allez, G., & Cervantes, C. (2010). Remote sensing of irrigated agriculture: Opportunities and challenges. *Remote Sensing, 2*(9), 2274–2304. doi:10.3390/rs2092274

Pawara, P., Okafor, E., Surinta, O., Schomaker, L., & Wiering, M. (2017, February). *Comparing Local Descriptors and Bags of Visual Words to Deep Convolutional Neural Networks for Plant Recognition.* ICPRAM. doi:10.5220/0006196204790486

Picon, A., Alvarez-Gila, A., Seitz, M., Ortiz-Barredo, A., Echazarra, J., & Johannes, A. (2018). Deep convolutional neural networks for mobile capture device-based crop disease classification in the wild. *Computers and Electronics in Agriculture.* doi:10.1016/j.compag.2018.04.002

Rahnemoonfar, M., & Sheppard, C. (2017). Deep count: Fruit counting based on deep simulated learning. *Sensors (Basel), 17*(4), 905. doi:10.339017040905 PMID:28425947

Ramcharan, A., Baranowski, K., McCloskey, P., Ahmed, B., Legg, J., & Hughes, D. P. (2017). Deep learning for image-based cassava disease detection. *Frontiers in Plant Science, 8*, 1852. doi:10.3389/fpls.2017.01852 PMID:29163582

Reyes, A. K., Caicedo, J. C., & Camargo, J. E. (2015, September). Fine-tuning Deep Convolutional Networks for Plant Recognition. CLEF (Working Notes).

Rydahl, P., Jensen, N. P., Dyrmann, M., Nielsen, P. H., & Jørgensen, R. N. (2017). RoboWeedSupport-Presentation of a cloud based system bridging the gap between in-field weed inspections and decision support systems. *Advances in Animal Biosciences, 8*(2), 860–864. doi:10.1017/S2040470017001054

Sa, I., Ge, Z., Dayoub, F., Upcroft, B., Perez, T., & McCool, C. (2016). Deepfruits: A fruit detection system using deep neural networks. *Sensors (Basel), 16*(8), 1222. doi:10.339016081222 PMID:27527168

Sladojevic, S., Arsenovic, M., Anderla, A., Culibrk, D., & Stefanovic, D. (2016). Deep neural networks based recognition of plant diseases by leaf image classification. *Computational Intelligence and Neuroscience*. PMID:27418923

Teke, M., Deveci, H. S., Haliloğlu, O., Gürbüz, S. Z., & Sakarya, U. (2013, June). A short survey of hyperspectral remote sensing applications in agriculture. In *Recent Advances in Space Technologies (RAST), 2013 6th International Conference on* (pp. 171-176). IEEE. 10.1109/RAST.2013.6581194

Too, E. C., Yujian, L., Njuki, S., & Yingchun, L. (2018). A comparative study of fine-tuning deep learning models for plant disease identification. *Computers and Electronics in Agriculture*. doi:10.1016/j.compag.2018.03.032

Tyagi, A. C. (2016). Towards a second green revolution. *Irrigation and Drainage*, *65*(4), 388–389. doi:10.1002/ird.2076

Wang, J., Chen, L., Zhang, J., Yuan, Y., Li, M., & Zeng, W. (2018, August). CNN Transfer Learning for Automatic Image-Based Classification of Crop. In *Image and Graphics Technologies and Applications: 13th Conference on Image and Graphics Technologies and Applications, IGTA 2018, Beijing, China, April 8–10, 2018, Revised Selected Papers* (*Vol. 875*, p. 319). Springer. 10.1007/978-981-13-1702-6_32

Weaver, C., & Marr, E. T. (2013). White vegetables: a forgotten source of nutrients: Purdue roundtable executive summary. *Advances in Nutrition*, *4*(3), 318S–326S. doi:10.3945/an.112.003566 PMID:23674800

Xue, J., Zhang, H., & Dana, K. (2018, March). Deep Texture Manifold for Ground Terrain Recognition. In *Proceedings of the IEEE Conference on Computer Vision and Pattern Recognition* (pp. 558-567). IEEE. 10.1109/CVPR.2018.00065

Zhang, S., Huang, W., & Zhang, C. (2018). Three-channel convolutional neural networks for vegetable leaf disease recognition. *Cognitive Systems Research*.

Chapter 8

Delay Tolerant Networks Architecture, Protocols, and Its Application in Vehicular Ad–Hoc Networks

Vijander Singh
Amity University Rajasthan, India

Linesh Raja
https://orcid.org/0000-0002-3663-1184
Amity University Rajasthan, India

Deepak Panwar
Amity University Rajasthan, India

Pankaj Agarwal
Amity University Rajasthan, India

ABSTRACT

Due to the high mobility of vehicular nodes in VANETs, there are high chances of partitions in the network. In such a situation, the protocols developed for VANETs cannot work well and an alternative network known as DTN (delay tolerant network) is capable enough to deal with VANET characteristics. The network which does not need any immediate data delivery and can wait for time and delivery of data is known as DTN. The concept of hold and forward the message is exploited by DTN. In this chapter, the authors are providing characteristics, architecture, and applications of delay tolerant vehicular ad-hoc networks.

DOI: 10.4018/978-1-5225-9096-5.ch008

INTRODUCTION

Due to high mobility of vehicular nodes in VANETs there are high chances of partitions in the network. In such situation the protocols developed for VANETs cannot work well and an alternative network known as DTN (Delay Tolerant Network) (Tornell, Calafate, Cano, & Manzoni, 2015; Singh, V, 2018) is capable enough to deal with VANET characteristics. This chapter describes the various features of DTN concentrating on those which effect most to the routing and forwarding protocols implementation e.g. path selection, network architectures and end node resource constraints.

Background

VANET routing protocols are categorized in two categories: geographic routing and topology-based. The former routing also known as DTN based routing protocols which uses neighboring location information for packet forwarding. The later on other researchers used the information about routes that exist in the network for packet forwarding. The FFRDV (Yu & Ko, 2009), DAER (Huang, Shu, Li & Wu 2008), VADD (Zhao & Cao 2008) and GeOpps (Leontiadis, I., & Mascolo, C. 2007) etc. are the important examples of DTN based VANET routing protocols. The violation of speed limit is a common issue on highways. The frequent network partitioning and infrastructure free environment (Little, T. D., & Agarwal, A. 2005) caused by high speed of vehicles poses a serious challenge to communication in VANET. To have a sigh of relief, the movement of motion can be predicted by the roads and digital city map in VANETs. The focus of the present study aims to provide an efficient routing technique for Delay Tolerant Vehicular Ad-hoc Networks. The network which do not need any immediate data delivery and can wait for time and delivery of data are known as DTN. The concept of hold & forward the message (Karimzadeh, M. 2011, Shen, J., Moh, S., & Chung, I. 2008, Bernsen, J., & Manivannan, D. 2008) is exploited by DTN.

According to the literature review study, most of the researchers focused on the traditional ad-hoc network based routing, while some others focused on delay/ disruption tolerant enabled protocols (Benamar, N., Benamar, M., & Bonnin, J. M. 2012) in VANETs.

In the year of 2012 Ashish Agarwal et al. in their paper (Agarwal, A., Starobinski, D., & Little, T. D. 2012) identified that when multihop connection is present, messages travel at the speed of radio over routed vehicles. On the other hand, when vehicles are not in the range of each other, messages are carried by vehicles and travel at vehicle's speed. The objective is to analyze and determine what benefits are gained by "DTN" architecture and under what circumstances, using the average message propagation speed as the primary metric of interest.

In the year of 2007, Z. Zhang, Q.Zhang in their research paper (Zhang, Z., & Zhang, Q. 2007) stated that routing is one of the most important components in "DTNs" and a lot of attention has been paid to the message ferry (MF) approach which ultimately supports routing in "DTNs". An overview on latest techniques including multicast support, message ferrying, transport layer issues and inter-region routing etc. has been provided in this research paper.

L.R. Amondaray and J.S. Pascual presented a framework for simulation (Romero Amondaray, L., & Seoane Pascual, J. 2008) of the "DTN" architecture and discovered the applicability of "DTN" to real scenarios found in projects of the Spanish-American Health Link Program ("EHAS").

Delay Tolerant Networks (DTNs) are applied in several working situation, including those which are subjected to disconnection and disruption as well as one with long delay, like Vehicular ad-hoc networks. Messages in DTNs are delivered to receiver in absence of end-to-end connection through retransmission, store and forward for the application which are capable enough to tolerate the delay. The choice of selecting a routing algorithm for DTN is still under study. The primary aim of routing protocol in DTN is to increase the possibility of deliver a packet (PDF) to receiver, while decrease end-to-end delay . Vehicular ad-hoc networks are different from Mobile ad-hoc network in the manner that in VANETs several independent nodes are moving with rich external helping data available and higher mobility in presence of managed and defined pattern, dynamically alteration of network topology, rapid partitioning of network and different behavior factor of driver. Mobile hosts also need to operate as router in order to maintain network connectivity without the presence of centralized entities like base station. Thus, various protocols for VANETs have been developed but only few studies were based on how the specific mobility pattern of vehicles may affect the application and performance of protocols.

Among available several applications in VANETs, many important applications including safety of traffic and auto pilot cars applications demand time restraint communication in ad-hoc wireless networks. These applications are generally termed as real-time applications. The non-real time applications like reservation at parking area, traffic management, information propagation related to any incident and query for queue length at nearby petrol pump/filling station are implemented over DTNs. Nodes with higher mobility without central administrative control are responsible for collide of packets in wireless medium and frequent disconnection of network in the communication of VANETs which causes frequent delays in delivery of packets and dropping of packets on contention medium. It is easy to discourage the real-time communication in this environment (Jerbi, M., Senouci, S. M., & Ghamri-Doudane, Y. 2006). Hence, there is an indeed requirement to propose an efficient technology to minimize end-to-end delay for time-sensitive applications over the DTNs.

CHARACTERISTICS OF DTNS

To discuss the routing problem, there is a need of a model capturing the most important characteristics (Karimzadeh, M. 2011) of a DTN network. This section describes the various features of DTN concentrating on those which effect most to the routing and forwarding protocols implementation e.g. path selection, network architectures and end node resource constraints.

Connections Are Not Steady

One of the most essential attributes of DTNs is that, there is no end to end association exists between source and destination. Usually the reason for such connections which are not steady may be a fault in a network or not. If the disconnection is not by fault occurrence then in mobile environment it can be due to i) mobility and ii) short duty cycle of system in operation. Intermittent connection as a result of mobility depends on predictability or can be fully opportunistic. In the latter case nodes come to the coverage area of each other due to their random movement or due to movement of other objects (Shen, J., Moh, S., & Chung, I. 2008, Bernsen, J., & Manivannan, D. 2008).

End-to-End Delay and Low Data Rate

End-to-End Delay is the total time taken by the source to place the packet on the link and the successful reception of the packet at its destination. There are number of applications having advantages by using short delivery times. This end-to-end delay comprises of transmission, processing, propagation time over all connections and additionally delays in queues at every hop along the way. In DTNs, transmission rates are often relatively small and End-to-End delay can be large. Additionally, data transmission rates can also be largely asymmetric in uplinks and downlinks.

Queuing Delay

The queuing delay is the time it takes to deplete the queue of messages ahead of the labeled one. The queuing delay relies on upon data rate and the measure of traffic traversing network. In "DTNs" where it is rather common that there is a disconnected end-to-end path, the queuing time could be very long, e.g. several minutes, several hours or even several days.

Resource Limitation

Nodes in "DTNs" often have extremely restricted energy sources either due to their mobile nature or on the grounds that the power grid is not available in their general vicinity of area. End system expends energy by sending, receiving, storing of messages and by performing route discovering and processing.

Limited Longevity

In some "DTNs", end nodes may be deployed in unfriendly situations. This is particularly valid for sensor systems, military utilizations of "DTNs" and interconnected devices used by emerged personnel. In such cases, interconnected nodes may be separated and not be supposed to survive for long duration. Reviewing that the end-to-end path between any source and destination may not exist for a large amount of time, there could be the situation when the delay of message transmission/delivery may surpass the lifetime of a transmitter node. As a result the end system should not be made responsible for reliable delivery of data using classic transport layer protocols such as TCP.

Security

"DTNs" are unprotected against numerous evil and bring various new security and safety challenges. The exceptional possibilities for security attacks including impairing information integrity, authenticity, user privacy and system performance are happen by the use of intermediate nodes as relay nodes. The use of specific routing mechanisms including flooding-based ones may even increase the risks associated with inserting false information into the network. Extra traffic injected by malicious nodes creates another serious threat due to resource scarcity of DTNs in some application scenarios.

DTN ARCHITECTURE

To support the delay tolerant applications there should be an architecture which must be followed by all the nodes and intermediate networks. As V.Cerf et al. proposed in (Cerf, V., Burleigh, S., Hooke, A., Torgerson, L., Durst, R., Scott, K. & Weiss, H. 2007), the RFC4838 (regarding DTN Architecture) is a general architecture to prevail over all the earlier challenges based on store-and-forward strategy. Architecture of DTN is depends on asynchronous messaging and uses the basic service model of the postal mail for delivery semantics. It provides a new approach to ensure end-to-end reliability in frequently partitioned networks and proposes a secure network infrastructure model which prevents unauthorized access.

Blocks of applications data, known as bundles, are transmitted from the source to storage memory of another intermediate node, which take the accountability for reliable delivery of the bundle to its destination or another intermediate node, these nodes are called custodians. The bundle may move along a path of custodians that finally reaches the destination as shown in Figure 1.

- **Source:** The node which originates data is known as source.
- **Custodian:** The intermediate node which helps in forwarding the data is known as custodian node. Custodians allow the source, or the previous custodian, to free their resources (such as bandwidth, memory etc.) soon because the next custodian gets the responsibility of retransmission. As shown in Figure 2, it is not necessary that all the

Figure 1. Bundle movement in DTN

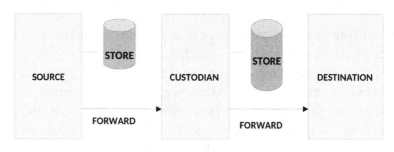

Figure 2. DTN Layers

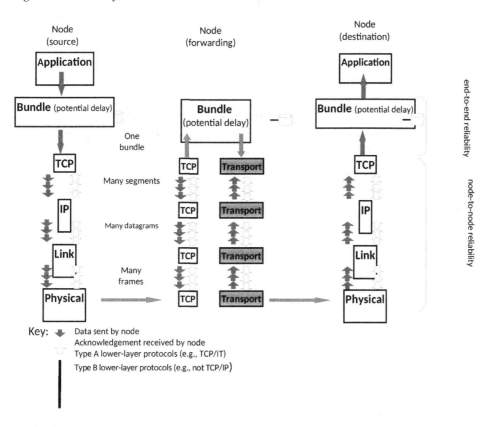

nodes in a DTN should accept custody. Having a custody means one need to share some resources related to retransmission, may be for a long duration of time. Some nodes may not have enough resources to take the custody of a bundle and would only act as forwarders.

- **Destination:** The node to which data must be reached is called destination node.
- **Store:** Any intermediate node or source node can store data if the next node is not present/ready immediately.
- **Bundles:** The bundle layer over the transport layer as shown in Figure 2, provides store-and-forward service using intermediate nodes as storage, and provides similar functionality as provided by the network layer of gateways. It differs from network layer because it is layer-atheist and focuses on bundle forwarding instead of packet switching. DTN architecture provides interoperability between underlying networks and protocols specific to each network. Underlying networks can have their own protocol stack. The convergence layer is defined by DTN protocols.

Bundle Protocol (BP)

The situation in the networks where frequent network partitions and congestion occurs, a DTN is the solution which provides communication through its end-to-end architecture. Networking environment suffering with congestion include those with variable or large delay, broken connectivity and high bit error rates. BP (Warthman Forrest. 2003, Cerf V., Burleigh S., Hooke A., Torgerson L., Durst R., Scott K. & Weiss H. 2007) and (Scott, K., & Burleigh, S. 2007) resides at the application layer of constituent internets, forming a store-carry-and-forward overlay network. Key potentials of Bundle Protocol (BP) include:

Figure 3. Custody may not be hop-by-hop

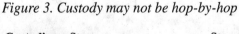

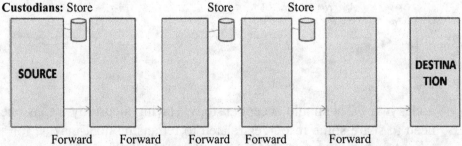

- **Retransmission:** Custody-based
- **Synchronization:** Possible with intermittent connectivity
- BP can take continuous connectivity
- Delay in binding of overlay network endpoint identifiers to constituent internet addresses.

Bundle Format

The format of a bundle and its specifications are described in RFC 5050 (Scott, K., & Burleigh, S. 2007). According to this RFC each bundle consists of a linked sequence of block structures, there should be at least two blocks in a bundle. The first block must be a primary bundle block in this sequence. There cannot be more than one primary bundle block in a single bundle. More support to the bundle protocol can be provided through Bundle Security Protocol (BSP), additional bundle protocol blocks of other types by following the primary block. At a time only one of the blocks may be a payload block. The last block must have the "last block" flag (in its block processing control flags) set to 1. This flag must be set to "0" for every other block in the bundle after the primary block.

Bundle Processing Control Flags

As K.Scott et.al. proposed the RFC 5050 in (Scott, K., & Burleigh, S. 2007) about Bundle Processing Control flags, that the bundle processing control flags field as shown in Table 1 is an SDNV (self-delimiting numeric values) in the primary bundle block of each bundle. A string of bits encoded in this SDNV is used to invoke selected bundle processing control features.

The bits in positions 0 through 20 given in Table 1 and characterize the bundle as follows (Table 2).

Table 1. Bundle Processing Control Flags Bit Layout

20 19 18 17 16 15 14 13 12 11 10 9 8 7 6 5 4 3 2 1 0		
Status Report	Class of Service	General

Table 2. Bundle Processing Control Flags Bit Description

Bit Group	Group Name	Bit	Description
0-6	Flags	0	Bundle is fragmented
		1	Unit of application is an administrative record
		2	Bundle should avoid fragmented
		3	Request for custody transfer
		4	Destination endpoint is a singleton
		5	Request for acknowledgement by application
		6	Can be used in future
7-13	Class of service of bundle	7,8	Priority of bundle 00-Bulk 01-Normal 10-Expediated 11-Reserved for future use
		9-13	Reserved for future use
14-20	Status report request flags	14	Request reporting of bundle reception
		15	Request reporting of custody acceptance
		16	Request reporting of bundle forwarding
		17	Request reporting of bundle delivery
		18	Request reporting of bundle deletion
		19,20	Reserved for future use

Block Processing Control Flags

The block processing control flags field as shown in Table 3 (Scott, K., & Burleigh, S. 2007) in each block is an SDNV excluding the primary bundle block. A string of bits encoded in this SDNV is used to invoke selected block processing control features.

The bit positions and their description is given in Table 4.

Table 3. Block Processing Control Flags Bit Layout

6 5 4 3 2 1 0						
Flags						

Table 4. Block Processing Control Flags Bit Description

Bit	Description
0	Block must be replicated in every fragment.
1	Transmit status report if block cannot be processed.
2	Delete bundle if block cannot be processed.
3	Last block.
4	Discard block if it cannot be processed.
5	Block was forwarded without being processed.
6	Block contains and EID-reference field.

Formats of Bundle Blocks

The format of the two basic BP blocks is shown in Table 6 and Table 7 and field description is given in Table 5.

The bundle payload block is divided into four different blocks (Zhang, Z., & Zhang, Q. 2007), which are shown in Table 7 and its field description is given in Table 8.

IMPORTANCE OF DTN IN VEHICULAR AD-HOC NETWORKS

Delay tolerant Networks (DTNs) are the networks where continuous end-to-end connectivity cannot be assumed. DTN protocols often employ a store-and-carry forwarding strategy. Using such a strategy, vehicles do not drop the packets when the connection is broken. Instead, they continue to carry the packet while moving and wait for a suitable node to forward the packet i.e., a packet is forwarded and stored from host to host along a path until the packet reaches its destination. Since more delays are incurred in DTNs due to the store-carry-forward mechanism, it becomes quite important for a current vehicle to select the next suitable intermediate vehicle that can deliver a packet to its destination as soon as possible without any further delay.

In many commercial applications and in road safety systems, vehicular delay-tolerant networks have been envisioned to be useful. The Delay-Tolerant Networking Research Group (DTNRG) was created to address the architectural

Table 5. Primary Bundle Block fields description

Name of field	Description regarding the value(s) the field contains.
Version	1-Byte field indicate the version of the bundle protocol. The present bundle protocol version is 0x06
Processing Flags	It contains the bundle processing control flags.
Block Length	It holds the value of the aggregate length of all remaining fields of the block.
Destination Scheme Offset	It contains the offset within the dictionary byte array of the scheme-name of the endpoint ID of the bundle's destination that is the endpoint containing the node(s) at which the bundle is to be delivered.
Destination SSP Offset	It contains the offset within the dictionary byte array of the scheme-specific part of the endpoint ID of the destination of the bundle.
Source Scheme Offset	It contains the offset within the dictionary byte array of the scheme name of the endpoint ID of the nominal source of the bundle.
Source SSP Offset	It contains the offset within the dictionary byte array of the scheme-specific part of the endpoint ID of the nominal source of the bundle.
Report-to SSP Offset	It contains the offset within the dictionary byte array of the scheme-specific part of the ID of the endpoint to which status report pertaining to the forwarding and delivering of this bundle are to be transmitted.
Custodian Scheme Offset	It contains the offset within the dictionary byte array of the scheme name of the current custodian endpoint ID.
Custodian SSP Offset	It contains the offset within the dictionary byte array of the scheme-specific part of the current custodian endpoint ID.
Creation Timestamp	It contains the creation time and sequence number of the bundle.
Lifetime	It contains the time at which payload of bundle will no longer be useful
Dictionary Length	It contains the length of the dictionary byte array.
Dictionary	It is an array of bytes formed by concatenating the null-terminated scheme names and SSPs of all endpoint IDS.
Fragment Offset	Indicate the offset from the start of the original application data unit at which the byte comprising the payload of this bundle were located.
Total Application Data Unit Length	Total length of the original application data unit of which this bundle's payload is a part.

and protocol design principles needed for interconnecting networks operating in environments where continuous end-to-end connectivity is sporadic. Although most of the existing work on vehicle networks is limited to 1-hop or short range multihop communication, vehicular delay-tolerant networks are useful to other scenarios. Vehicle delay-tolerant networks have many applications, such as delivering advertisements and announcements regarding sale information or remaining stocks at a department store. Information such as the available parking spaces in a parking lot, the meeting schedule at a conference room, and the estimated bus arrival time at a bus stop can also be

Table 6. Primary Bundle Block

31 30 29 28 27 26 25 24 23 22 21 20 19 18 17 16 15 14 13 12 11 10 9 8 7 6 5 4 3 2 1 0	
Version	Proc. Flags
Block Length	
Destination scheme offset	Destination Scheme Specific Part (SSP) offset
Source scheme offset	Source SSP offset
Report-to scheme	Report-to SSP offset
Custodian scheme offset	Custodian SSP offset
Creation Timestamp time	
Creation Timestamp sequence number	
Lifetime	
Dictionary Length	
Dictionary byte array (variable)	
Fragment offset	
Total application data unit length	

Table 7. Bundle Payload Block

31 30 29 28 27 26 25 24 23 22 21 20 19 18 17 16 15 14 13 12 11 10 9 8 7 6 5 4 3 2 1 0		
Block Type	Proc. Flags	Block Length
Bundle Payload (Variable)		

Table 8. Bundle Payload Block field description

Block Partition	Description
Block Type	1-Byte field indicate the type of block
Block Processing Control Flags	It contains the block processing control flags
Block Length	It contains the aggregate length of all remaining fields of the block (Bundle Payload).
Bundle Payload	Application data carried by this bundle

delivered by vehicle delay-tolerant networks. With a vehicular delay-tolerant network, the requester can send the query to the broadcast site and get a reply from it. In these applications, the users can tolerate up to a minute of delay as long as the reply eventually returns.

DTNS APPLICATIONS

Delay tolerant networks are used in variety of applications (Tornell, S. M., Calafate, C. T., Cano, J., & Manzoni, P. 2015). Some of the applications particularly in "VANETs" are discussed as follows:

- **Peer-to-Peer Communication:-**All communication systems must be able to allow the users to communicate with each other through exchange of messages. So most of the communication applications emphasize on P2P architecture. For the use of geographic protocols (Cao, Y., & Sun, Z. 2013) for P2P communication it is important for the sender to have information about the location of the receiver, which is possible by using location service. E-mail system is the best example of P2P communication by which clients communicate through message exchange. But user of the e-mail system application is small as compared to vehicular network. To ensure the delivery in VN, V2V and V2I combination is best approach for P2P application. The sender to receiver delivery can be divided into two parts i) routing from source to RSUs and ii) routing from another RSU to the destination. This can be done by deployment of RSUs which are further connected to backbone of a network.
- **V2I and Environment Sensing Application:-** In VANETs source to destination delivery can be done in 2 parts V2V and V2I delivery. Handovering packet between 2 vehicles is V2V message delivery and deliver a message from a vehicle to an RSU is V2I delivery. An RSU can use (Zhao, W., Ammar, M., & Zegura, E. 2004) the received information to identify geographic location of the source, order a large number of goods in a shop, traffic management, road security, road status, weather information, plan routes of taxis, to provide the way to emergency vehicles and analyze pollution in cities etc.
- **Dissemination Application:-**This application emphasizes the flooding of messages and tries to deliver the information quickly to maximum number of vehicles. Due to high delay DTN can be adopted for above mentioned applications. The advantage can be taken in accident scenario to avoid the route where accident has taken place, to avoid further cascading vehicle crashes and to help the police to manage the situation.

- **Cooperative Connect Downloading Application:-** The direction of information flow is from RSU to vehicle in such types of applications. Normally the information to be transferred from RSU to vehicle may be too large to transfer in a single contact (As contact time is quite low). This problem can be solved by introducing the DTN network protocols.

Figure 4 shows distributed networks which forms DTN network. The DTN network can use different networks as underlying technology (Warthman, Forrest. 2003). The satellite networks, wireless networks, telephone networks and general internet can be used to make a DTN enabled network. (as given in Figure 4).

Figure 4. DTN networks

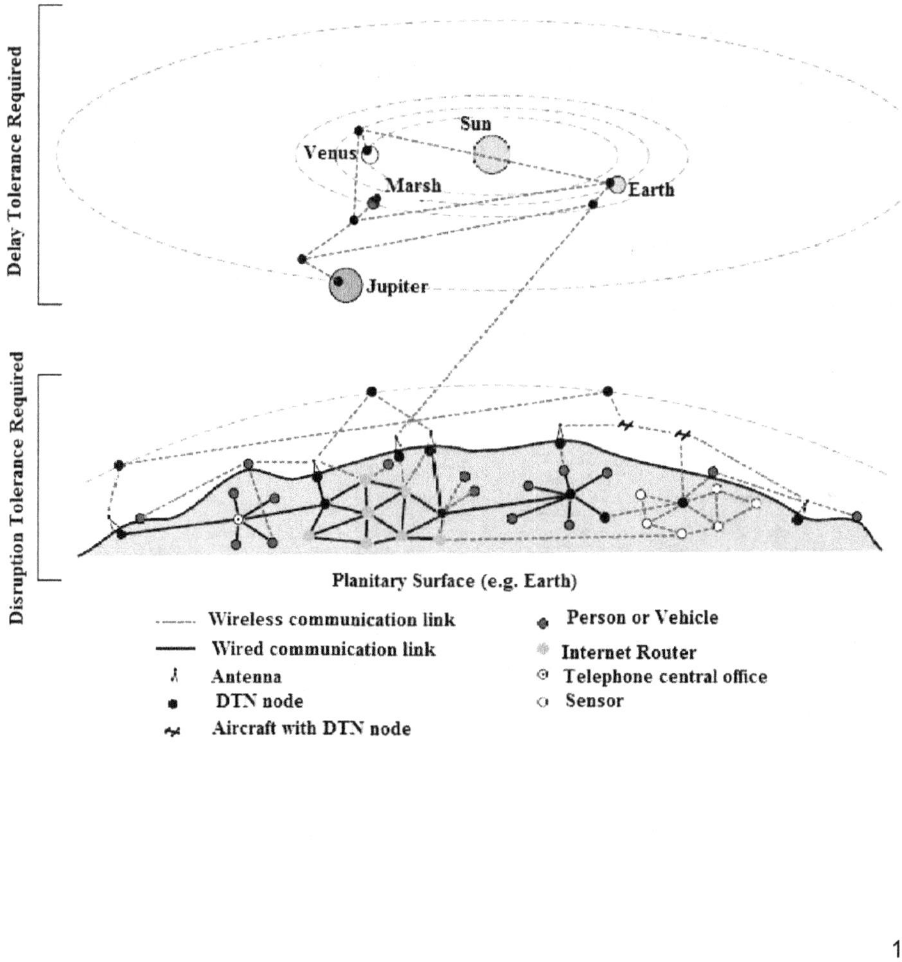

DTN ROUTING PROTOCOLS

VANET is built to offer more comfort and safety to the passengers. Every VANET device in a vehicle works as a node in the ad-hoc network to create more reliable communication through wireless network.

The main characteristics of VANET provide more customization to develop new services. However safety and comfort are two most important and relevant areas (Yousefi, S., Mousavi, M. S., & Fathy, M. 2006) of the device as shown in Figure 5 are as follows (Singh, V., & Saini, G. L. 2018, Mobile Communications, Schiller, 2008):

1. **Comfort Applications:** These applications provide traveler more comfort and traffic efficiency during traveling. For example a comfort application inform you about: traffic information system, nearest or next petrol/ gas station, GPRS location tracking, weather information as well as enjoying internet, music or movies during the journey. This particular application is directly related to DTNs.
2. **Safety Applications:** This type of applications works to enhance safety of passengers. They work in different manner such as exchanging safety relevant information via IVC. Drivers are motivated to use these

Figure 5. Categories of VANETs

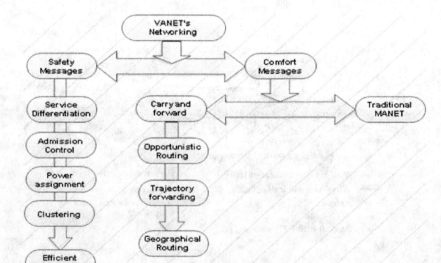

applications to get maximum safety during travel. Few examples of safety applications are emergency warning system, traffic sign/signal violation warning, lane-changing assistant, interaction coordination. These applications are required direct vehicle-to-vehicle communication due to stringent delay necessities.

Highly increasing number of vehicles on roads have made driving more challenging, tough and dangerous task. However total road area available to drive has not increased in ratio of increasing vehicles. To sort out this problem world's top automobile companies are working with concerned government agencies. Their joint efforts are focused to help driver on the road by escaping bad traffic area or hazardous events. These efforts invent WAVE (Wireless Access for Vehicle Environment) technology, one of superior kind of wireless access to make a smart vehicle-to-vehicle and vehicle-to-road communication.

VANET can use multiple ad-hoc networking technologies including *Bluetooth, WiFi, WiMAX 802.16, IEEE 802.11 b/g, IRA, Zigbee for smart, effective, accurate and easy communication between vehicles.* Moreover VANET improves safety features (Kohli, S., Kaur, B., & Bindra, S. 2010) in vehicle providing real time communication between vehicles, infotainment and telematics.

VANET safety features resemble the operation technology of MANET while processing for self-management, self-organization, low bandwidth and share radio transmission. However the key hindrance in operation of VANET provides high speed and uncertain mobility (in contrast to MANET) of the mobile nodes (vehicles) on the road. To utilize efficient routing protocol service MANET architecture should be upgraded to that it can accommodate the fast mobile of the VANET nodes optimistically. Thus working on the process gives more research challenges to design appropriate routing protocol mechanism.

VANETS ROUTING PROTOCOLS

A timeline of the currently available routing protocols (Bernsen J., & Manivannan D. 2008) for VANETs is as follow given in Figure 7. These protocols are compared on the basis of three sets of specifications: requirement, design approaches and objectives. Few of them target building vehicle-to-vehicle network, other are focused on vehicle-to-roadside communication.

Figure 6. VANETs routing algorithm timeline (Tornell S. M., Calafate C. T., Cano J. & Manzoni P. 2015) and potential influence

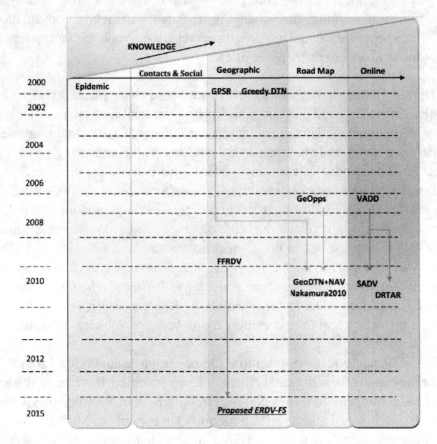

Similarly other protocols are designed to create communication in delay tolerant networks. Simply there are QoS oriented protocols, some of which connects vehicles to Internet. Routing protocols are categorized in two streams topology-based and geographic routing. The information used by the Topology-based routing is about the links which are already exist in the network to perform packet forwarding whereas geographic routing is developed to use location of neighboring node. Here topology-bases routing has to suffer from routing route breaks because highly changing frequency of link information.

To sort out this major error, nodes keep the packets with themselves and carry until they came into the range of another node, and now the carrying

Figure 7. Types of Routing Protocols in VANETs

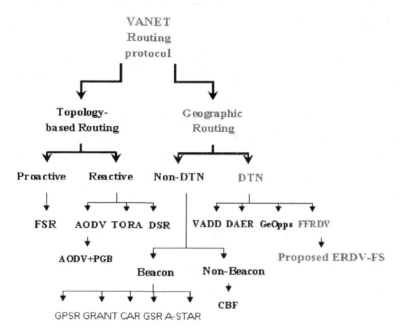

node forward the packets following some protocol based on characteristics of neighbor's node (called carry-and- forward strategy). This strategy is known as DTN technology and improves the packet delivery by store-carry and forward.

ROUTING PROTOCOLS IN DELAY TOLERANT NETWORKS

DTN is developed to mainly maximize the probability of message delivery. Besides this, DTN minimizes resources *(i.e. network bandwidth, buffer size and battery energy)* consumption. Moreover while DTNs applications are designed to tolerate of delay, this does not benefit DTNs utilities to get benefit from the decreased delay but helps to reduce the delivery latency. The notable DTN vehicular routing protocols (Lee, K. C., Lee, U., & Gerla, M. 2010) and (Dhamal, P., Nagaraj, U., & Devotale, D. 2011) are VADD (Vehicle-Assisted Data Delivery), GeOpps (Geographical Opportunistic Routing), DAER, and FFRDV as shown in figure 7. These protocols are discussed as follows:

VADD (Zhao, J., & Cao, G. 2008): Vehicle-Assisted Data Delivery

VADD works on the process of carry and forward. Using predicable mobility, VADD differs from existing carry and forwarding applications to avoid dependency on traffic pattern and road layout. For example, a vehicle's driving speed is controlled by the traffic density of the road as well as the speed limit of the vehicle. Its driving direction can be predicated easily observing road pattern and the acceleration of the engine speed. In this scenario, a vehicle decides at the nearest junctions to select the next forwarding path to minimize packet delivery delay. It is supposed that vehicles are equipped with pre-loaded digital maps including steel-level map with traffic statistics i.e. vehicle speed, traffic density and other data related to roads at different times of the day.

VADD had developed to sparse connected network to that vehicle can try to utilize wireless communications channel effortlessly. It allows vehicles to race with faster speed, else VADD model is disciplined by following principles:

1. If the packet has to be carried through selected roads, it should choose the road with lower traffic density and higher speed
2. It should transmit through wireless channel as much as possible
3. As the characteristics of vehicular ad-hoc networks is unpredictable, it cannot be expected that the packet to be routed successfully on the same path which is identified previously as an optimal path. To improve performance, the dynamic algorithm for the selection of path must be executed throughout the packet forwarding process continuously.

VADD has three types of modes for packet forwarding: *StraightWay, Intersection and Destination*. These modes are completely dependent on the position of packet carrier (i.e. *the vehicle that has the packet*). The packet carrier selects the best packets forwarding path by switching between different packet modes. Moreover intersection mode is the most critical, efficient, critical and complicated choice, it allows vehicles more choices at the intersection.

GeOpps (Leontiadis I. & Mascolo C. 2007): Geographical Opportunistic Routing

GeOpps is a novel delay tolerant routing algorithm which exploits the availability of information from the Navigation System (NS) to optimize opportunistically route a data packet to a certain geographical location. It uses advantages of the vehicle's NS suggested routes to select path and vehicle that can carry the information closer to the targeted destination of the packets. It uses suggested routes of vehicle's navigation system to choose vehicle to get nearest the final destination of a packet. GeOpps consumes information from the navigation system to efficiently route packets. It supposes that vehicles are equipped with navigation systems having informations of the geographical locations of the nearby infostations (*access points to the Backbone*). A navigation system may have different types of sensors including acceleration sensor and speed sensor. It contains maps also to evaluate the present traffic conditions of a special road segment. This information is communicated to the nearest infostations. However, it does not provide constant connectivity between info stations (*mainly in remote areas*) and vehicle; other vehicles are assumed to perform as data mules from the sensing vehicle to get accurate geographical location of the nearest info station.

A centralized system combines all the information gathered from various sources to estimate the current traffic conditions on the road. Later, it generates traffic warning for the concerned specific road segment and suggests alternative paths to vehicles as per their requirements. Afterwards, traffic management centre dispatches this information to the vehicle to warn the drivers. Very firstly warning is sent to the nearest information, from where they are channelized to the affected road segments using the maps of the vehicle networks. While this information reaches to the affected area, local message dissemination techniques (*such as localized epidemic or constrained flooding*) are employed to spread the information to nearby vehicles. After receiving this information, the navigation system of vehicles evaluates the information in order to recalculate a route to avoid road segments with highly dense traffic and lower speed.

DAER (Huang H., Shu W., Li M. & Wu M. Y. 2008): Distance Aware Epidemic Routing

In DAER the packets which need to be forwarded from n_i to n_j are categorized according to the distance from the neighbor node n_j and the destination of packet: $d(\Psi(n_j, t), \Psi(dest(b_k),t))$ given that it is smaller than the current distance $d(\Psi(n_i, t), (dest(b_k),t))$, where $d(\Psi1,\Psi2)$ has been defined as the geographical distance between $\Psi1$ and $\Psi2$. A bundle b_k with the greatest $d(\Psi(n_i, t), \Psi(dest(b_k),t)) - d(\Psi(n_j, t), (dest(b_k),t))$ is chosen for forwarded first. This is called greedy distance forwarding. Once a bundle b_k at node n_i is forwarded to its neighbor node n_j, if b_k still remains in buffer at n_i, it contains the same probability with other bundles in the buffer to be forward again while the nodes meet with another neighbors. Using this practice, the duplication tree expands immediately. In order to improve the effectiveness of duplication, every time when a bundle is newly forwarded, a decision is made whether the bundle will be pruned off from node n_i. The decision is based on the bundle's geographical tendency of approaching to its destination. It compares the current distance $d(\Psi(n_i, t), \Psi(dest(b_k),t))$ to the distance $d(\Psi(n_i, t'), \Psi(dest(b_k),t'))$ recorded at the time b_k arrived at n_i. If bundle b_k diffuses away from its destination with node n_i, it will be pruned, that is, deleted from the buffer at node n_i. This process is named anti-diffusion pruning in the algorithm. Similarly, for the buffer replacement, a bundle compares its current distance to its destination and the targeted value when it first arrived at current node to determine whether it is approaching to or diffusing from its destination. If the bundle diffuses away from its set destination, it contains higher priority to be replaced by a newly arrived bundle. The whole process is called anti-diffusion buffer replacement. This mechanism is introduces due to two reasons. First, a bundle must travel on a node which is moving toward its destination. Else it must be dropped to avoid unnecessary consumption of the limited connection time. Secondly, when bundle is near to the destination, it should make more copies to expedite the delivery.

FFRDV (Yu, D., & Ko, Y. B. 2009): Fastest Ferry Routing in DTN VANETs

The FFRDV utilizes the concept of transmitting data (*from one node vehicle to other node vehicle on highways*) for applications which can be able to tolerate delay, over fastest ferry where ferry is a reliable source for communication and transmission of messages between nodes. The "FFRDV" considers that the road is divided into lanes and further lanes are divided into logical blocks of some fixed size (between 2 consecutive milestones). While entering the block the ferries which carrying the data, broadcast a HELLO message. All ferries within the block reply to that HELLO with their speed and coordinates. The ferry which holds data is called Current Ferry (CF). After receiving HELLO messages from all in-block ferries, CF compares its own speed from the speed received in reply HELLO messages. Now, CF elects the fastest ferry (*the ferry having highest speed*) among all ferries running within the block. This elected fastest ferry becomes Designated Ferry (DF). The CF sends Bundle having with it to the elected DF and discards the Bundle after receiving acknowledgment from DF. Now the CF after discarding Bundle becomes normal ferry.

Comparison of DTN Routing Protocols (Tornell, S. M., Calafate, C. T., Cano, J., & Manzoni, P. 2015):

The above discussed DTN enabled Vehicular ad-hoc network routing protocols can be summarized in Table 9. The VN specific field indicates whether the protocol is for vehicular network or not.

Table 9. Characteristics of DTN Routing protocols

Protocol	Year	VN Specific	Application	Group	Routing Metrics	Optimization		
						Reliability	Redundancy	Message Priority
GeOpps	2007	Yes	P2P/V2I	Road Map	Nearest point ETA	No	No	No
DAER	2008	Yes	P2P/V2I	Zero Knowledge	Distance	No	Multicopy	Distance
VADD	2008	Yes	P2P/V2I	Online	Loc+Density+Speed	No	No	No
FFRDV	2009	Yes	Dissemination	Geographic Loc	Speed	HopAck	No	No

CONCLUSION

This chapter described applications of DTN networks, DTN architecture, DTN protocols overview, general characteristics and types of the routing protocols of VANETs. DTN architecture includes bundle protocol, bundle format, bundle processing control flags and specifications of bundle protocol. The role of DTN in VANET was also discussed in the chapter. A brief introduction of GeOpps, DAER, VADD and FFRDV is given and taken into consideration for the proposed research. A detail description of DTN enabled VANETs routing protocols are explained and summarized their characteristics.

REFERENCES

Agarwal, A., Starobinski, D., & Little, T. D. (2012). Phase transition of message propagation speed in delay-tolerant vehicular networks. *IEEE Transactions on Intelligent Transportation Systems*, *13*(1), 249–263. doi:10.1109/TITS.2011.2168954

Benamar, N., Benamar, M., & Bonnin, J. M. (2012, May). Routing protocols for DTN in vehicular environment. In *Multimedia Computing and Systems (ICMCS), 2012 International Conference on* (pp. 589-593). IEEE. 10.1109/ICMCS.2012.6320307

Bernsen, J., & Manivannan, D. (2008, August). Greedy routing protocols for vehicular ad hoc networks. In *Wireless Communications and Mobile Computing Conference, 2008. IWCMC'08. International* (pp. 632-637). IEEE. 10.1109/IWCMC.2008.109

Cao, Y., & Sun, Z. (2013). Routing in delay/disruption tolerant networks: A taxonomy, survey and challenges. *IEEE Communications Surveys and Tutorials*, *15*(2), 654–677. doi:10.1109/SURV.2012.042512.00053

Cerf, V., Burleigh, S., Hooke, A., Torgerson, L., Durst, R., Scott, K. & Weiss, H. (2007). *Delay-tolerant networking architecture* (No. RFC 4838).

Dhamal, P., Nagaraj, U., & Devotale, D. (2011). *Study of various routing protocols in VANET*. Academic Press.

Huang, H., Shu, W., Li, M., & Wu, M. Y. (2008, March). Performance evaluation of vehicular dtn routing under realistic mobility models. In *Wireless Communications and Networking Conference, 2008. WCNC 2008. IEEE* (pp. 2206-2211). IEEE.

Jerbi, M., Senouci, S. M., & Ghamri-Doudane, Y. (2006). Towards efficient routing in vehicular Ad Hoc networks. *Proceedings of the 3rd IEEE international workshop on Mobile Computing and Networking*.

Karimzadeh, M. (2011). *Efficient routing protocol in delay tolerant networks (DTNs)*. Academic Press.

Kohli, S., Kaur, B., & Bindra, S. (2010). A comparative study of Routing Protocols in VANET. *Proceedings of ISCET*, 173-177.

Lee, K. C., Lee, U., & Gerla, M. (2010). Survey of routing protocols in vehicular ad hoc networks. In *Advances in vehicular ad-hoc networks: Developments and challenges* (pp. 149–170). IGI Global. doi:10.4018/978-1-61520-913-2.ch008

Leontiadis, I., & Mascolo, C. (2007). *GeOpps: Geographical opportunistic routing for vehicular networks*. Academic Press.

Little, T. D., & Agarwal, A. (2005, September). An information propagation scheme for VANETs. In *Proc. IEEE Intelligent Transportation Systems* (pp. 155-160). IEEE.

Romero Amondaray, L., & Seoane Pascual, J. (2008, September). Delay tolerant network simulation with vnuml. In *Proceedings of the third ACM workshop on Challenged networks* (pp. 109-112). ACM. 10.1145/1409985.1410006

Scott, K., & Burleigh, S. (2007). *Bundle protocol specification* (No. RFC 5050).

Shen, J., Moh, S., & Chung, I. (2008, July). Routing protocols in delay tolerant networks: A comparative survey. In *The 23rd International Technical Conference on Circuits/Systems, Computers and Communications (ITC-CSCC 2008)* (pp. 6-9). Academic Press.

Singh, V., & Saini, G. L. (2018). DTN-Enabled Routing Protocols and Their Potential Influence on Vehicular Ad Hoc Networks. In *Soft Computing: Theories and Applications* (pp. 367–375). Singapore: Springer. doi:10.1007/978-981-10-5687-1_33

Tornell, S. M., Calafate, C. T., Cano, J., & Manzoni, P. (2015). DTN Protocols for Vehicular Networks: An Application Oriented Overview. *IEEE Communications Surveys and Tutorials*, *17*(2), 868–887. doi:10.1109/COMST.2014.2375340

Warthman, F. (2003). *Delay-Tolerant Networks: A Tutorial*. Academic Press.

Yousefi, S., Mousavi, M. S., & Fathy, M. (2006, June). Vehicular ad hoc networks (VANETs): challenges and perspectives. In *ITS Telecommunications Proceedings, 2006 6th International Conference on* (pp. 761-766). IEEE.

Yu, D., & Ko, Y. B. (2009, February). FFRDV: fastest-ferry routing in DTN-enabled vehicular ad hoc networks. In *Advanced Communication Technology, 2009. ICACT 2009. 11th International Conference on* (Vol. 2, pp. 1410-1414). IEEE.

Zhang, Z., & Zhang, Q. (2007). Delay/disruption tolerant mobile ad hoc networks: Latest developments. *Wireless Communications and Mobile Computing, 7*(10), 1219–1232. doi:10.1002/wcm.518

Zhao, J., & Cao, G. (2008). VADD: Vehicle-assisted data delivery in vehicular ad hoc networks. *IEEE Transactions on Vehicular Technology, 57*(3), 1910–1922. doi:10.1109/TVT.2007.901869

Zhao, W., Ammar, M., & Zegura, E. (2004, May). A message ferrying approach for data delivery in sparse mobile ad hoc networks. In *Proceedings of the 5th ACM international symposium on Mobile ad hoc networking and computing* (pp. 187-198). ACM. 10.1145/989459.989483

Chapter 9
Digital Image Classification Techniques:
A Comprehensive Review

Utkarsh Shrivastav
Lovely Professional University, India

Sanjay Kumar Singh
Lovely Professional University, India

ABSTRACT

Image classification is a technique to categorize an image in to given classes on the basis of hidden characteristics or features extracted using image processing. With rapidly growing technology, the size of images is growing. Different categories of images may contain different types of hidden information such as x-ray, CT scan, MRI, pathologies images, remote sensing images, satellite images, and natural scene image captured via digital cameras. In this chapter, the authors have surveyed various articles and books and summarized image classification techniques. There are supervised techniques like KNN and SVM, which classify an image into given classes and unsupervised techniques like K-means and ISODATA for classifying image into a group of clusters. For big images, deep learning networks can be employed that are fast and efficient and also compute hidden features automatically.

DOI: 10.4018/978-1-5225-9096-5.ch009

INTRODUCTION TO DIGITAL IMAGE

An image is a copy of a subject that is visibly similar to that object. An image a 2D representation of any certain object. There can be many examples of an image, people go to some places or cherish some moments and take pictures. So it can be concluded that images show similarity or resemblances from the reality. In current scenario mostly digital images are being captured and used. Digital images is a representation of an image in form of numbers, normally binary, of a two-dimensional image. These images are generally captured with the help of a digital camera and then they are transferred to any system having processing probabilities for further processing of image. The processing on any digital image is known as digital image processing. The processing may consist of different functionalities to achieve some particular characteristics of an image like image enhancement, color transformation, spatial transformation. (Gonzalez & Woods, 2008)

Image Enhancement

In digital image, it may happen that there may be some sort noise or disturbance that is included in the image. It may be due to the poor camera quality, camera movement, bad light conditions. So to remove that, people often use image processing so that those minor yet affecting impurities can be removed or minimized. (Khamparia & Pandey, 2015) The image enhancement functionalities may include functions like: enhancing the contrast, brightness, sharpness of an image, removing red light affect on any image. Figure 1 is

Figure 1. Image Enhancement

showing before and after effects of image processing. figure 1(a) shows, the image is dark also contrast is high and figure 1(b) shows that after applying image processing image quality has improved.

Color Transformation

In the past, there were Mechanical cameras in which the negative images were produced and it was impossible to make changes in the color or type of the image. (Khamparia & Pandey, 2017) But now, digital images gives freedom to change image of one type into image of another type for example a color image can be converted into a black and white image. also any video can be converted into any format. In the Indian film industries there are movies like "Mughal-e-azam" which was earlier released in black and white form but then it was re-released in color format. (Unnithan,2004)

Figure 2 shows color transformation in a sample image, which was RGB earlier and then converted to grayscale image.

Spatial Transformation

Sometimes, it may require to bring structural transformation of image like crop, resize, rotate, scale etc. Image processing allows someone to perform such transformations. One can perform such operations with various tools.

Figure 2. Color Transformation

*For a more accurate representation see the electronic version.

Image processing addresses the problems like resolution fixing, focusing, color saturation fixing, hue fixing etc. As fast as technology is growing the use and demand of image processing is also growing. Like for criminal detection or border security the use of cctv cameras are used. Similarly, for weather forecasting (Deeprasertkul & Praikan,2016) and even in medical uses (Birare & Chakkawar,2018) the use of image processing is growing day by day.

Further more this chapter has been divided into 4 sections, section 2 discusses about the various types of images. Section 3 describes about the classification and various techniques used for image classification purpose. Section 4 talks about deep learning concepts and some of the very popular deep learning networks like convolutional neural network and autoencoders.

TYPE OF DIGITAL IMAGES

A digital image may be of different types. And most amazing thing about digital images is they can be convert image of one type into image of another type. The types of images are binary image, grayscale image, RGB or True color image and indexed color image.

Binary Image

As the name represents itself, a binary image is made up of only 2 colors black and white. The matrix of any binary image consists of only two numbers these are: 0 and 1, where 0 means black and 1 means white. Because of this behaviour these type of images is known as black and white images. In binary image there is no grayscale values in between. The size of binary images is 1-bit/pixel.(Wu, Tang & Lin,2000)

In the figure 3, Figure 3(b) shows a binary image created with the help of image processing, and figure 3(a) shows the matrix of the concerned image.

Grayscale Image

In grayscale images, they can have different color shades of grey ranging from 0-255, where 255 means white and 0 means black. The lower the range will be darker the image will be produced and vice-versa. And then one can check the grayscale image by viewing the Histogram of any image. The size of these type of images is 8-bits. (Saravanan,2010)

Figure 3. Binary Image

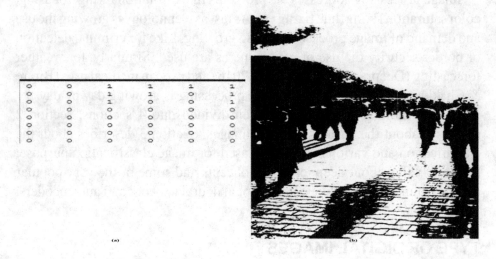

Histogram of an image is a bar chart showing the different grayscale levels in an image. In the figure 4 below there are three images. Figure 4(a) shows the grayscale image on the top. Figure 4(b) shows the histogram of the image. And figure 4(c) shows the matrix of the image.

Figure 4. Grayscale Image

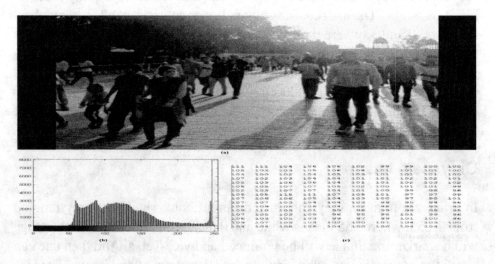

RGB Image

This type of images also known as coloured images. As these images are consist of 24-bit size. As the name implies it consist of 3 different colors: RED, GREEN, BLUE. Each color element is of 8 bit each hence 24-bit collectively. (Saravanan,2010)

In figure 5, figure 5(b) shows an sample RGB image distribution model in its various components Red, Green and Blue, and figure 5(a) shows an sample RGB image.

Indexed Image

An indexed image is also a color image. But its color depends upon the color map that has been chosen for the creation of an image. The size of the image also varies, it is generally less than the RGB images as it save those colors which are required for the creation of an image. So the size of the image depends upon the number of colors being used in the image.(Yeh & Kuo,2002)

Figure 6 (Mathwork,2018) shows the compressed matrix in an indexed image, this shows the size reduction of an image because of less use of colors.

Figure 5. RGB Image

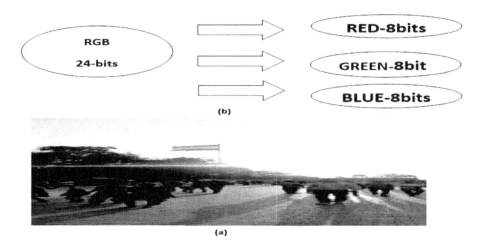

For a more accurate representation see the electronic version.

Figure 6. Indexed Image

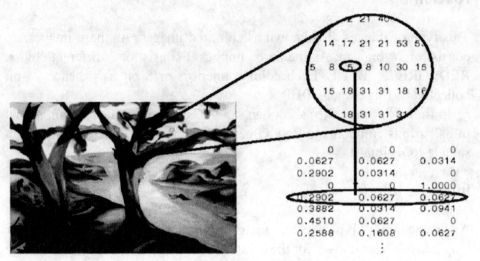

*For a more accurate representation see the electronic version.

CLASSIFICATION TECHNIQUES

Image classification is the process of categorising pixels of images into a group of predefined classes (Beaula et al.,2016). This concept is known as image classification. In order to achieve this classification between image and the classes, one needs to understand the relationship between them appropriately. It is one of the most fascinating task in image processing. A system must be trained in order to achieve classification.

Generally, in image classification the features of an image are identified on the basis of various properties. (Sisodia et al.,2014) These features may vary according to different techniques being used for the image classification. These features show variance in an image, with the help of which some sort of patterns can be identified and finally an image can be classified. There are different techniques for image classification. But on a broader scale these techniques can further be divided into two types, supervised and Unsupervised Techniques.

Supervised Techniques

This approach is also known as the supervised approach for image classification. In supervised classification, (Rani, 2017) firstly representative samples for each class is selected. (e.g. Land cover information) Supervised classification uses the insubstantial marks defined in the training set. These techniques are mostly used for remote sensing. The features are generally the boundary information fetched from the image and then other internal factors of images plays important role in detecting various features for the image. Some of the most famous supervised techniques are: Maximum likelihood (Jia,2002), K-Nearest Neighbours (Khanal & Sampio,2018), Linear Vector Quantization (Omatu,2001) and SVM (Janadri et al.,2017).

K-Nearest Neighbours

K-Nearest Neighbour is a most famous supervised technique for performing classification as well as regression. In this technique there are two things provided. Basically, there are training samples, given to analyse the properties and put them accordingly in to the classes (Kawattikul & Chomphuwiset,2018) and training sets are also provided, with which the comparison will take place. In KNN, "K" stands for the number of nearest neighbours from the training sample. This whole algorithm based on the concept of Euclidean distance.

It is calculated by

$$D = \sqrt{\left(x_2 - x_1\right)^2 + \left(y_2 - y_1\right)^2}$$

Where, (x_1, y_1) and (x_2, y_2) are the coordinates for training sample and training sets respectively. (Khanal & Sampio, 2018)

1. Suppose there is a training sample "x" that needs to be classified. In this case the first step is to find out the Euclidean distance of the training sample from all the other training data sets provided.
2. The next step is to specify the number of nearest neighbours required. It is a random process and may vary according to the uses.
3. Once the number of nearest neighbours has been specified, the nearest K neighbours will be pointed out. The training data set having minimum Euclidean distance from the training sample will be termed as the nearest neighbours.
4. After the Nearest neighbours have been specified, next step is to carefully observe the class of those neighbours. The neighbours representing a

class in majority will be termed as resultant class. And hence the training sample "x" will be allotted to that class only.

5. The results of KNN may vary according to number of 'k'. So, it is always advised to specify k optimally.

Khanal et al. (2018) presented a paper in which they introduced various techniques to classify intensity of exercise using facial expressions. They took an HD video as an input captured from an static camera. The images extracted from the video were based on the time slot varies based on increment in the heart rate. The face expressions were detected in two phases, first was to identify the facial expression points and second was to classify them. For classification KNN and SVM were used. KNN presented 100% accuracy in few classes. Few researchers presented their work in a paper in which, they used classification techniques for optimally predicting the diseases with the help of analysing medical reports using KNN, (Singh et al.,2018) decision tree and Naive Bayes classifiers in which the results extracted using KNN were best. This technique was generally useful for predicting diseases at the time when there is no proper medical expertise available.

Support Vector Machine

In this technique a plane is divided into various classes and then the training sample has to be classified into one or other class. The main task that an SVM does, it creates a hyperplane in a high dimensional space, with the help of which not only classification can be performed but also other tasks like regression or outlier detection can be performed as well. With the help of this hyperplane a good amount separation is achieved between the classes. (Janadri et al.,2017) The area should be maximised to the nearest data point of any class. In general the class is divided in an equal part with the help of a single line.(Khamparia & Pandey, 2018) The margin between both the classes should be maximised, it is believed that the higher the margin the lesser will be the error in classification. SVM is the most relevant technique when it comes to the choice use by researchers. While it may happen that a problem is not linearly separable in this case the cover's theorem is applicable, where it states that any non linearly separable problem is separable if the size of dimension is increased.

In the figure 7, there are two classes circles and stars separated by three hyperplanes A,B and C. It is visible that the distance between nearest member of both the classes is appropriately equal. It means that the region of

Figure 7. Classification using SVM

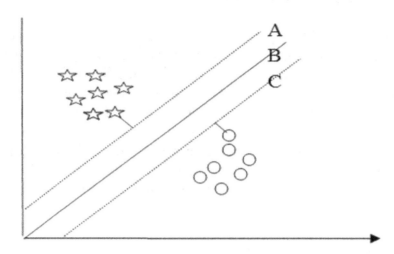

classification is maximized. The hyperplane B is separating the two classes in the best possible way, and hence the classification achieved is optimal.

Joshi & Mukherjee (2018) presented their work in which they have taken multispectral satellite images as an input for the purpose of high-level content based image retrieval in this they have used high level feature extraction techniques such as SIFT and Gabor, and then the accuracy is further increased by using SVM. Birare & Chakkarwar (2018) introduced their noble work, In which they discussed a technique to automatically detect brain tumour cells using SVM. They have used K-means clustering and Otsu method for segmentation purpose of the reports and further by using text based extracted features, they have used SVM for classification and achieved an accuracy of 98.51%. Two researchers introduced a technique named as SIFRS, which was a facial recognition system and very helpful for visually disabled persons. (Dixit & Satpute,2018) This technique was basically using feature extraction and classification techniques for matching the faces and if someone was trying to bluff physically impaired person. This system sends an alert message as well. It was implemented with the help of SVM and worked quite well. The KNN widely used in extraction of features and classifying them. SVM can be used for classification as well as regression. It is much better in terms of accuracy as compared to the KNN as it provides an equal opportunity for all the datasets to get classify with equal chances. The SVM is widely used in pattern recognition.

Unsupervised Techniques

In this technique unlike supervised techniques, there is no concept of classes. Clustering is performed on the basis of features and pixels persisting similar properties and kept together in a cluster. And hence there is no training set present in the unsupervised techniques. In this technique the most difficult task is to identify the number of clusters that is required. Because it may happen that during clustering the researchers come across few features which are meaningless. For example: From a bunch of people it is needed to separate out vegetarian people from the non-vegetarians, two clusters are required for the same. The most widely used unsupervised techniques are: K-means clustering (Wu et al., 2015), ISODATA(El-Rahman,2016) technique for clustering.

K Means Clustering

The K means clustering also works on the Euclidean distance principle similar to that of k nearest neighbour technique (Khanal & Sampio,2018), but here no one talks about the classes instead, there are anonymous group of data and with the help of Euclidean distance, the clusters are created and then put data members into the clusters.(Miranda et al., 2016)

1. first of all, it is necessary to determine initial number of clusters, The K in the name K means clustering represents the number of clusters, that needs to be initialized.
2. Once K random centroids for K clusters has been identified the next step is to find the Euclidean distance from all the data points to each centroid.
3. Once the distances have been calculated, the data points will be assigned to the cluster which having minimum Euclidean distance between them.
4. Now as the data points have been assigned to a cluster, new centroids of the clusters is find out by calculating mean of all the data points in a cluster.
5. This process is repeated until there is a halt in the continuous change in cluster or it can be said that, the algorithm comes to a halt when there will be no new centroid detected.

In figure 8 there are three clusters and the dark data points are the clusters for the centroids.

Figure 8. Clustering using K-Means

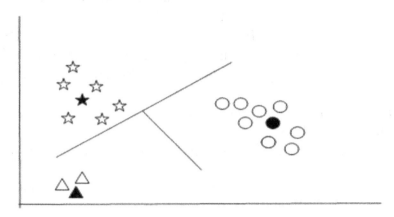

Wu et al. (2015) presented a technique for remote sensing image classification based on color feature classification. Basically, features were extracted using HSV color features and then the k-means clustering technique was applied on the image. The results were better than traditional k-means clustering. Kavya & Padmaja (2017) presented their work of glaucoma detection using texture feature detection, Fundus image is used as the input and then using hough transformation the required area from the image is extracted. Then they have applied k-means clustering for the segmentation purpose which provided around 84% accuracy and then finally SVM classifier is used for classification which provided 86% of accuracy. Detti et al. (2018) presented a paper for polymer electrolyte membrane fuel cell diagnosis, in this approach a voltage signal is processed by fast fourier transformation to provide total harmonic distortion which was further used for fault detection. The defects were identified using k-means and KNN.

ISODATA Technique

Another widely used clustering algorithm is ISODATA (Kar & Kelkar,2013) technique, this technique is ideal when there is a huge variance in type of clusters. Unlike K means or other clustering method, there is no need to predefine the number of clusters. (Papadopoulos et al., 2008) In this technique the user effort require is also very less, that is the main reason of its popularity among researchers. The ISODATA algorithm basically work on the Divide and Unified approach. Hence there are two main phases for ISODATA technique, divide phase and unification phase. (Ramya & Praveen,2015)

1. Firstly, sample points are put on a plane and roughly there are divided into different clusters separated by few distance.

2. In the next phase, identify clusters having very few pixel points (sample points) and do nothing but eliminate those clusters. Because such clusters are generally nothing but outliers, which do nothing but increase the overhead.

3. Once the elimination is performed, the very next step is a step called unification. In this step the clusters which are situated very close to each other and separated by a negligible distance are unified and converted into a group of big large cluster.

4. After the unification is performed the next phase again comes that of dividing phase. In this phase large clusters are identified and divided into new clusters.

5. This process repeats itself again and again till the clusters with required properties have not been occupied.

In the figure 9, the division phase and unification phase have been shown. In figure 9(a) the division phase is visible. Where the clusters are separated by a straight line and there are 4 clusters, however after unification there are only two clusters, C1 and C2 visible in figure 9(b).

El-Rahman (2016) presented his work to classify hyperspectral images using ISODATA. He has used a dataset from Florida extracted using SAMSON sensor. The images were firstly processed through principal component analysis

Figure 9. ISODATA technique

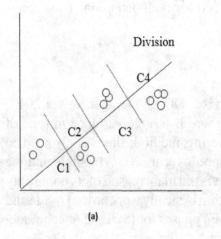 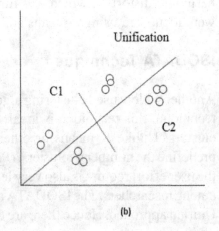

and then through ISODATA. The overall accuracy was 75.6187%. Li et al. (2010) presented their work to cluster remote sensing images using a parallel ISODATA clustering technique. The technique is used on the MapReduce platform instead of MPI. For better results instead of RGB, CIELAB color space is used. K-means clustering has managed to perform quite satisfactory in every field such as in medical imaging, chemical engineering and also in geographical images as well. The isodata is not a very famous technique as compared to kmeans technique, probably because of its complexity to use. However, this technique specially manages to perform well with geographical images.

DEEP LEARNING

Deep learning is a sub field of study in machine learning. Deep learning is a technique to teach computer something that comes to human mind automatically. (Courville et al.,2015) The deep learning techniques has revolutionised the way of training a network. The traditional learning was all about information processing, (Gurney, 1997) where the system was trained to enable them doing few things which human could do easily. But deep learning is beyond that. In deep learning one is simply not only training the networks, but also teaching them to train itself. It is simply not mean by only emulating human mind. But now with the help of deep learning approaches one can surely find the similarities between machine and human minds. With the help of deep learning the feature detection and extraction has become very convenient. (Khamparia & Pandey, 2017) With the help of deep learning the feature detection can be done automatically, which is the most important things for performing any image processing task. (Komleh, & Joudaki, 2017)

Deep learning was first introduced in a paper by Hinton (2007). In general, Deep learning is nothing but the advancement of traditional learning where the algorithm was more inspired by the human minds and were based on the Artificial neural networks. If someone look at the networks introduced under the name of deep learning. One big difference was that, the networks that use in deep learning have more number of layers as compared to that of traditional networks. (Mahapatra,2018) More number of layers simply mean that the data needed to train the network was very high. It leads to extension in execution time as well. Which obviously provided better results.

If someone look at the algorithms being used today in deep learning, most of them are supervised and uses labelled data which is huge in amount. (Khamparia & Pandey, 2017)

In addition to these advantages one most important benefit provided by deep learning is that, deep learning models have ability to perform automatic feature extraction from unprocessed data. This phenomenon is often termed as feature learning. However, because there are so many similarities from the artificial neural networks, there are still many researchers who have shown their dissatisfaction of deep networks being termed as deep learning networks and not only artificial neural networks. The most important type of deep neural networks are convolutional neural networks and autoencoder.

Convolutional Neural Networks

Convolutional neural networks are very similar to the traditional neural networks as the structure of the network is very similar to that of the traditional networks. (Wilkinson, 2004) The connectivity patterns in CNN is inspired by the connectivity patterns in animal virtual cortex. In animal virtual cortex the neurons are arranged in such a manner that they respond to the overlapping region of the visual fields. The network is made up of multiple neurons present at different levels. Each neuron has some weights and bias on it. The whole network seems like a big function and at the last layer softmax function (Shi et al., 2018) is applicable. The CNN operates in multiple phases, each phase have their own specific work or task. The convolutional network is fully connected that makes is different from the other networks. (Khamparia & Pandey, 2016) As the level of output achieved via this network is already a enhanced version. There are few phases or layers, in which CNN operates these are convolutional layer, pooling layer, and fully connected layer.

Convolutional Layer

The convolutional layer operates in two steps. In the first step, divide the input image that is provided in the form a matrices (0 and 1, where 0 means black part of the image and 1 means white part of the image) into a form of sub matrices. Suppose there is a 5*5 matrix for an image, then in the next step all the possible 3*3 matrices of the image is fetched out. The 3*3 matrix will be used as a mask and will be moved over the image to fetch the separated sub matrices, this process will be repeated till all the sub matrices have been find out.(Patidar et al.,2014)

Once all the sub matrices have been captured out of the input matrix, the next step comes into play, In this one by one each sub matrix feed to the network separately, which results into the output x1, x2, x3 and so on. The term convolution generally means by reduce the dimensionality with the help of introducing sub matrices. And hence the execution time for the image will be faster.

In the Figure 10, firstly the input image was divided into the sub matrices by applying a mask of 3*3 size, it was moved over the entire image and shifted to 1 place further, this process was repeated till whole image was not covered.

And then in figure 11 they were passed to the network. After which a optimized and filtered image with reduced dimensionality was found for the further processing.

Pooling Layer

After the convolutional layer, it further need to reduce the dimensionality of the image. This thing is achieved by performing pooling. Pooling is a layer in which sampling is performed. This is used for reducing the size of the image. In this operation row wise operation is performed on the resultant image.

Figure 10. Convolution layer (applying filter)

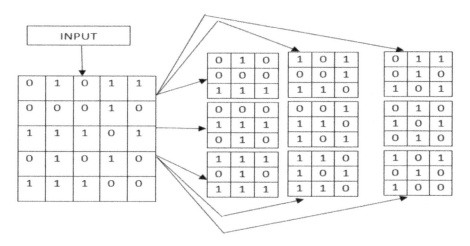

Figure 11. Further dimensionality reduction

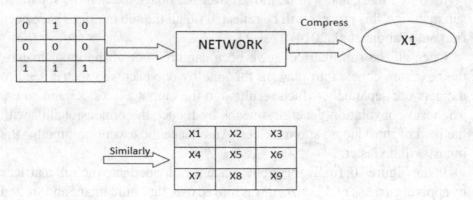

The pooling is of generally two types. Max pooling and Mean pooling. In the max pooling the maximum value out of each row is selected, whereas in Mean pooling, The mean value is selected as the representative value for that particular row.

In Figure 12, The max pooling is applied over the resultant image which was fetched after the convolution layer and a more precise image was fetched.

Fully Connected Layer

Once the pooling layer is finished the last stage is to sum up the output from previous layer and feeding it to the network. This is the sample working of Convolutional Neural Network. (Vakharia et al.,2017)

Figure 12. Max Pooling

Figure 13 shows that the output fetched after pooling is feed to a feed forward network. this process can repeat to a number of times depending upon the quality of result required.

DaQin & Haiyan (2018) presented a paper in which they discussed about the algorithm for large image, huge datasets. In this paper they have used deep convolutional network with a huge dataset and with the help of their work they have successfully achieved a accuracy up to 80%. Vo et al.. (2017) proposed a paper work on the classification online advertisement using CNN, they have used two parameters, numbers of layers(n) and number of filters(m) in convolution layer. The number of n and m varies. The output comes in YES or NO. This algorithm was to check if the online images(ads) are clearly visible or not. The accuracy was 86%. Han & Lee (2018) proposed an image classification technique based on CNN using a multithread GPU. The GPU had 256 threads which was limit for the each layer. The result was generating fast in terms of speed. So, it was a time efficient technique.

Autoencoder

It may be defined as, it is an enhanced version of convolutional neural network. This neural network work on the phenomenon of compression and reconstruction. In some cases it is observed that the neural network has lossy output in terms of information due to the compression, the network generally loss some of the information while performing compression. The autoencoder has two phases compression and decompression.

The input layer takes an image of any size as the input. In the next phase, it works same as the convolution layer as in convolutional neural network. First of all a filter of random size is applied on the image and then the image is divided into the submatrices. This was exactly the same work that was

Figure 13. Feeding the network

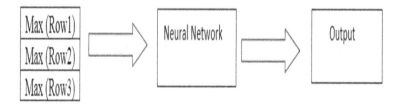

Figure 14. Autoencoder sample model

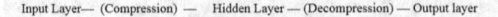

Input Layer— (Compression) —   Hidden Layer — (Decompression) — Output layer

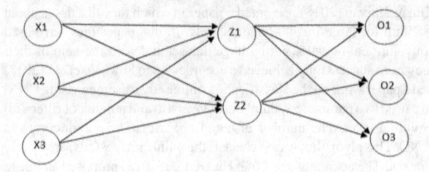

being done in the first phase of convolution layer, again the pooling is applied on the image to reduce its size more. And on that reduced part of image the feature extraction is performed.

The next part is known as decompression or reconstruction as the image, which was compressed earlier is recover in this phase. In figure 14, a sample autoencoder network is discussed. However, because of the compression the image recreated at the end, is quite blurry. This is because, some of the information is lost during the phase. The autoencoder is used for image classification, encoding, image reconstruction, denoising, pattern recognition etc.

Ding & Zhou (2017) presented a paper for enhancing the level accuracy in land use classification in a remote sensing image using stacked autoencoder. The network was trained through Greedy layer algorithm and then the network was optimized using back propagation network, which gave an output accuracy better than that of SVM and back propagation network. Ozdemir et al. (2017) proposed an paper in remote sensing domain for hyperspectral classification of highly dimensional image. They understood that deep autoencoder network is highly qualified for performing classification on an huge image. They have used stacked autoencoder for the same. They have used labelled data and soft-max activation function for hyperspectral classification. The results were impressive. CNN can be is used in many fields such as medical imaging, remote sensing images, blurry images, text and pattern recognition. Time taken by CNN can be more than that of traditional techniques but the results achieved are mostly better. The autoencoder is a deep learning neural network, which is almost similar to that CNN but here reverse process also takes place, this network is mostly used in classifying features and recognizing patterns.

CONCLUSION AND DISCUSSION

Image classification is the most popular tasks used in daily life. The chapter discussed about digital image and their types, classification techniques. Supervised techniques are used for classification, unsupervised techniques perform really well for performing clustering and when the size of images are very big than deep networks can be employed.

In this chapter the authors studied and discussed about some of the widely used classification techniques. It was very obvious from the chapter that almost all the classification techniques performs satisfactory with almost all kind of images, but with some specific images few techniques works extra ordinary. However, the accuracy and efficiency can be improved by enhancing the hardware or merging the algorithms. Still it would be unfair to say which technique is the best technique as the parameter for selecting a suitable technique may vary from person to person and heavily depends upon the kind of use.

REFERENCES

Beaula, A. R. S. R., Marikkannu, P., Sungheetha, A., & Sahana, C. (2016). Comparative study of distinctive image classification techniques. *2016 10th International Conference on Intelligent Systems and Control (ISCO)*, 1-8. doi: 10.1109/ICSGEA.2018.00064

Birare, G., & Chakkarwar, V. A. (2018). Automated detection of brain tumour cell using support vector. In *9th International Conference on Computing, Communication and Networking Technologies (ICCCNT)*. Bangalore: IEEE. doi: 10.1109/ICCCNT.2018.8494133

Courville, A., Goodfellow, A., & Bengio, Y. (2015). *Deep Learning*. Cambridge, MA: MIT Press.

Daqin, W., & Haiyan, H. (2018). The Algorithm Research of Image Classification Based on Deep Convolutional Network. *2018 International Conference on Smart Grid and Electrical Automation (ICSGEA)*, 231–233.10.1109/ICSGEA.2018.00064

Deeprasertkul, P., & Praikan, W. (2016). A rainfall forecasting estimation using image processing technology. *2016 International Conference on Information and Communication Technology Convergence (ICTC)*, 371-376. 10.1109/ICTC.2016.7763499

Detti, A. H., Jemei, S., Morando, S., & Steiner, N. Y. (2018). Classification Based Method Using Fast Fourier Transform (FFT) and Total Harmonic Distortion (THD) Dedicated to Proton Exchange Membrane Fuel Cell (PEMFC) Diagnosis. *2017 IEEE Vehicle Power and Propulsion Conference. VPPC, 2017*, 1–6. doi:10.1109/VPPC.2017.8331040

Ding, A., & Zhou, X. (2017). Land-Use Classification with Remote Sensing Image Based on Stacked Autoencoder. *Proceedings - 2016 International Conference on Industrial Informatics - Computing Technology, Intelligent Technology, Industrial Information Integration, ICIICII 2016*, (1), 145–149. 10.1109/ICIICII.2016.0044

Dixit, A., & Satpute, V. R. (2018). SIFRS: Spoof Invariant Facial Recognition System. *2018 9th International Conference on Computing, Communication and Networking Technologies (ICCCNT)*, 1–7.

El-Rahman, S. A. (2016). Hyperspectral imaging classification using ISODATA algorithm: Big data challenge. *Proceedings - 2015 5th International Conference on e-Learning, ECONF 2015*, 247–250. 10.1109/ECONF.2015.39

Gonzalez, R. C., & Woods, R. E. 1. (2008). Digital image processing (3rd ed.). Upper Saddle River, NJ: Prentice Hall.

Gurney, K. (1997). *Introduction to neural networks* (1st ed.). London: University College London Press. doi:10.4324/9780203451519

Han, S. H., & Lee, K. Y. (2018). Implemetation of image classification CNN using multi thread GPU. *Proceedings - International SoC Design Conference 2017, ISOCC 2017*, 296–297. 10.1109/ISOCC.2017.8368904

Hinton, G. E. (2007). Learning multiple layers of representation. *Trends in Cognitive Sciences, 11*(10), 428–434. doi:10.1016/j.tics.2007.09.004 PMID:17921042

Janadri, C. S., Sheeparamatti, B. G., & Kagawade, V. (2017). Multiclass classification of kirlian images using SVM technique. *2017 International Conference on Advances in Computing, Communications and Informatics, ICACCI 2017*, 2246–2250. 10.1109/ICACCI.2017.8126180

Jia, X. (2002). Simplified maximum likelihood classification for hyperspectral data in cluster space. *IEEE International Geoscience and Remote Sensing Symposium*, 2578-2580. doi: 10.1109/IGARSS.2002.1026706

Joshi, C., & Mukherjee, S. (2018). Empirical analysis of SIFT, Gabor and fused feature classification using SVM for multispectral satellite image retrieval. *2017 4th International Conference on Image Information Processing, ICIIP 2017*, 542–547. 10.1109/ICIIP.2017.8313776

Kar, S. A., & Kelkar, V. V. (2013). Classification of Multispectral satellite images. *International Conference on Advances in Technology and Engineering, ICATE 2013*, 115. 10.1109/ICAdTE.2013.6524747

Kavya, N., & Padmaja, K. V. (2017). Glaucoma detection using texture features extraction, *2017 51st Asilomar Conference on Signals, Systems, and Computers*, 1471-1475. doi: 10.1109/ACSSC.2017.8335600

Kawattikul, K., & Chomphuwiset, P. (2018). A simple text detection in document images using classification-based techniques. *IEEE 4th International Conference on Soft Computing and Machine Intelligence, ISCMI 2017*, 119–122. 10.1109/ISCMI.2017.8279610

Khamparia, A., & Pandey, B. (2015). Knowledge and intelligent computing methods in e-learning. *Int. J. Technol. Enhanc. Learn.*, 7(3), 221–242. doi:10.1504/IJTEL.2015.072810

Khamparia, A., & Pandey, B. (2016). Threat driven modeling framework using petri nets for e-learning system. *SpringerPlus*, 5(1), 446. doi:10.118640064-016-2101-0 PMID:27119050

Khamparia, A., & Pandey, B. (2017). Comprehensive analysis of semantic web reasoners and tools: A survey. *Education and Information Technologies*, 22(6), 3121–3145. doi:10.100710639-017-9574-5

Khamparia, A., & Pandey, B. (2017). A novel method of case representation and retrieval in CBR for e-learning. *Education and Information Technologies, Vol*, 22(1), 337–354. doi:10.100710639-015-9447-8

Khamparia, A., & Pandey, B. (2017). Effects of visual mapping placed game-based learning on students learning performance in defence-based courses. *Int. J. Technology Enhanced Learning*, 9(1), 37–50. doi:10.1504/IJTEL.2017.084083

Khamparia, A., & Pandey, B. (2018). SVM and PCA Based Learning Feature Classification Approaches for E-Learning System. *International Journal of Web-Based Learning and Teaching Technologies*, 13(2), 32–45. doi:10.4018/IJWLTT.2018040103

Khastavaneh, H., Ebrahimpour-Komleh, H., & Joudaki, M. (2017). Face image quality assessment based on photometric features and classification techniques. *2017 IEEE 4th International Conference on Knowledge-Based Engineering and Innovation (KBEI)*, 289–293. 10.1109/KBEI.2017.8324988

Li, B., Zhao, H., & Lv, Z. (2010). Parallel ISODATA clustering of remote sensing images based on MapReduce. *Proceedings - 2010 International Conference on Cyber-Enabled Distributed Computing and Knowledge Discovery, CyberC 2010*, 380–383. 10.1109/CyberC.2010.75

Mahapatra, S. (2018). *Why deep learning over machine learning*. Retrieved from https://towardsdatascience.com/why-deep-learning-is-needed-over-traditional-machine-learning-1b6a99177063

Mathwork. (2018). *Indexed image representation*. Retrieved from https://in.mathworks.com/help/matlab/creating_plots/image-ypes.html

Miranda, E., Aryuni, M., & Irwansyah, E. (2016). A survey of medical image classification techniques. *2016 International Conference on Information Management and Technology (ICIMTech)*, 56–61. 10.1109/ICIMTech.2016.7930302

Omatu, S., Fujinaka, T., Kosaka, T., Yanagimoto, H., & Yoshioka, M. (2001). Italian Lira classification by LVQ. *IJCNN'01. International Joint Conference on Neural Networks. Proceedings (Cat. No.01CH37222)*, 2947-2951. 10.1109/IJCNN.2001.938846

Ozdemir, A. O. B., Gedik, B. E., & Çetin, C. Y. Y. (2017). Hyperspectral classification using stacked autoencoders with deep learning. *Workshop on Hyperspectral Image and Signal Processing, Evolution in Remote Sensing.* 10.1109/WHISPERS.2014.8077532

Papadopoulos, G. T., Chandramouli, K., Mezaris, V., Kompatsiaris, I., Izquierdo, E., & Strintzis, M. G. (2008). A Comparative Study of Classification Techniques for Knowledge-Assisted Image Analysis. *2008 Ninth International Workshop on Image Analysis for Multimedia Interactive Services*, 4–7. 10.1109/WIAMIS.2008.36

Patidar, D., Jian, N., & Parikh, A. (2014). Performance Analysis of Artificial Neural Network and K Nearest Neighbors Image Classification Techniques with Wavelet features. *IEEE International Conference on Computer Communication and Systems(ICCCS'14), Chennai, INDIA*, 191–194. 10.1109/ICCCS.2014.7068192

Ramya, M., & Praveen, K. (2015). Performance comparison of content based and ISODATA clustering based on news video anchorperson detection. *2015 International Conference on Innovations in Information, Embedded and Communication Systems (ICIIECS)*, 1-5. 10.1109/ICIIECS.2015.7193105

Rani, N. S. (2017). Region Based Image Classification using Watershed Transform Techniques. *Intelligent Computing and Control (I2C2), 2017 International Conference on Intelligent Computing and Control*, 1-5.

Saravanan, C. (2010). Color Image to Grayscale Image Conversion. *2010 Second International Conference on Computer Engineering and Applications*, 196-199. 10.1109/ICCEA.2010.192

Shi, W., Gong, Y., Tao, X., Cheng, D., & Zheng, N. (2018). Fine-Grained Image Classification Using Modified DCNNs Trained by Cascaded Softmax and Generalized Large-Margin Losses. *IEEE Transactions on Neural Networks and Learning Systems*, 1–12. doi:10.1109/TNNLS.2018.2852721 PMID:30047915

Singh, C., Cheggoju, N., & Satpute, V. R. (2018). Implementing Classification algorithms in Medical Report Analysis for helping Patient during unavailability of Medical expertise. *2018 9th International Conference on Computing, Communication and Networking Technologies (ICCCNT)*, 1–5.

Sisodia, P. S., Tiwari, V., & Kumar, A. (2014). A comparative analysis of remote sensing image classification techniques. *2014 International Conference on Advances in Computing, Communications and Informatics (ICACCI)*, 1418–1421. 10.1109/ICACCI.2014.6968245

Unnithan, S. (2004, July 19). Epic movie Mughale-Azam returns in colour cinemascope, digital sound. *India Today Magzine.* Retrieved from https://www.indiatoday.in/magazine/society-the-arts/films/story/20040719-epic-movie-mughale-azam-returns-in-colour-digital-sound-789831-2004-07-19

Vakharia, V., Kiran, M. B., Dave, N. J., & Kagathara, U. (2017). Feature extraction and classification of machined component texture images using wavelet and artificial intelligence techniques. *2017 8th International Conference on Mechanical and Aerospace Engineering (ICMAE)*, 140–144. 10.1109/ICMAE.2017.8038631

Vo, A. T., Tran, H. S., & Le, T. H. (2017). Advertisement image classification using convolutional neural network. *Proceedings - 2017 9th International Conference on Knowledge and Systems Engineering*, 197–202. 10.1109/KSE.2017.8119458

Wilkinson, G. G. (2004). Are Remotely Sensed Image Classification Techniques Improving? Results of a Long Term Trend Analysis. *IEEE Workshop on Advances in Techniques for Analysis of Remotely Sensed Data*, 30-34.doi: 10.1109/WARSD.2003.1295169

Wu, M., Tang, E., & Lin, B. (2000). Data hiding in digital binary image. *2000 IEEE International Conference on Multimedia and Expo. ICME2000. Proceedings. Latest Advances in the Fast Changing World of Multimedia (Cat. No.00TH8532)*, 393-396. 10.1109/ICME.2000.869623

Wu, S., Chen, H., Zhao, Z., Long, H., & Song, C. (2015). An improved remote sensing image classification based on K-means using HSV color feature. *Proceedings - 2014 10th International Conference on Computational Intelligence and Security, CIS 2014*, 201–204. 10.1109/CIS.2014.90

Yeh, C. H., & Kuo, C. J. (2002). Image segmentation through index images. *2002 IEEE International Symposium on Circuits and Systems. Proceedings.* doi: 10.1109/ISCAS.2002.1010930

Chapter 10
Intelligent Medical Diagnostic System for Diabetes

Jimmy Singla
Lovely Professional University, India

ABSTRACT

In this chapter, the neuro-fuzzy technique has been used for the diagnosis of different types of diabetes. It has been reported in the literature that triangular membership functions have been deployed for Mamdani and Sugeno fuzzy expert systems that have been used for diagnosis of different types of diabetes. The Gaussian membership functions are expected to give better results. In this context, Gaussian membership functions have been attempted in the neuro-fuzzy system for the diagnosis of different types of diabetes in the research work, and improved results have been obtained in terms of different parameters like sensitivity, specificity, accuracy, precision. Further, for the comparative study, the dataset used for neuro-fuzzy expert system developed in this research work has been considered on Mamdani fuzzy expert system as well as Sugeno fuzzy expert system, and it has been confirmed that the result parameters show better values in the proposed model.

DOI: 10.4018/978-1-5225-9096-5.ch010

INTRODUCTION

Diabetes occurs due to lack of insulin. The body uses glucose through the help of a hormone called insulin. But this hormone cannot be produced by the diabetic person properly. So, due to lack of insulin the glucose level in the blood increases and it results in high blood sugar. The main causes of diabetes are health and environmental factors. Diabetes can be diagnosed by some blood tests like RBS, AIC test, PP test etc. There are mainly three types of diabetes. These three types are type1 diabetes, type2 diabetes and pre diabetes. The destruction of cells of the pancreatic tissue is the major reason of diabetes known as the islets of langerhans. Type 1 diabetes arises mostly due to autoimmune disorder or strong genetic components. Type1 diabetes arises mostly in children and adults. It will increase the blood glucose level of the body. 5 to 10 percent of the persons are affected by type1 diabetes. The warning signs of type 1 diabetes are regular urination, disproportionate dehydration and tetchiness, severe starvation accompanied by loss of weight, sickness, queasiness and tiredness. Type 2 Diabetes is another category of diabetes which occurs due to genetic links, lack of sleep, poor diet, obesity, stress, etc. Rate of type 2 diabetic patients has increased markedly since 1960. In 1985, it was approximately 30 million people and in 2010 it was approximately 285 million people. 20 to 40 percent of population is affected by type 2 diabetes. Type2 diabetes is developed in a person having age in between forty five to sixty five. The main reasons of type2 diabetes are obesity and family history. Other symptoms of type 2 diabetes are lack of sensation in hands or feet, gum or bladder infectivity, exhaustion, imprecise vision, frequent urination, excessive thirst, excessive irritability. Pre Diabetes is like a wakeup call that human is on the path of diabetes. In Prediabetes the level of blood glucose is higher than normal. Pre Diabetes makes patient more likely to get heart disease or have a stroke. But patient can also take actions to lower those risks. Prediabetes can also lead to type 2 diabetes.

There are several factors affecting diabetes. In this study we have considered following factors for the diagnosis of diabetes:

- Age
- Obesity
- RBS
- Family health history

Age is the length of time during which a human being has existed. As said by the organization of american diabetes, about 5090 citizens below the age of 20 are diagnosed with type 2 diabetes annually.

Obesity is a state where an individual has gathered so much body fat that it might have a harmful result on the health. The community is normally considered overweight or obese when their BMI is more than 30 kg/m2.

Random blood sugar test is performed on a sample of blood to measure level of glucose in blood. It is performed to confirm diabetes mellitus.

Family health history is a significant parameter with which a number of serious diseases occurred, even including type 2 diabetes. In truth, mostly individuals with type 2 diabetes have same disease in their blood relations like father, mother, brother and sister.

Need of the Study

Though India is a developed country yet the death rate increases day by day because of the different diseases such as kidney failure, cardiovascular disease, skin problem and cancer. Most of these diseases occur due to diabetes. Today, in India there are more than 62 million diabetic persons. IDF identifies that, almost 52% of Indian persons are distressed from diabetes and they do not know about disease. According to IDF in 2011 nearly 10 lacs Indian were affected by diabetes and by 2030 the numbers are expected to cross 100 million. Nearly 44 lacs adults aged (20 to 79 years) are affected by the diabetes. The reason behind the increase in death rate is unawareness among individuals. Another reason is the carelessness of individuals regarding their lifestyle that increases the diseases and results in a high death rate. It concludes that the medical expert systems are required to overcome the burden due to diabetes. This study is about the classification of diabetes by using intelligent systems. This study focuses on detection of all kinds of diabetes like type1, type2 and prediabetes by using Mamdani FIS and Sugeno FIS. In this research work, Neuro-fuzzy expert system has been proposed and better results have been obtained.

Artificial Intelligence

The intelligence exhibited by the machine or software is called artificial intelligence. Artificial intelligence means not a natural intelligence. It is an interdisciplinary field that covers science, mathematics, neuroscience and computer science. Reasoning, knowledge, planning, natural language processing are the main goals of artificial intelligence. To fulfill these goals and to learn about intelligence, a machine called artificial intelligent machine is used. The intelligent systems react to the inputs and in response give appropriate directions. They accumulate knowledge in their memory, analyze them using certain framed rules and update their capabilities. AI technologies have been effectively explored to their complete levels in the problem solving domains. They provide reasons about the problems as well as solutions by using different concepts and methods for building programs. The expansion of expert systems for decision making is the most commonly used AI applications.

Intelligent System

In intelligent system, the executive capabilities of an individual expert are emulated by a computer system. Expert systems are the part of artificial intelligence. These are the computer programs which deal with incomplete and uncertain data. Expert Systems represent domain specific knowledge. The expert systems can consider the problems to take out new information. They can achieve the knowledge from practice and make the predictions by using processes like natural evolution. The expert systems allow some probable results to be chosen with different grade of confidence. The output of an expert system may be informative, a lesson or a risk ruling. An expert system consists of two parts. These parts are the 1) knowledge base 2) inference engine. The facts and rules are characterized by the knowledge base. The inference engine applies rules to the facts and it has an explanation and debugging capabilities. For building an expert system, the knowledge is always provided by the domain professional. The knowledge engineer encodes the information to the knowledge base. It is having the knowledge of the system. It behaves like an intelligent assistant as human expert. The Inference Engine draws a conclusion from the knowledge contained by the knowledge-base. It is responsible for getting the final solution from the initial information.

Simple Rule Based Medical Expert System

The medical diagnosis is the significant application of intelligent system. The most important objective of every medical diagnostic expert system is classification of ailment. A medical diagnostic intelligent system is a combination of medical knowledge base with programs. The results got from medical diagnostic expert system are same as the results provided by specialist in that problem domain. Medical Knowledge of dedicated physician or expert is very important for the development of medical diagnostic intelligent system. The facts are composed in two stages. In the initial stage, the medical situation of disease is recorded in personal interactions with patients and experts. After this in the second stage, rules are generated where each rule is having two components IF and THEN. IF component contains symptoms and THEN component contains disease.

Fuzzy Logic

It is a technique for computing supported on partial truth values. The partial truth values are always among the completely false and completely true.

Fuzzy Expert System

Fuzzy medical expert systems are grouping of rules and membership functions. Fuzzy systems are sloping towards mathematical processing. Fuzzy logic is a developing tool for its modeling using real values taken from structured range. It is likely to maintain as many features of classical logic as feasible. Fuzzy logic is based on data processing methodology that is extremely suitable when seeking to form indefinite information and to formulate coherent judgments in an uncertain environment. The fuzzy expert system is based on three walks. In the first walk, the non fuzzy set is transformed into fuzzy set. It is known as fuzzification. In the next walk, the input set is transformed into output fuzzy set. In the third walk, the fuzzy set value is converted into concrete value.

Mamdani-Type Fuzzy Inference System

Mamdani model confines the knowledge of an expert. It allows us to demonstrate the knowledge in more understanding and human oriented way.

Most of the computational troubles can be held by Mamdani fuzzy system. In Mamdani fuzzy system, the outcome is evaluated via the process known as defuzzification. Mamdani fuzzy system is largely applied in decision support applications. In this research, The Mamdani fuzzy model is implemented for the identification of diabetes.

Sugeno-Type Fuzzy Inference System

Sugeno model does its work in a finer manner with better adjustment of the membership functions in order to tremendously mold the data. The differentiation among Sugeno and Mamdani system is in the approach in which their crisp outcome is produced from the fuzzy participation. The outcome is designed by evaluating the weighted average of input values. The considerable control of Mamdani output is not offered in the Sugeno fuzzy system as the output of the set of rules is either constant or linear in Sugeno fuzzy system.

Neural Network

It is an in order processing representation that is stimulated by the way in which biological nervous systems like brain processes information. The major component of this model is the new arrangement of the processing system. It is a collection of a huge number of extremely high interconnected processing elements running in unity to answer specific problems. Neural Network discovers by examples. It is configured for a particular application through a learning process. The adjustments to the synaptic connections are involved in learning phase of the biological systems. These adjustments do exist between the neurons. Neural networks have significant capability to develop meanings from complex or indefinite data. They can be applied to take out patterns and identify movements that are also difficult to be observed by either human beings or other principles. A trained neural network can be considered as a professional in the class of information that has been assigned to it for the purpose of study and analysis.

Neuro-Fuzzy System

From the time when the fuzzy systems are accepted in medical applications, the society recognized that the expansion and growth of a fuzzy expert system having outstanding performance is not a simple task. The problems occur in discovery of membership functions and suitable set of rules and it is a very exhausting procedure of errors. This shows the way that learning algorithms should be applied to fuzzy expert systems. The neural networks have been offered as an option to computerize or to carry the improved systems. The mainstream of the beginning application of these systems was in process control. It is relevant for all the regions of the information like data classification, data analysis, defect detection and hold to assessment making etc. Neural networks and fuzzy systems can join their benefits and to cure the human sickness. Thus, the shortcomings of the fuzzy expert systems are remunerated by the capability of neural network. These practices are corresponding to each other, which justify their use together.

BACKGROUND

L E. Egede et al. (2010) described the correlation among diabetes and depression. A wide seek of the literature was made on Medline commencing 1966 to 2009. The diabetes and depression coexistly affect the mortality, health care costs, decreased adherence to treatment, increase complication rates, decreased superiority of existence and enlarged danger of demise. The depression and diabetes are having some common symptom. These are cold hands and feet, numbness in hands, polyuria, abnormal thirst and daytime sleepiness. Ahmad A Al-Hajji (2012) developed a system for detection of neurological disarray. More than 10 types of neurological infections are identified by the proposed system. Due to the nervous system disorders, there are often unusual attacks to the humans and this system gives recommendations to the humans regarding these attacks. The production rules were constructed on the symptoms of every kind of neurological disease and they were proposed using decision tree and inferred using backward chaining method. The knowledge base includes information that is collected from practitioners or experts from neurology department of different hospitals. T S Zeki et al. (2012) presented a rule based expert system. The main objective of this paper is to diagnose all types of diabetes. Diagnosis of diabetes is done on the bases of Patient's age, patient's situation, symptoms like headache, over thirst, feeling hungry, overweight, family history, etc. The aim of this paper is to provide information and treatment advices to the patients. Jimmy Singla

(2013) implemented a medical diagnostic expert system to recognize the lung infections between the users. The decision is given using the symptoms that can be experienced by the user. This medical expert system assists the medical professionals or users in making the suitable diagnosis of the patient. There are many common and uncommon symptoms for the lung diseases. This generates much difficulty for the medical professionals to arrive at a correct conclusion. This expert system can remove this difficulty and it is having knowledge of thirty two lung diseases. Its accuracy is 70%. A Keles et al. (2008) analyzed the thyroid disease by using the expert system. In important organs of the body the thyroid gland is one of them. As the thyroid sometime produces too much hormone and sometime does not produce enough hormones, which affect the energy rate of the body. This is the reason, the body of thyroid patient does not work properly. ESTDD system is basically designed for the doctors who are not using the advanced computer applications. The authors applied Neuro fuzzy method to diagnose the accuracy of the system. The accuracy achieved with ESTDD is 95.33%. B Pandey et al. (2009) provided a knowledge based system and intelligent computing system (ICS) for planning, diagnosis and treatment in medicine. KBS is the combination of rule based reasoning, case based reasoning, and model based reasoning and ICS is the combination of genetic algorithm, artificial neural network (ANN) and fuzzy logic. So the aim of this paper is to represent the development and deployment of various expert system methodologies. Mohammed Abbas Kadhim et al. (2011) proposed a medical diagnostic expert system for detection of back pain diseases using fuzzy logic. The input parameters for this medical diagnostic expert system are body mass index, age, gender of patient etc. On the basis of these input factors, this medical diagnostic expert system formulates appropriate decision on back pain diseases and also offers suggestions to the patient. The accuracy of this fuzzy expert system is 90%. X.Y. Djam and Y. H. Kimbi (2011) stated that the hypertension is one of the most dangerous diseases and there is a requirement to manage this disease using fuzzy logic. Everybody is concerned with hypertension in some ways. For example - one can be a patient, a patient's relative or a wise counselor. In this research work, a medical diagnostic expert system is developed for the management of hypertension. This medical diagnostic expert system diagnoses the likelihood of the disease and its strictness using fuzzy logic. Fuzzy logic approach offers an easy method to reach at a specific conclusion from ambiguous or noisy data using linguistic variables. In order to accomplish this, a study of the knowledge based system for the management of hypertension was undertaken. The proposed system uses the concept of forward chaining method in performing deductions and the root sum square of drawing inference was engaged to infer the data from the developed production rules. The centroid approach is used for the defuzzification. The proposed system is simulated in the in MATLAB 7.10.0. The proposed system is applied on the data of 30 patients and performance of the proposed system is calculated. The calculated results were in the range of the predefined limits by the medical professionals. The proposed system has 85% accuracy. M F Ganji and M S Abadeh (2011) described the system by integrating ant colony optimization and fuzzy system called FCS-ANTMINER. The system is designed for the diagnosis of diabetes disease based on the input variables such as age, plasma glucose concentration, oral glucose tolerance test, BMI. The parameter accuracy, precision, recall and f-square are calculated based on the given input variables. In FCS-ANTMINER, first of all ACO is applied to generate fuzzy rules during the training process and then these rules are tested to calculate the result of the system. The accuracy obtained with the system is 84.24%. Vishali Bhandari and Rajeev Kumar (2015) stated that diabetes is a condition in which a body can not produce insulin, which is compulsory to manage glucose. Diabetes will also affect the heart infection, kidney infection, nerve injure, and blood vessel harm. This study exercises Mamdani and Sugeno intelligent systems for the detection of diabetes. Fuzzy intelligent system is a grouping of membership functions and rules. This research work summarizes the necessary dissimilarity among the Mamdani and Sugeno intelligent systems with different input parameters. They proved that the Sugeno fuzzy systems have better results than Mamdani fuzzy systems.

Summary of Background Work

The simple rule based expert systems do not tell the probability that the diagnosis is close to reality. They are often implemented in PROLOG. The fuzzy logic should be incorporated with the simple rule based approach. With fuzzy logic, the system will be able to compute the probability that the diagnosis is close to the reality. So it is concluded here that the fuzzy logic can be incorporated in the research work. But the problem still arise is there is need to formulate the rules and membership functions manually. These membership functions and rules are generated with the knowledge taken from doctors. So learning algorithms of neural network are applied to the fuzzy system so that these membership functions and rules can be generated automatically and it is expected that the automatically generated membership functions and rules can give better results than the manually generated rules and membership functions. In the literature, the authors have diagnosed all kinds of diabetes using Mamdani and Sugeno systems. They concluded that the performance of Sugeno fuzzy system is better than the Mamdani fuzzy system. In this research work, the authors have developed membership functions and rules manually. In this work, the learning algorithms of neural network have been incorporated with fuzzy logic for the detection of all types of diabetes. So all the membership functions and rules have been generated automatically and performance is found to be better than the fuzzy systems. In our work, we have also implemented the Mamdani and Sugeno models and compared the performance with neuro fuzzy system.

Development of Neuro-Fuzzy System

The medical diagnostic intelligent system for detection of all types of diabetes is developed using neuro fuzzy technique. The input variables used in this research are age, obesity, RBS, family history and output variable is type of diabetes. All these input and output parameters are described in introduction section. The data pertaining above input variables has been acquired from experts in medical assessments on patients of diabetes. Further fuzzy expert system is generated through four inputs plus one output. The four inputs have been assigned the variable names input1, input2, input3, input4 and output has been assigned the variable name output. The formation of the proposed neuro-fuzzy intelligent system for detection of all types of diabetes is shown in Figure 1.

Membership Functions

Gaussian membership functions are taken for each input. Input1 and input3, each is having three Gaussian membership functions. Input2 and input4, each is having two Gaussian membership functions. For example for variable

Figure 1. Structure of Neuro-fuzzy System

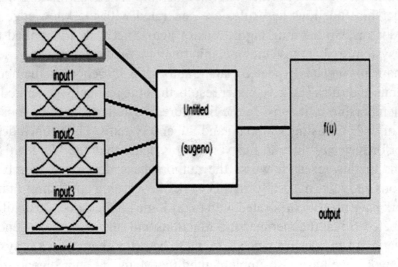

one that is age, it has been divided into three groups, young, middle and old (Automatically generated from training the dataset). Each of these three groups will become three membership functions of variable AGE. Likewise for others, we have corresponding membership functions depending upon the range automatically taken from the dataset during the training phase. The membership functions for input1, input2, input3, input4 are shown in Figure 2, Figure 3, Figure 4, Figure 5 respectively. When ANFIS model is used,

Figure 2. Membership function for input1 i.e. Age

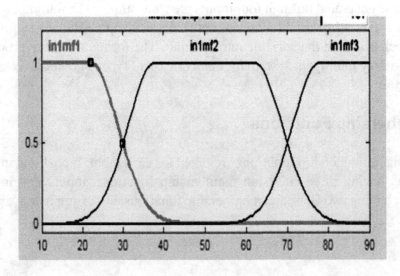

Figure 3. Membership functions for input2 i.e. Obesity

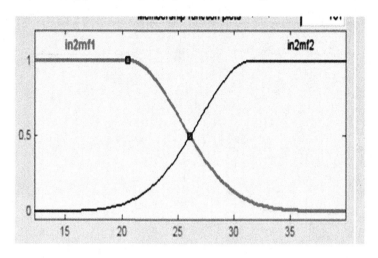

Figure 4. Membership functions for input3 i.e. RBS

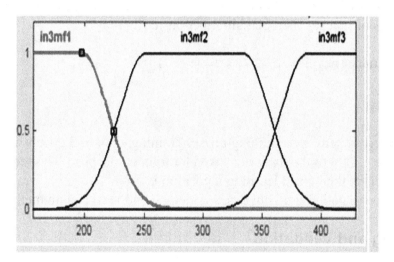

both membership functions and rules are automatically generated. They are identified from training set. These are not externally defined.

Rules

Rules are developed using membership functions taking all the possible combinations and it will result in 36 numbers of rules. Total number of rules =

Figure 5. Membership functions for input4 i.e. Family History

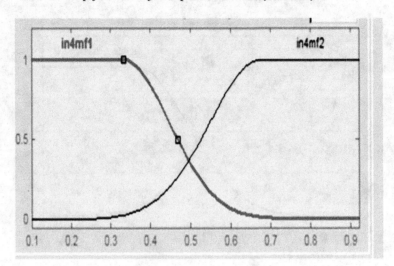

membership functions of input1*membership functions of input2*membership functions of input3* membership functions of input4.

Total number of rules=$3*2*3*2=36$

Training

The expert system is on training phase. Training error at 5 epochs is shown in Figure 6. 70% of the dataset is taken for training purpose. To speed up the convergence, the hybrid learning algorithm is used. This is an arrangement of back propagation gradient descent method and least square method.

Testing and Validation

Testing of dataset is done after the training at different epochs. The data which is not a part of training dataset is to be tested to validate the accuracy of the system. 30% of the dataset is taken for testing and validation purpose. Validation dataset is the dataset offered to the qualified fuzzy inference system to observe how intelligent the system guesses the subsequent dataset outcome values. The dataset is also not a part of training dataset.

Figure 6. Training error at 5 epochs

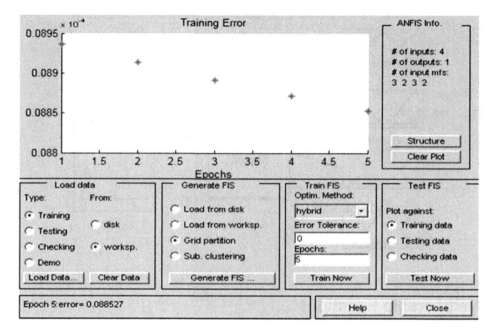

Development of Mamdani Fuzzy System

The Mamdani system is validated for the dataset taken for detection of special types of diabetes. The input variables that is symptoms and output that is resultant type of diabetes used in this model are taken exactly same as taken in the neuro-fuzzy model for diagnosis of different types of diabetes. The knowledge acquired from experts while development of neuro fuzzy intelligent system is used here for validation of Mamdani system for all special types of diabetes.

Fuzzy Expert System

Mamdani fuzzy expert system is validated for four inputs plus one output. The four inputs are age, obesity, RBS, family history and output is type of diabetes. The structure of the Mamdani fuzzy intelligent system for detection of all special types of diabetes is shown in Figure 7.

Figure 7. Fuzzy Logic Structure

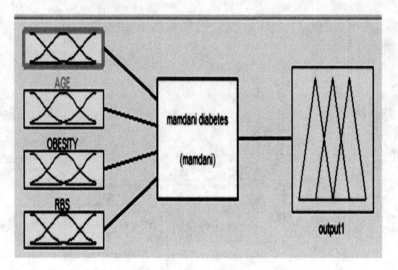

Membership Functions

Triangular membership functions are taken for each input. Age and RBS, each is having three triangular membership functions. Obesity and family history, each is having two triangular membership functions. The output type of diabetes has three triangular membership functions. The membership functions for Age, obesity, RBS, Family history and type of diabetes are shown in Figure 8, Figure 9, Figure 10, Figure 11 and Figure 12 respectively.

Figure 8. Membership functions for Age

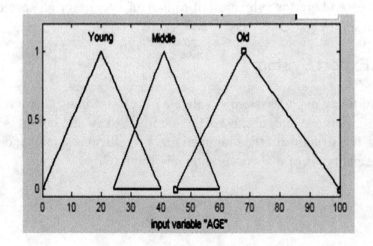

Figure 9. Membership functions for Obesity

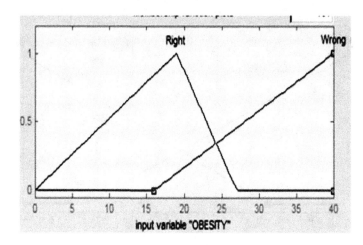

Figure 10. Membership functions for RBS

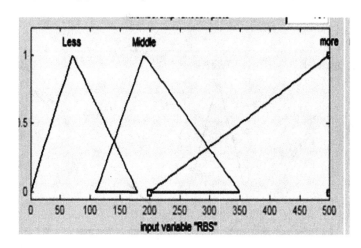

Rules

Rules are designed with the help of knowledge taken from experts. These are shown in Figure 13.

Development of Sugeno Fuzzy System

The Sugeno model is also validated for dataset taken for diagnosis of special categories of diabetes. The development of Sugeno system is almost same

Figure 11. Membership functions for family history

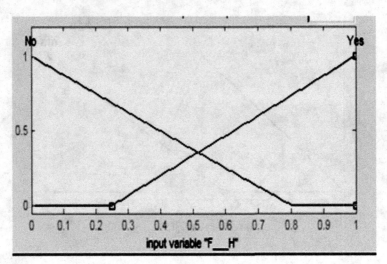

Figure 12. Membership functions for Type of diabetes

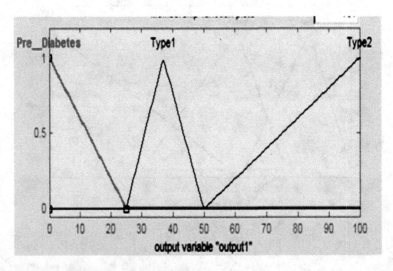

as the Mamdani system. The output membership functions are only different in both systems. The output using Sugeno model can vary from 0 to 1 and output membership functions are here taken as constant. So for pre-diabetes, constant value 0 is considered and for type1diabetes, it is 0.5 and for type2 diabetes, it is 1.

Figure 13. Rules in Mamdani Fuzzy System

1. If (AGE is Young) and (OBESITY is Right) and (RBS is Less) and (F___H is No) then (output1 is Pre_Diabetes) (1)
2. If (AGE is Young) and (OBESITY is Right) and (RBS is Less) and (F___H is Yes) then (output1 is Pre_Diabetes) (1)
3. If (AGE is Young) and (OBESITY is Right) and (RBS is Middle) and (F___H is No) then (output1 is Pre_Diabetes) (1)
4. If (AGE is Young) and (OBESITY is Right) and (RBS is Middle) and (F___H is Yes) then (output1 is Type1) (1)
5. If (AGE is Young) and (OBESITY is Right) and (RBS is more) and (F___H is No) then (output1 is Type1) (1)
6. If (AGE is Young) and (OBESITY is Right) and (RBS is more) and (F___H is Yes) then (output1 is Type1) (1)
7. If (AGE is Young) and (OBESITY is Wrong) and (RBS is Less) and (F___H is No) then (output1 is Pre_Diabetes) (1)
8. If (AGE is Young) and (OBESITY is Wrong) and (RBS is Less) and (F___H is Yes) then (output1 is Pre_Diabetes) (1)
9. If (AGE is Young) and (OBESITY is Wrong) and (RBS is Middle) and (F___H is No) then (output1 is Type1) (1)
10. If (AGE is Young) and (OBESITY is Wrong) and (RBS is Middle) and (F___H is Yes) then (output1 is Type1) (1)
11. If (AGE is Young) and (OBESITY is Wrong) and (RBS is more) and (F___H is No) then (output1 is Type1) (1)
12. If (AGE is Young) and (OBESITY is Wrong) and (RBS is more) and (F___H is Yes) then (output1 is Type2) (1)
13. If (AGE is Middle) and (OBESITY is Right) and (RBS is Less) and (F___H is No) then (output1 is Pre_Diabetes) (1)
14. If (AGE is Middle) and (OBESITY is Right) and (RBS is Less) and (F___H is Yes) then (output1 is Pre_Diabetes) (1)
15. If (AGE is Middle) and (OBESITY is Right) and (RBS is Middle) and (F___H is No) then (output1 is Type1) (1)
16. If (AGE is Middle) and (OBESITY is Right) and (RBS is Middle) and (F___H is Yes) then (output1 is Type1) (1)
17. If (AGE is Middle) and (OBESITY is Right) and (RBS is more) and (F___H is No) then (output1 is Type1) (1)
18. If (AGE is Middle) and (OBESITY is Right) and (RBS is more) and (F___H is Yes) then (output1 is Type2) (1)

RESULTS

Now throughout evaluating the output of the intelligent system, the professional expert organize adequately and inadequately detected patient folders by evaluating decisions made by the intelligent system with the professional expert decisions made on similar patients cases and different presentation factors are calculated with different models as given in Table 1.

CONCLUSION AND FUTURE SCOPE

This neuro-fuzzy expert system can help the expert and inexpert to determine the different types of diabetes. This system is like a supporting tool that

Table 1. Performance of different fuzzy models

S. No.	Disease	Model	Membership function	Sensitivity (%)	Specificity (%)	Precision (%)	Accuracy (%)
1	Types of Diabetes	Neuro-fuzzy	Gaussian	96.67	98.33	98.31	97.5
2		Mamdani	Triangular	91.67	90	90.16	90.83
3		Sugeno	Triangular	93.33	91.67	91.8	92.5

helps the expert in his prescription to keep the patient stable. Mamdani and Sugeno fuzzy models have also been validated for the same data set. The performance of each medical expert system is calculated in the form of different parameters like accuracy, precision, specificity and sensitivity. From the parameters, this is concluded that the neuro-fuzzy intelligent system is more accurate as compared to Mamdani system, Sugeno fuzzy and simple rule based systems. There is a need of only computer system and MATLAB software to implement this research work. So this system may also be used in hospitals. This type of system is much beneficial in developing counties where the number of deaths imputed to different diseases is very high.

With the passage of time, medical study and research will identify more parameters that effect on the identification of different types of diabetes. These parameters can be incorporated into the neuro-fuzzy models being undertaken in the research work.

REFERENCES

Abdullah, A. A., Zakaria, Z., & Mohammad, N. F. (2011). Design and Development of Fuzzy Expert System for Diagnosis of Hypertension. *Proc. 2nd International Conference on Intelligent Systems, Modeling and Simulation*, 113-117. 10.1109/ISMS.2011.27

Al-Hajji, A. A. (2012). Rule Based Expert System for Diagnosis of Neurological Disorders. *Proc. International Conference on Communications and information Technology.*

Al-Malaise Al-Ghamdi, A., Wazzan, M. A., Mujallid, F. M., & Bakhsh, N. K. (2011). An Expert System of Determining Diabetes Treatment Based on Cloud Computing Platforms. *International Journal of Computer Science and Information Technologies*, 2(5), 1982–1987.

Alonso-Amo, F., Pérez, A. G., Gómez, G. L., & Montes, C. (1995). An expert system for homeopathic glaucoma treatment (SEHO). *Expert Systems with Applications*, 8(1), 89–99. doi:10.1016/S0957-4174(94)E0001-B

Bhandari, V., & Kumar, R. (2015). Comparative Analysis of Fuzzy Expert Systems for Diabetic Diagnosis. *International Journal of Computers and Applications*, 132(6), 8–14. doi:10.5120/ijca2015907424

Bojestig, M., Arnqvist, H. J., Hermanson, G., Karlberg, B. E., & Ludvigsson, J. (1994). Declining Incidence of Nephropathy in Insulin Dependent Diabetes Mellitus. *The New England Journal of Medicine*, 330(1), 15–18. doi:10.1056/NEJM199401063300103 PMID:8259139

Djam, X. Y., & Kimbi, Y. H. (2011). A Medical Diagnostic Support System for the Management of Hypertension. *Journal of Sciences and Multidisciplinary Research*, 3, 16–30.

Egede, L. E., & Ellis, C. (2010). Diabetes and Depression: Global Perspectives. *Diabetes Research and Clinical Practice*, 87(3), 302–312. doi:10.1016/j.diabres.2010.01.024 PMID:20181405

Ganji, M. F., & Abadeh, M. S. (2011). A Fuzzy Classification System Based on Ant Colony Optimization for Diabetes Disease Diagnosis. *Expert Systems with Applications*, 38(12), 14650–14659. doi:10.1016/j.eswa.2011.05.018

Kadhim, M. A., Alam, A., & Kaur, H. (2011). Design and Implementation of Fuzzy Expert System for Back Pain Diagnosis. International. *Journal of Innovative Technology & Creative Engineering, 1*(9), 16–22.

Kalpana, M., & Kumar, A. V. S. (2011). Fuzzy Expert System for Diabetes Using Fuzzy Verdict Mechanism. *International Journal of Advanced Networking and Applications, 3*(2), 1128–1134.

Keles, A., & Keles, A. (2008). ESTDD: Expert System for Thyroid Diseases Diagnosis. *Expert Systems with Applications, 34*(1), 242–246. doi:10.1016/j. eswa.2006.09.028

Khamparia, A., & Pandey, B. (2015). Knowledge and intelligent computing methods in e-learning. *Int. J. Technol. Enhanc. Learn., 7*(3), 221–242. doi:10.1504/IJTEL.2015.072810

Khamparia, A., & Pandey, B. (2016). Threat driven modeling framework using petri nets for e-learning system. *SpringerPlus, 5*(1), 446. doi:10.118640064-016-2101-0 PMID:27119050

Khamparia, A., & Pandey, B. (2017, January). A novel method of case representation and retrieval in CBR for e-learning. *Education and Information Technologies, Vol, 22*(1), 337–354. doi:10.100710639-015-9447-8

Khamparia, A., & Pandey, B. (2017). Effects of visual mapping placed game-based learning on students learning performance in defence-based courses. *Int. J. Technology Enhanced Learning, 9*(1), 37–50. doi:10.1504/IJTEL.2017.084083

Khamparia, A., & Pandey, B. (2017). Comprehensive analysis of semantic web reasoners and tools: A survey. *Education and Information Technologies, 22*(6), 3121–3145. doi:10.100710639-017-9574-5

Khamparia, A., & Pandey, B. (2018). SVM and PCA Based Learning Feature Classification Approaches for E-Learning System. *International Journal of Web-Based Learning and Teaching Technologies, 13*(2), 32–45. doi:10.4018/IJWLTT.2018040103

Khamparia, A., & Pandey, B. (2018, February). Effects of visual map embedded approach on students learning performance using BriggsMyers learning style in word puzzle gaming course. *Computers & Electrical Engineering, 66*(C), 531–540. doi:10.1016/j.compeleceng.2017.12.041

Miller, R. A. (1994). Medical Diagnostic Decision Support Systems - Past, Present, and Future: A Threaded Bibliography and Brief Commentary. *Journal of the American Medical Informatics Association*, *1*(1), 8–27. doi:10.1136/jamia.1994.95236141 PMID:7719792

Pandey, B., & Mishra, R. B. (2009). Knowledge and Intelligent Computing System in Medicine. *Computers in Biology and Medicine*, *39*(3), 215–230. doi:10.1016/j.compbiomed.2008.12.008 PMID:19201398

Remuzzi, G., Schieppati, A., & Ruggenenti, P. (2002). Nephropathy in Patients with Type 2 Diabetes. *The New England Journal of Medicine*, *346*(15), 1145–1151. doi:10.1056/NEJMcp011773 PMID:11948275

Singla, J. (2013). The diagnosis of Some Lung Diseases in a Prolog Expert System. *International Journal of Computers and Applications*, *78*(15), 37–40. doi:10.5120/13603-1435

Sproule, B. A., Naranjo, C. A., & Turksen, I. B. (2002). Fuzzy pharmacology: Theory and Applications. *Trends in Pharmacological Sciences*, *23*(9), 412–417. doi:10.1016/S0165-6147(02)02055-2 PMID:12237153

Srinivas, Y., Timmons, W. D., & Durkin, J. (2001). A Comparative Study of the three Expert Systems for Blood Pressure Control. *Expert Systems with Applications*, *20*(3), 267–274. doi:10.1016/S0957-4174(00)00065-8

Zadeh, L. A. (1975). The Concept of a Linguistic Variable and Its Application to Approximate Reasoning-I. *Information Sciences*, *8*(3), 199–249. doi:10.1016/0020-0255(75)90036-5

Zeki, T. S., Malakooti, M. V., Ataeipoor, Y., & Tabibi, S. T. (2012). An Expert System for Diabetes Diagnosis. *American Academic and Scholarly Research Journal Special Issue*, *4*(5), 1–13.

Compilation of References

Abdullah, A. A., Zakaria, Z., & Mohammad, N. F. (2011). Design and Development of Fuzzy Expert System for Diagnosis of Hypertension. *Proc. 2nd International Conference on Intelligent Systems, Modeling and Simulation*, 113-117. 10.1109/ISMS.2011.27

Adamic, L. A., & Adar, E. (2003). Friends and neighbors on the web. *Social Networks*, *25*(3), 211–230. doi:10.1016/S0378-8733(03)00009-1

Agarwal, A., Starobinski, D., & Little, T. D. (2012). Phase transition of message propagation speed in delay-tolerant vehicular networks. *IEEE Transactions on Intelligent Transportation Systems*, *13*(1), 249–263. doi:10.1109/TITS.2011.2168954

Ahmad, A., Whitworth, B., Zeshan, F., Bertino, E., & Friedman, R. (2017). Extending social networks with delegation. In *Computers & Security* (Vol. 70, pp. 546–564). Elsevier.

Airoldi, E. M., Anderson, A. G., Fienberg, S. E., & Skinner, K. K. (2006, June). Ronald Reagan's radio addresses? *Bayesian Analysis*, *1*(2), 289–320. doi:10.1214/06-BA110

Al-Hajji, A. A. (2012). Rule Based Expert System for Diagnosis of Neurological Disorders. *Proc. International Conference on Communications and information Technology*.

Al-Janabi, Al-Shourbaji, Shojafar, & Shamshirband. (2017). Survey of main challenges (security and privacy) in wireless body area networks for healthcare applications. *Egyptian Informatics Journal, 18*(2), 113-122.

Al-Malaise Al-Ghamdi, A., Wazzan, M. A., Mujallid, F. M., & Bakhsh, N. K. (2011). An Expert System of Determining Diabetes Treatment Based on Cloud Computing Platforms. *International Journal of Computer Science and Information Technologies*, *2*(5), 1982–1987.

Alonso-Amo, F., Pérez, A. G., Gómez, G. L., & Montes, C. (1995). An expert system for homeopathic glaucoma treatment (SEHO). *Expert Systems with Applications*, *8*(1), 89–99. doi:10.1016/S0957-4174(94)E0001-B

Amara, J., Bouaziz, B., & Algergawy, A. (2017). A Deep Learning-based Approach for Banana Leaf Diseases Classification. In BTW (Workshops) (pp. 79-88). Academic Press.

Amelkin, V., Bullo, F., & Singh, A. K. (2017). Polar Opinion Dynamics in Social Networks. *IEEE Transactions on Automatic Control*, *62*(11), 5650–5665. doi:10.1109/TAC.2017.2694341

Bachrach, Y., Kosinski, M., Graepel, T., Kohli, P., & Stillwell, D. (2012, June). Personality and patterns of Facebook usage. In *Proceedings of the 4th annual ACM web science conference* (pp. 24-32). ACM. 10.1145/2380718.2380722

Balagani, K. S., Phoha, V. V., Ray, A., & Phoha, S. (2011). On the discriminability of keystroke feature vectors used in fixed text keystroke authentication. *Pattern Recognition Letters*, *32*(7), 1070–1080. doi:10.1016/j. patrec.2011.02.014

Banga, K. (2016, October). Big Data Healthcare Market to reach $27.6bn by 2021. *Future Analytics World*. Retrieved from http://fusionanalyticsworld. com/big-data-healthcare-market-reach-27-6bn-2021/

Barabasi, A., & Albert, R. (1999). Emrgance of scaling in random networks. *Science*, *286*(5439), 509–512. doi:10.1126cience.286.5439.509 PMID:10521342

Barbedo, J. G. A. (2018). Impact of dataset size and variety on the effectiveness of deep learning and transfer learning for plant disease classification. *Computers and Electronics in Agriculture*, *153*, 46–53. doi:10.1016/j. compag.2018.08.013

Basco, J. A. (2017, November). Real-time analysis of healthcare using big data analytics. *IOP Conference Series. Materials Science and Engineering*, *263*(4), 042056. doi:10.1088/1757-899X/263/4/042056

Beaula, A. R. S. R., Marikkannu, P., Sungheetha, A., & Sahana, C. (2016). Comparative study of distinctive image classification techniques. *2016 10th International Conference on Intelligent Systems and Control (ISCO)*, 1-8. doi: 10.1109/ICSGEA.2018.00064

Benamar, N., Benamar, M., & Bonnin, J. M. (2012, May). Routing protocols for DTN in vehicular environment. In *Multimedia Computing and Systems (ICMCS), 2012 International Conference on* (pp. 589-593). IEEE. 10.1109/ICMCS.2012.6320307

Bernsen, J., & Manivannan, D. (2008, August). Greedy routing protocols for vehicular ad hoc networks. In *Wireless Communications and Mobile Computing Conference, 2008. IWCMC'08. International* (pp. 632-637). IEEE. 10.1109/IWCMC.2008.109

Bhandari, V., & Kumar, R. (2015). Comparative Analysis of Fuzzy Expert Systems for Diabetic Diagnosis. *International Journal of Computers and Applications*, *132*(6), 8–14. doi:10.5120/ijca2015907424

Bharghavan, V., Demers, A., Shenker, S., & Zhang, L. (1994). MACAW: A Media Access Protocol for Wireless LAN. *Proceedings of ACM SIGCOM '94*, 212-225. 10.1145/190314.190334

Biggs, N. L., Lloyd, K. E., & Wilson, R. J. (1986). Graph Theory (2nd ed.). New York, NY: The Clarendon Press.

Birare, G., & Chakkarwar, V. A. (2018). Automated detection of brain tumour cell using support vector. In *9th International Conference on Computing, Communication and Networking Technologies (ICCCNT)*. Bangalore: IEEE. doi: 10.1109/ICCCNT.2018.8494133

Bo, C., Zhang, L., Li, X. Y., Huang, Q., & Wang, Y. (2013, September). Silentsense: silent user identification via touch and movement behavioral biometrics. In *Proceedings of the 19th annual international conference on Mobile computing & networking* (pp. 187-190). ACM.

Bojestig, M., Arnqvist, H. J., Hermanson, G., Karlberg, B. E., & Ludvigsson, J. (1994). Declining Incidence of Nephropathy in Insulin Dependent Diabetes Mellitus. *The New England Journal of Medicine, 330*(1), 15–18. doi:10.1056/NEJM199401063300103 PMID:8259139

Bond, Chykina, & Jones. (2017). Social network effects on academic achievement. *The Social Science Journal, 54*(4), 438-449. doi:10.1016/j.soscij.2017.06.001

Brin, S., & Page, L. (1998). The anatomy of a large-scale hypertextual Web search engine. *Proceedings of the 7th International Conference on World Wide Web*, 107-117. 10.1016/S0169-7552(98)00110-X

Brown, N., Cambruzzi, J., Cox, P. J., Davies, M., Dunbar, J., Plumbley, D., & Sheppard, D. W. (2018). Big Data in Drug Discovery. *Progress in Medicinal Chemistry, 57*, 277–356. doi:10.1016/bs.pmch.2017.12.003 PMID:29680150

Campisi, P., Maiorana, E., Bosco, M. L., & Neri, A. (2009). User authentication using keystroke dynamics for cellular phones. *IET Signal Processing, 3*(4), 333–341. doi:10.1049/iet-spr.2008.0171

Cao, Y., & Sun, Z. (2013). Routing in delay/disruption tolerant networks: A taxonomy, survey and challenges. *IEEE Communications Surveys and Tutorials, 15*(2), 654–677. doi:10.1109/SURV.2012.042512.00053

Cerf, V., Burleigh, S., Hooke, A., Torgerson, L., Durst, R., Scott, K. & Weiss, H. (2007). *Delay-tolerant networking architecture* (No. RFC 4838).

Cesana, M., Maniezzo, D., Bergamo, P., & Gerla, M. (2003). Interference Aware (IA) MAC: an Enhancement to IEEE802.11b DCF. *Proceedings of IEEE Vehicular Technology Conference*. 10.1109/VETECF.2003.1286110

Chang, T. Y., Tsai, C. J., & Lin, J. H. (2012). A graphical-based password keystroke dynamic authentication system for touch screen handheld mobile devices. *Journal of Systems and Software, 85*(5), 1157–1165. doi:10.1016/j.jss.2011.12.044

Chen, H., Engkvist, O., Wang, Y., Olivecrona, M., & Blaschke, T. (2018). The rise of deep learning in drug discovery. *Drug Discovery Today, 23*(6), 1241–1250. doi:10.1016/j.drudis.2018.01.039 PMID:29366762

Chen, R., Liu, X., Jin, S., Lin, J., & Liu, J. (2018). Machine Learning for Drug-Target Interaction Prediction. *Molecules (Basel, Switzerland)*, *23*(9), 2208. doi:10.3390/molecules23092208 PMID:30200333

Chen, W., Paik, I., & Hung, P. C. K. (2015). Constructing a Global Social Service Network for Better Quality of Web Service Discovery. *IEEE Transactions on Services Computing*, *8*(2), 284–298. doi:10.1109/TSC.2013.20

Chen, X., Proulx, B., Gong, X., & Zhang, J. (2015). Exploiting Social Ties for Cooperative D2D Communications: A Mobile Social Networking Case. *IEEE/ACM Transactions on Networking*, *23*(5), 1471–1484. doi:10.1109/TNET.2014.2329956

Choudhury, R. R., & Vaidya, N. (2004). Deafness: A MAC Problem in Ad Hoc Networks when using Directional Antennas. Proc. of IEEE ICNP. doi:10.1109/ICNP.2004.1348118

Chow & Leung. (1999). *Performance of IEEE 802.11 medium access control protocol over a wireless local area network with distributed radio bridges.* WCNC 1999, New Orleans, LA.

Colwell, L. J. (2018). Statistical and machine learning approaches to predicting protein-ligand interactions. *Current Opinion in Structural Biology*, *49*, 123–128. doi:10.1016/j.sbi.2018.01.006 PMID:29452923

Courville, A., Goodfellow, A., & Bengio, Y. (2015). *Deep Learning.* Cambridge, MA: MIT Press.

Crawford, H., & Ahmadzadeh, E. (2017, July). Authentication on the go: assessing the effect of movement on mobile device keystroke dynamics. In *Thirteenth Symposium on Usable Privacy and Security* (pp. 163-173). Academic Press.

Crops. (n.d.). Retrieved from https://www.plantvillage.org/en/crops

Dávideková, M., & Greguš, M. (2017). Social Network Types: An Emergency Social Network Approach - A Concept of Possible Inclusion of Emergency Posts in Social Networks through an API. *2017 IEEE International Conference on Cognitive Computing (ICCC)*, 40-47. 10.1109/IEEE.ICCC.2017.13

Deeprasertkul, P., & Praikan, W. (2016). A rainfall forecasting estimation using image processing technology. *2016 International Conference on Information and Communication Technology Convergence (ICTC)*, 371-376. 10.1109/ICTC.2016.7763499

Detti, A. H., Jemei, S., Morando, S., & Steiner, N. Y. (2018). Classification Based Method Using Fast Fourier Transform (FFT) and Total Harmonic Distortion (THD) Dedicated to Proton Exchange Membrane Fuel Cell (PEMFC) Diagnosis. *2017 IEEE Vehicle Power and Propulsion Conference. VPPC, 2017*, 1–6. doi:10.1109/VPPC.2017.8331040

Dhamal, P., Nagaraj, U., & Devotale, D. (2011). *Study of various routing protocols in VANET*. Academic Press.

Dimitri, G. M., & Lió, P. (2017). DrugClust: A machine learning approach for drugs side effects prediction. *Computational Biology and Chemistry, 68*, 204–210. doi:10.1016/j.compbiolchem.2017.03.008 PMID:28391063

Ding, A., & Zhou, X. (2017). Land-Use Classification with Remote Sensing Image Based on Stacked Autoencoder. *Proceedings - 2016 International Conference on Industrial Informatics - Computing Technology, Intelligent Technology, Industrial Information Integration, ICIICII 2016*, (1), 145–149. 10.1109/ICIICII.2016.0044

Dixit, A., & Satpute, V. R. (2018). SIFRS: Spoof Invariant Facial Recognition System. *2018 9th International Conference on Computing, Communication and Networking Technologies (ICCCNT)*, 1–7.

Djam, X. Y., & Kimbi, Y. H. (2011). A Medical Diagnostic Support System for the Management of Hypertension. *Journal of Sciences and Multidisciplinary Research, 3*, 16–30.

Dyrmann, M., Jørgensen, R. N., & Midtiby, H. S. (2017). RoboWeedSupport-Detection of weed locations in leaf occluded cereal crops using a fully convolutional neural network. *Advances in Animal Biosciences, 8*(2), 842–847. doi:10.1017/S2040470017000206

Egede, L. E., & Ellis, C. (2010). Diabetes and Depression: Global Perspectives. *Diabetes Research and Clinical Practice, 87*(3), 302–312. doi:10.1016/j.diabres.2010.01.024 PMID:20181405

El-Rahman, S. A. (2016). Hyperspectral imaging classification using ISODATA algorithm: Big data challenge. *Proceedings - 2015 5th International Conference on e-Learning, ECONF 2015*, 247–250. 10.1109/ECONF.2015.39

Faloutsos, M., Faloutsos, P., & Faloutsos, C. (1999). On power-law relationships of the Internet topology. In *Proceedings of the conference on Applications, technologies, architectures, and protocols for computer communication (SIGCOMM '99)*. ACM. 10.1145/316188.316229

Ferdousi, R., Safdari, R., & Omidi, Y. (2017). Computational prediction of drug-drug interactions based on drugs functional similarities. *Journal of Biomedical Informatics*, *70*, 54–64. doi:10.1016/j.jbi.2017.04.021 PMID:28465082

Ferentinos, K. P. (2018). Deep learning models for plant disease detection and diagnosis. *Computers and Electronics in Agriculture*, *145*, 311–318. doi:10.1016/j.compag.2018.01.009

Fetterly, M., Manasse, M., Najork, M., & Wiener, J. L. (2004). A large-scale study of the evolution of web pages. *Software, Practice & Experience*, *34*(2), 213–237. doi:10.1002pe.577

Ganji, M. F., & Abadeh, M. S. (2011). A Fuzzy Classification System Based on Ant Colony Optimization for Diabetes Disease Diagnosis. *Expert Systems with Applications*, *38*(12), 14650–14659. doi:10.1016/j.eswa.2011.05.018

Gao, F., Musial, K., Cooper, C., & Tsoka, S. (2015). Link Prediction Methods and Their Accuracy for Different Social Networks and Network Metrics. Scientific Programming. doi:10.1155/2015/172879

Gao, X., & Guan, J. (2012). Network model of knowledge diffusion. *Scientometrics*, *90*(3), 749–762. doi:10.100711192-011-0554-z

Getoor, L. (2005). Link mining: A new data mining challenge. *SIGKDD Explorations*, *5*(1), 84–89. doi:10.1145/959242.959253

Ghani, S., Kwon, B. C., Lee, S., Yi, J. S., & Elmqvist, N. (2013). Visual Analytics for Multimodal Social Network Analysis: A Design Study with Social Scientists. *IEEE Transactions on Visualization and Computer Graphics*, *19*(12), 2032–2041. doi:10.1109/TVCG.2013.223 PMID:24051769

Giuffrida, C., Majdanik, K., Conti, M., & Bos, H. (2014, July). I sensed it was you: authenticating mobile users with sensor-enhanced keystroke dynamics. In *International Conference on Detection of Intrusions and Malware, and Vulnerability Assessment* (pp. 92-111). Springer. 10.1007/978-3-319-08509-8_6

Gonzalez, R. C., & Woods, R. E. 1. (2008). Digital image processing (3rd ed.). Upper Saddle River, NJ: Prentice Hall.

Gupta, P., & Kumar, P. R. (2000, March). The Capacity of Wireless Networks. *IEEE Transactions on Information Theory*, *46*(2), 388–404. doi:10.1109/18.825799

Gurney, K. (1997). *Introduction to neural networks* (1st ed.). London: University College London Press. doi:10.4324/9780203451519

Haas, Z. J., & Deng, J. (2002). Dual Busy Tone Multiple Access (DBTMA): A Multiple Access Control Scheme for Ad Hoc Networks. *IEEE Transactions on Communications*, *50*(6), 975–985. doi:10.1109/TCOMM.2002.1010617

Hage, P., & Harary, F. (1995). Eccentricity and centrality in networks social networks. Elsevier.

Hall, D., McCool, C., Dayoub, F., Sunderhauf, N., & Upcroft, B. (2015, January). Evaluation of features for leaf classification in challenging conditions. In *Applications of Computer Vision (WACV), 2015 IEEE Winter Conference on* (pp. 797-804). IEEE. 10.1109/WACV.2015.111

Han, S. H., & Lee, K. Y. (2018). Implemetation of image classification CNN using multi thread GPU. *Proceedings - International SoC Design Conference 2017, ISOCC 2017*, 296–297. 10.1109/ISOCC.2017.8368904

Hanneman, R. (2001). *Introduction to Social Network Methods*. Retrieved from http://faculty.ucr.edu/~hanneman/nettext/networks.zip

Hargittai, E., & Sandvig, C. (2016). *Big Data, Big Problems, Big Opportunities: Using Internet Log Data to Conduct Social Network Analysis Research. In Digital Research Confidential:The Secrets of Studying Behavior Online* (p. 288). MIT Press.

Harnie, D., Saey, M., Vapirev, A. E., Wegner, J. K., Gedich, A., Steijaert, M., & De Meuter, W. (2017). Scaling machine learning for target prediction in drug discovery using apache spark. *Future Generation Computer Systems*, *67*, 409–417. doi:10.1016/j.future.2016.04.023

Hasan, M. A., & Zaki, M. J. (2011). A Survey of Link Prediction in Social Networks. In C. Aggarwal (Ed.), *Social Network Data Analytics*. Boston, MA: Springer. doi:10.1007/978-1-4419-8462-3_9

He, J., Kaleshi, D., Munro, A., Wang, Y., Doufexi, A., & McGeehan, J. (2005). Performance Investigation of IEEE 802.11 MAC in Multihop Wireless Networks. *Proceedings of the 8th ACM international symposium on Modeling, analysis and simulation of wireless and mobile systems*. 10.1145/1089444.1089487

He, Q., Cai, L., Shen, X., & Ho, P.-H. (2006). Improving TCP Performance over Wireless Ad Hoc Networks with Busy Tone Assisted Scheme. *EURASIP J. Wireless Comm. and Networking, Article ID*, *51610*, 11.

He, Z., Cai, Z., & Yu, J. (2018). Latent-Data Privacy Preserving With Customized Data Utility for Social Network Data. *IEEE Transactions on Vehicular Technology*, *67*(1), 665–673. doi:10.1109/TVT.2017.2738018

Hinton, G. E. (2007). Learning multiple layers of representation. *Trends in Cognitive Sciences*, *11*(10), 428–434. doi:10.1016/j.tics.2007.09.004 PMID:17921042

Hu, K., & Xiang, J. (n.d.). *Link Prediction in Complex Networks by Multi Degree Preferential-Attachment Indices*. Academic Press.

Hua, L. C., Anisi, M. H., Yee, P. L., & Alam, M. (2017). Social networking-based cooperation mechanisms in vehicular ad-hoc network—a survey. In *Vehicular Communications*. Elsevier. doi:10.1016/j.vehcom.2017.11.001

Huang, H., Shu, W., Li, M., & Wu, M. Y. (2008, March). Performance evaluation of vehicular dtn routing under realistic mobility models. In *Wireless Communications and Networking Conference, 2008. WCNC 2008. IEEE* (pp. 2206-2211). IEEE.

IEEE 802.11 WG, Part 11: Wireless LAN Medium Access Control (MAC) and Physical Layer (PHY) Specification, Standard, IEEE, Aug. 1999.

IEEE Standards Department. (1999). *ANSI///IEEE Standard 802.11.* IEEE Press.

Itzhaky, Y., Farjon, G., Khoroshevsky, F., Shpigler, A., & Hillel, A. B. (2018). *Leaf counting: Multiple scale regression and detection using deep cnns.* Academic Press.

Janadri, C. S., Sheeparamatti, B. G., & Kagawade, V. (2017). Multiclass classification of kirlian images using SVM technique. *2017 International Conference on Advances in Computing, Communications and Informatics, ICACCI 2017*, 2246–2250. 10.1109/ICACCI.2017.8126180

Jeanjaitrong, N., & Bhattarakosol, P. (2013, September). Feasibility study on authentication based keystroke dynamic over touch-screen devices. In *13th International Symposium on Communications and Information Technologies (ISCIT)*, (pp. 238-242). IEEE. 10.1109/ISCIT.2013.6645856

Jerbi, M., Senouci, S. M., & Ghamri-Doudane, Y. (2006). Towards efficient routing in vehicular Ad Hoc networks. *Proceedings of the 3rd IEEE international workshop on Mobile Computing and Networking.*

Jiang, F., Jiang, Y., Zhi, H., Dong, Y., Li, H., Ma, S. & Wang, Y. (2017). Artificial intelligence in healthcare: past, present and future. *Stroke and Vascular Neurology, 2*(4), 230-243.

Jiang, J., Wen, S., Yu, S., Xiang, Y., & Zhou, W. (2018). Rumor Source Identification in Social Networks with Time-Varying Topology. IEEE Transactions on Dependable and Secure Computing, 15(1), 166-179. doi:10.1109/TDSC.2016.2522436

Jia, X. (2002). Simplified maximum likelihood classification for hyperspectral data in cluster space. *IEEE International Geoscience and Remote Sensing Symposium*, 2578-2580. doi: 10.1109/IGARSS.2002.1026706

Johannes, A., Picon, A., Alvarez-Gila, A., Echazarra, J., Rodriguez-Vaamonde, S., Navajas, A. D., & Ortiz-Barredo, A. (2017). Automatic plant disease diagnosis using mobile capture devices, applied on a wheat use case. *Computers and Electronics in Agriculture, 138*, 200–209. doi:10.1016/j. compag.2017.04.013

Joshi, C., & Mukherjee, S. (2018). Empirical analysis of SIFT, Gabor and fused feature classification using SVM for multispectral satellite image retrieval. *2017 4th International Conference on Image Information Processing, ICIIP 2017*, 542–547. 10.1109/ICIIP.2017.8313776

Joshi, C., & Singh, U. K. (2017). Information security risks management framework – A step towards mitigating security risks in university network. *Journal of Information Security and Applications, 35*, 128-137.

Jurdak, R., Lopes, C. V., & Baldi, P. (2004). A Survey, Classification and. Comparative Analysis of Medium Access Control Protocols for Ad. Hoc Networks. *IEEE Communications Surveys and Tutorials, 6*(1), 2–16. doi:10.1109/COMST.2004.5342231

Kadhim, M. A., Alam, A., & Kaur, H. (2011). Design and Implementation of Fuzzy Expert System for Back Pain Diagnosis. International. *Journal of Innovative Technology & Creative Engineering, 1*(9), 16–22.

Kalpana, M., & Kumar, A. V. S. (2011). Fuzzy Expert System for Diabetes Using Fuzzy Verdict Mechanism. *International Journal of Advanced Networking and Applications, 3*(2), 1128–1134.

Kamilaris, A., Gao, F., Prenafeta-Boldú, F. X., & Ali, M. I. (2016, December). Agri-IoT: A semantic framework for Internet of Things-enabled smart farming applications. In *Internet of Things (WF-IoT), 2016 IEEE 3rd World Forum on* (pp. 442-447). IEEE. 10.1109/WF-IoT.2016.7845467

Kamilaris, A., Kartakoullis, A., & Prenafeta-Boldú, F. X. (2017). A review on the practice of big data analysis in agriculture. *Computers and Electronics in Agriculture, 143*, 23–37. doi:10.1016/j.compag.2017.09.037

Kamilaris, A., & Prenafeta-Boldú, F. X. (2018). Deep learning in agriculture: A survey. *Computers and Electronics in Agriculture, 147*, 70–90. doi:10.1016/j.compag.2018.02.016

Kanehisa, M., Goto, S., Furumichi, M., Tanabe, M., & Hirakawa, M. (2009). KEGG for representation and analysis of molecular networks involving diseases and drugs. *Nucleic Acids Research, 38*(suppl_1), D355-D360.

Karimzadeh, M. (2011). *Efficient routing protocol in delay tolerant networks (DTNs)*. Academic Press.

Karn, P. (1990). MACA - A New Channel Access Method for Packet Radio. *ARRL/CRRL Amateur Radio 9th Computer Networking Conference,* 134-140.

Kar, S. A., & Kelkar, V. V. (2013). Classification of Multispectral satellite images. *International Conference on Advances in Technology and Engineering, ICATE 2013,* 115. 10.1109/ICAdTE.2013.6524747

Kaur, S., & Rashid, M. (2016). Web News Mining using Back Propagation Neural Network and Clustering using K-Means Algorithm in Big Data. *Indian Journal of Science and Technology, 9*(41). doi:10.17485/ijst/2016/v9i41/95598

Kavya, N., & Padmaja, K. V. (2017). Glaucoma detection using texture features extraction, *2017 51st Asilomar Conference on Signals, Systems, and Computers,* 1471-1475. doi: 10.1109/ACSSC.2017.8335600

Kawattikul, K., & Chomphuwiset, P. (2018). A simple text detection in document images using classification-based techniques. *IEEE 4th International Conference on Soft Computing and Machine Intelligence, ISCMI 2017,* 119–122. 10.1109/ISCMI.2017.8279610

Keles, A., & Keles, A. (2008). ESTDD: Expert System for Thyroid Diseases Diagnosis. *Expert Systems with Applications, 34*(1), 242–246. doi:10.1016/j.eswa.2006.09.028

Khamparia, A., & Pandey, B. (2015). Knowledge and intelligent computing methods in e-learning. *Int. J. Technol. Enhanc. Learn., 7*(3), 221–242. doi:10.1504/IJTEL.2015.072810

Khamparia, A., & Pandey, B. (2016). Threat driven modeling framework using petri nets for e-learning system. *SpringerPlus, 5*(1), 446. doi:10.118640064-016-2101-0 PMID:27119050

Khamparia, A., & Pandey, B. (2017). A novel method of case representation and retrieval in CBR for e-learning. *Education and Information Technologies, 22*(1), 337–354. doi:10.100710639-015-9447-8

Khamparia, A., & Pandey, B. (2017). Comprehensive analysis of semantic web reasoners and tools: A survey. *Education and Information Technologies, 22*(6), 3121–3145. doi:10.100710639-017-9574-5

Khamparia, A., & Pandey, B. (2017). Effects of visual mapping placed game-based learning on students learning performance in defence-based courses. *Int. J. Technology Enhanced Learning*, *9*(1), 37–50. doi:10.1504/IJTEL.2017.084083

Khamparia, A., & Pandey, B. (2017). Effects of visual mapping placed game-based learning on students learning performance in defence-based courses. *Int. J. TechnologyEnhanced Learning*, *9*(1), 37–50.

Khamparia, A., & Pandey, B. (2018). Effects of visual map embedded approach on students learning performance using BriggsMyers learning style in word puzzle gaming course. *Computers & Electrical Engineering*, *66*(C), 531–540. doi:10.1016/j.compeleceng.2017.12.041

Khamparia, A., & Pandey, B. (2018). SVM and PCA Based Learning Feature Classification Approaches for E-Learning System. *International Journal of Web-Based Learning and Teaching Technologies*, *13*(2), 32–45. doi:10.4018/IJWLTT.2018040103

Khastavaneh, H., Ebrahimpour-Komleh, H., & Joudaki, M. (2017). Face image quality assessment based on photometric features and classification techniques. *2017 IEEE 4th International Conference on Knowledge-Based Engineering and Innovation (KBEI)*, 289–293. 10.1109/KBEI.2017.8324988

Kim, J., & Hastak, M. (2018). Social network analysis: Characteristics of online social networks after a disaster. *International Journal of Information Management, 38*(1), 86-96.

Kitzes, J., Wackernagel, M., Loh, J., Peller, A., Goldfinger, S., Cheng, D., & Tea, K. (2008). Shrink and share: Humanity's present and future Ecological Footprint. *Philosophical Transactions of the Royal Society of London. Series B, Biological Sciences*, *363*(1491), 467–475. doi:10.1098/rstb.2007.2164 PMID:17652075

Kohli, S., Kaur, B., & Bindra, S. (2010). A comparative study of Routing Protocols in VANET. *Proceedings of ISCET*, 173-177.

Kolachalama, V. B., & Garg, P. S. (2018). Machine learning and medical education. *NPJ Digital Medicine, 1*(1), 54.

Kumar, R., Novak, J., & Tomkin, A. (2006). Structure and Evolution of Online Social Networks. In *KDD'06*. ACM.

Kumar, R., Raghavan, P., Rajagopalan, S., & Tomkins, A. (1999). Trawling the Web for emerging cyber-communities. In *Proceedings of the eighth international conference on World Wide Web (WWW '99)*. Elsevier North-Holland, Inc.

Kumar, R., Novak, J., Raghavan, P., & Tomkins, A. (2004, December). Structure and evolution of blogspace. *Communications of the ACM, 47*(12), 35–39. doi:10.1145/1035134.1035162

Kunegis, J., Blattner, M., & Moser, C. (2013). Preferential attachment in online networks: measurement and explanations. *Proceedings of the 5th Annual ACM Web Science Conference (WebSci '13)*, 205-214. 10.1145/2464464.2464514

Lavecchia, A. (2015). Machine-learning approaches in drug discovery: Methods and applications. *Drug Discovery Today, 20*(3), 318–331. doi:10.1016/j.drudis.2014.10.012 PMID:25448759

LeCun, Y., & Bengio, Y. (1995). Convolutional networks for images, speech, and time series. The Handbook of Brain Theory and Neural Networks, 3361(10), 1995.

Lee, K. C., Lee, U., & Gerla, M. (2010). Survey of routing protocols in vehicular ad hoc networks. In *Advances in vehicular ad-hoc networks: Developments and challenges* (pp. 149–170). IGI Global. doi:10.4018/978-1-61520-913-2.ch008

Leicht, E. A., Holme, P., & Newman, M. E. J. (2006). Vertex similarit in networks. *Phys. Rev. E, 73*(2), 026120. doi:10.1103/PhysRevE.73.026120 PMID:16605411

Leontiadis, I., & Mascolo, C. (2007). *GeOpps: Geographical opportunistic routing for vehicular networks*. Academic Press.

Leppink, J., & Fuster, P. (2018). *Social Networks as an Approach to Systematic review*. Health Professions Education. doi:10.1016/j.hpe.2018.09.002

Li, B., Zhao, H., & Lv, Z. (2010). Parallel ISODATA clustering of remote sensing images based on MapReduce. *Proceedings - 2010 International Conference on Cyber-Enabled Distributed Computing and Knowledge Discovery, CyberC 2010*, 380–383. 10.1109/CyberC.2010.75

Liaghat, S., & Balasundram, S. K. (2010). A review: The role of remote sensing in precision agriculture. *American Journal of Agricultural and Biological Sciences*, 5(1), 50–55. doi:10.3844/ajabssp.2010.50.55

Liben-Nowell, D., & Kleinberg, J. (2003). The link prediction problem for social networks. In *Proceedings of the 12th ACM International Conference on Information and Knowledge Management (CIKM '03)* (pp. 556–559). ACM. 10.1145/956863.956972

Li, J., Blake, C., De Couto, D. S. J., Lee, H. I., & Morris, R. (2001). Capacity of Ad Hoc Wireless Networks. *7th ACM International Conference on Mobile Computing and Networking*, Rome, Italy.

Lima, A. N., Philot, E. A., Trossini, G. H. G., Scott, L. P. B., Maltarollo, V. G., & Honorio, K. M. (2016). Use of machine learning approaches for novel drug discovery. *Expert Opinion on Drug Discovery*, 11(3), 225–239. doi:10.1517/17460441.2016.1146250 PMID:26814169

Little, T. D., & Agarwal, A. (2005, September). An information propagation scheme for VANETs. In *Proc. IEEE Intelligent Transportation Systems* (pp. 155-160). IEEE.

Lo, Y. C., Rensi, S. E., Torng, W., & Altman, R. B. (2018). Machine learning in chemoinformatics and drug discovery. *Drug Discovery Today*, 23(8), 1538–1546. doi:10.1016/j.drudis.2018.05.010 PMID:29750902

Mady & Blumstein. (2017). Social security: are socially connected individuals less vigilant? *Animal Behaviour, 134*, 79-85.

Mahapatra, S. (2018). *Why deep learning over machine learning*. Retrieved from https://towardsdatascience.com/why-deep-learning-is-needed-over-traditional-machine-learning-1b6a99177063

Marche, Atzori, Iera, Militano, & Nitti. (n.d.). Navigability in Social Networks of Objects: The Importance of Friendship Type and Nodes' Distance. *IEEE Globecom Workshops (GC Workshops)*, 1-6.

Mathwork. (2018). *Indexed image representation*. Retrieved from https://in.mathworks.com/help/matlab/creating_plots/image-ypes.html

Matjaz, K., Jean, S. S., Riste S., & Zelealem, Y., (2018). *Eccentricity of networks with structural constraints*. Academic Press.

Meng, L., Hulovatyy, Y., Striegel, A., & Milenković, T. (2016). On the Interplay Between Individuals' Evolving Interaction Patterns and Traits in Dynamic Multiplex Social Networks. IEEE Transactions on Network Science and Engineering, 3(1), 32-43. doi:10.1109/TNSE.2016.2523798

Meng, F., Gong, X., Guo, L., Cai, X., & Zhang, Q. (2017). Software-Reconfigurable System Supporting Point-to-Point Data Communication Between Vehicle Social Networks and Marketers. *IEEE Access: Practical Innovations, Open Solutions, 5*, 22796–22803. doi:10.1109/ACCESS.2017.2764098

Meng, Y., Wong, D. S., & Schlegel, R. (2012, November). Touch gestures based biometric authentication scheme for touchscreen mobile phones. In *International Conference on Information Security and Cryptology* (pp. 331-350). Springer.

Merini, T. U., & Caldelli, R. (2017). Tracing images back to their social network of origin: A CNN-based approach. *IEEE Workshop on Information Forensics and Security (WIFS)*, 1-6.doi: 10.1109/WIFS.2017.8267660

Miller, R. A. (1994). Medical Diagnostic Decision Support Systems - Past, Present, and Future: A Threaded Bibliography and Brief Commentary. *Journal of the American Medical Informatics Association, 1*(1), 8–27. doi:10.1136/jamia.1994.95236141 PMID:7719792

Miranda, E., Aryuni, M., & Irwansyah, E. (2016). A survey of medical image classification techniques. *2016 International Conference on Information Management and Technology (ICIMTech)*, 56–61. 10.1109/ICIMTech.2016.7930302

Mitra, A., Paul, S., Panda, S., & Padhi, P. (2016). A Study on the Representation of the Various Models for Dynamic Social Networks. *Procedia Computer Science, 79*, 624-631.

Mohanty, S. P., Hughes, D. P., & Salathé, M. (2016). Using deep learning for image-based plant disease detection. *Frontiers in Plant Science, 7*, 1419. doi:10.3389/fpls.2016.01419 PMID:27713752

Nagasubramanian, K., Jones, S., Singh, A. K., Singh, A., Ganapathysubramanian, B., & Sarkar, S. (2018). *Explaining hyperspectral imaging based plant disease identification: 3D CNN and saliency maps.* arXiv preprint arXiv:1804.08831

Newman, M. E. J. (2001). *Clustering and preferential attachment in growing networks*. Physical Review Letters E. doi:10.1103/PhysRevE.64.025102

Nie, L., Song, X., & Chua, T.-S. (2016). *Learning from Multiple Social Networks. In Learning from Multiple Social Networks*. Morgan & Claypool.

Ntoulas, C. J., & Olston, C. (2004). What's new on the web? The evolution of the web from a search engine perspective. *13th WWW*, 1–12.

Omatu, S., Fujinaka, T., Kosaka, T., Yanagimoto, H., & Yoshioka, M. (2001). Italian Lira classification by LVQ. *IJCNN'01. International Joint Conference on Neural Networks. Proceedings (Cat. No.01CH37222)*, 2947-2951. 10.1109/IJCNN.2001.938846

Ozdemir, A. O. B., Gedik, B. E., & Çetin, C. Y. Y. (2017). Hyperspectral classification using stacked autoencoders with deep learning. *Workshop on Hyperspectral Image and Signal Processing, Evolution in Remote Sensing*. 10.1109/WHISPERS.2014.8077532

Ozdogan, M., Yang, Y., Allez, G., & Cervantes, C. (2010). Remote sensing of irrigated agriculture: Opportunities and challenges. *Remote Sensing*, 2(9), 2274–2304. doi:10.3390/rs2092274

Pandey, B., & Mishra, R. B. (2009). Knowledge and Intelligent Computing System in Medicine. *Computers in Biology and Medicine*, 39(3), 215–230. doi:10.1016/j.compbiomed.2008.12.008 PMID:19201398

Panteleev, J., Gao, H., & Jia, L. (2018). Recent applications of machine learning in medicinal chemistry. *Bioorganic & Medicinal Chemistry Letters*, 28(17), 2807–2815. doi:10.1016/j.bmcl.2018.06.046 PMID:30122222

Papadopoulos, G. T., Chandramouli, K., Mezaris, V., Kompatsiaris, I., Izquierdo, E., & Strintzis, M. G. (2008). A Comparative Study of Classification Techniques for Knowledge-Assisted Image Analysis. *2008 Ninth International Workshop on Image Analysis for Multimedia Interactive Services*, 4–7. 10.1109/WIAMIS.2008.36

Patidar, D., Jian, N., & Parikh, A. (2014). Performance Analysis of Artificial Neural Network and K Nearest Neighbors Image Classification Techniques with Wavelet features. *IEEE International Conference on Computer Communication and Systems (ICCCS'14), Chennai, INDIA*, 191–194. 10.1109/ICCCS.2014.7068192

Pawara, P., Okafor, E., Surinta, O., Schomaker, L., & Wiering, M. (2017, February). *Comparing Local Descriptors and Bags of Visual Words to Deep Convolutional Neural Networks for Plant Recognition.* ICPRAM. doi:10.5220/0006196204790486

Peng, S., Zhou, Y., Cao, L., Yu, S., Niu, J., & Jia, W. (2018). Influence analysis in social networks: A survey. *Journal of Network and Computer Applications, 106,* 17-32. doi:10.1016/j.jnca.2018.01.005

Picon, A., Alvarez-Gila, A., Seitz, M., Ortiz-Barredo, A., Echazarra, J., & Johannes, A. (2018). Deep convolutional neural networks for mobile capture device-based crop disease classification in the wild. *Computers and Electronics in Agriculture.* doi:10.1016/j.compag.2018.04.002

Poorin Mohammad, N., Hamedi, J., & Moghaddam, M. H. A. M. (2018). Sequence-based analysis and prediction of lantibiotics: a machine learning approach. *Computational Biology and Chemistry.*

Quick, D., & Choo, K.-K. R. (2017). Pervasive social networking forensics: Intelligence and evidence from mobile device extracts. *Journal of Network and Computer Applications, 86,* 24-33. doi:10.1016/j.jnca.2016.11.018

Rahnemoonfar, M., & Sheppard, C. (2017). Deep count: Fruit counting based on deep simulated learning. *Sensors (Basel), 17*(4), 905. doi:10.339017040905 PMID:28425947

Ramcharan, A., Baranowski, K., McCloskey, P., Ahmed, B., Legg, J., & Hughes, D. P. (2017). Deep learning for image-based cassava disease detection. *Frontiers in Plant Science, 8,* 1852. doi:10.3389/fpls.2017.01852 PMID:29163582

Ramya, M., & Praveen, K. (2015). Performance comparison of content based and ISODATA clustering based on news video anchorperson detection. *2015 International Conference on Innovations in Information, Embedded and Communication Systems (ICIIECS),* 1-5. 10.1109/ICIIECS.2015.7193105

Rani, N. S. (2017). Region Based Image Classification using Watershed Transform Techniques. *Intelligent Computing and Control (I2C2), 2017 International Conference on Intelligent Computing and Control,* 1-5.

Rashid, M., & Chawla, R. (2013). Securing Data Storage by Extending Role Based Access Control. *International Journal of Cloud Applications and Computing*, *3*(4), 28–37. doi:10.4018/ijcac.2013100103

Rath, M., & Panda, M. R. (2017). MAQ system development in mobile ad-hoc networks using mobile agents. *IEEE 2nd International Conference on Contemporary Computing and Informatics (IC3I)*, 794-798.

Rath, M., & Pattanayak, B. (2018). Technological improvement in modern health care applications using Internet of Things (IoT) and proposal of novel health care approach. *International Journal of Human Rights in Healthcare*. doi:10.1108/IJHRH-01-2018-0007

Rath, M., & Pattanayak, B. K. (2014). A methodical survey on real time applications in MANETS: Focussing On Key Issues. *International Conference on, High Performance Computing and Applications (IEEE ICHPCA)*, 1-5, 22-24. 10.1109/ICHPCA.2014.7045301

Rath, M., & Pattanayak, B. K. (2018). Monitoring of QoS in MANET Based Real Time Applications. Smart Innovation, Systems and Technologies, 84, 579-586. doi:10.1007/978-3-319-63645-0_64

Rath, M., Pati, B., & Pattanayak, B. K. (2016). Inter-Layer Communication Based QoS Platform for Real Time Multimedia Applications in MANET. Wireless Communications, Signal Processing and Networking (IEEE WiSPNET), 613-617. doi:10.1109/WiSPNET.2016.7566203

Rath, Pati, & Pattanayak. (2018). An Overview on Social Networking: Design, Issues, Emerging Trends, and Security. *Social Network Analytics: Computational Research Methods and Techniques*, 21-47.

Rath, M. (2017). Resource provision and QoS support with added security for client side applications in cloud computing. *International Journal of Information Technology*, *9*(3), 1–8.

Rath, M., & Pati, B. (2017). *Load balanced routing scheme for MANETs with power and delay optimization. International Journal of Communication Network and Distributed Systems, 19*.

Rath, M., Pati, B., Panigrahi, C. R., & Sarkar, J. L. (2019). QTM: A QoS Task Monitoring System for Mobile Ad hoc Networks. In P. Sa, S. Bakshi, I. Hatzilygeroudis, & M. Sahoo (Eds.), *Recent Findings in Intelligent Computing Techniques. Advances in Intelligent Systems and Computing* (Vol. 707). Singapore: Springer. doi:10.1007/978-981-10-8639-7_57

Rath, M., Pati, B., & Pattanayak, B. K. (2017). Cross layer based QoS platform for multimedia transmission in MANET. *11th International Conference on Intelligent Systems and Control (ISCO)*, 402-407. 10.1109/ISCO.2017.7856026

Rath, M., & Pattanayak, B. (2017). MAQ: A Mobile Agent Based QoS Platform for MANETs. *International Journal of Business Data Communications and Networking, IGI Global, 13*(1), 1–8. doi:10.4018/IJBDCN.2017010101

Rath, M., & Pattanayak, B. K. (2018). SCICS: A Soft Computing Based Intelligent Communication System in VANET. Smart Secure Systems – IoT and Analytics Perspective. *Communications in Computer and Information Science, 808*, 255–261. doi:10.1007/978-981-10-7635-0_19

Rath, M., Pattanayak, B. K., & Pati, B. (2017). *Energetic Routing Protocol Design for Real-time Transmission in Mobile Ad hoc Network. In Computing and Network Sustainability, Lecture Notes in Networks and Systems* (Vol. 12). Singapore: Springer.

Rathore, S., Sharma, P. K., Loia, V., Jeong, Y.-S., & Park, J. H. (2017). Social network security: Issues, challenges, threats, and solutions. *Information Sciences, 421*, 43-69. doi:10.1016/j.ins.08.063

Rau, R. (2017). Social networks and financial outcomes. *Current Opinion in Behavioral Sciences, 18*, 75-78.

Ravasz, E., Somera, A. L., Mongru, D. A., Oltvai, Z. N., & Barabasi, A.-L. (2002). Hierarchical Organization of Modularity in Metabolic Networks. *Science, 297*(5586), 1553. doi:10.1126cience.1073374 PMID:12202830

Remuzzi, G., Schieppati, A., & Ruggenenti, P. (2002). Nephropathy in Patients with Type 2 Diabetes. *The New England Journal of Medicine, 346*(15), 1145–1151. doi:10.1056/NEJMcp011773 PMID:11948275

Reyes, A. K., Caicedo, J. C., & Camargo, J. E. (2015, September). Fine-tuning Deep Convolutional Networks for Plant Recognition. CLEF (Working Notes).

Romero Amondaray, L., & Seoane Pascual, J. (2008, September). Delay tolerant network simulation with vnuml. In *Proceedings of the third ACM workshop on Challenged networks* (pp. 109-112). ACM. 10.1145/1409985.1410006

Rtah, M. (2018). Big Data and IoT-Allied Challenges Associated With Healthcare Applications in Smart and Automated Systems. *International Journal of Strategic Information Technology and Applications*, *9*(2). doi:10.4018/IJSITA.201804010

Rydahl, P., Jensen, N. P., Dyrmann, M., Nielsen, P. H., & Jørgensen, R. N. (2017). RoboWeedSupport-Presentation of a cloud based system bridging the gap between in-field weed inspections and decision support systems. *Advances in Animal Biosciences*, *8*(2), 860–864. doi:10.1017/S2040470017001054

Saevanee, H., & Bhattarakosol, P. (2009, January). Authenticating user using keystroke dynamics and finger pressure. *In Consumer Communications and Networking Conference* (pp. 1-2). IEEE. 10.1109/CCNC.2009.4784783

Sa, I., Ge, Z., Dayoub, F., Upcroft, B., Perez, T., & McCool, C. (2016). Deepfruits: A fruit detection system using deep neural networks. *Sensors (Basel)*, *16*(8), 1222. doi:10.339016081222 PMID:27527168

Saini, B. S., Kaur, N., & Bhatia, K. S. (2018). Authenticating Mobile Phone Users Based on Their Typing Position Using Keystroke Dynamics. In *Proceedings of 2nd International Conference on Communication, Computing and Networking* (pp. 25-33). Springer.

Sajadi, S. H., Fazli, M., & Habibi, J. (2018). The Affective Evolution of Social Norms in Social Networks. IEEE Transactions on Computational Social Systems, 5(3), 727-735. doi:10.1109/TCSS.2018.2855417

Santi. (2012). Mobile Social Network Analysis. In *Mobility Models for Next Generation Wireless Networks: Ad Hoc, Vehicular and Mesh Networks*. Wiley Telecom. doi:10.1002/9781118344774.ch19

Sapountzi, A., & Psannis, K. E. (2018). Social networking data analysis tools & challenges. *Future Generation Computer Systems, 86*, 893-913. doi:10.1016/j.future.2016.10.019

Saravanan, C. (2010). Color Image to Grayscale Image Conversion. *2010 Second International Conference on Computer Engineering and Applications*, 196-199. 10.1109/ICCEA.2010.192

Sarwar Kamal, M. (2017). De-Bruijn graph with MapReduce framework towards metagenomic data classification. *International Journal of Information Technology, 9*(1), 59–75. doi:10.100741870-017-0005-z

Schlegel, R., Chow, C. Y., Huang, Q., & Wong, D. S. (2017). Privacy-Preserving Location Sharing Services for Social Networks. *IEEE Transactions on Services Computing, 10*(5), 811–825. doi:10.1109/TSC.2016.2514338

Schneier, B. (2010). A Taxonomy of Social Networking Data. *IEEE Security and Privacy, 8*(4), 88–88. doi:10.1109/MSP.2010.118

Schork, N. J. (2015). Personalized medicine: Time for one-person trials. *Nature, 520*(7549), 609–611. doi:10.1038/520609a PMID:25925459

Scott, K., & Burleigh, S. (2007). *Bundle protocol specification* (No. RFC 5050).

Scott, J. (1988). Social Network Analysis. *Sociology, 22*(1), 109–127. doi:10.1177/0038038588022001007

Serrat, O. (2017). Social Network Analysis. In *Knowledge solutions*. Singapore: Springer. doi:10.1007/978-981-10-0983-9_9

Sethi, K. K., Mishra, D. K., & Mishra, B. (2012). KDRuleEx:A Novel Approach for Enhancing User comrehensibility using rule extraction. *Third international conference on intelligent systems modelling and simulation.*

Shen, J., Moh, S., & Chung, I. (2008, July). Routing protocols in delay tolerant networks: A comparative survey. In *The 23rd International Technical Conference on Circuits/Systems, Computers and Communications (ITC-CSCC 2008)* (pp. 6-9). Academic Press.

Shi, W., Gong, Y., Tao, X., Cheng, D., & Zheng, N. (2018). Fine-Grained Image Classification Using Modified DCNNs Trained by Cascaded Softmax and Generalized Large-Margin Losses. *IEEE Transactions on Neural Networks and Learning Systems*, 1–12. doi:10.1109/TNNLS.2018.2852721 PMID:30047915

Silawan, T., & Aswakul, C. (2017). SybilVote: Formulas to Quantify the Success Probability of Sybil Attack in Online Social Network Voting. IEEE Communications Letters, 21(7), 1553-1556.

Singh, C., Cheggoju, N., & Satpute, V. R. (2018). Implementing Classification algorithms in Medical Report Analysis for helping Patient during unavailability of Medical expertise. *2018 9th International Conference on Computing, Communication and Networking Technologies (ICCCNT)*, 1–5.

Singh, V. K., Mani, A., & Pentland, A. (2014). Social Persuasion in Online and Physical Networks. *Proceedings of the IEEE, 102*(12), 1903–1910. doi:10.1109/JPROC.2014.2363986

Singh, V., & Saini, G. L. (2018). DTN-Enabled Routing Protocols and Their Potential Influence on Vehicular Ad Hoc Networks. In *Soft Computing: Theories and Applications* (pp. 367–375). Singapore: Springer. doi:10.1007/978-981-10-5687-1_33

Singla, J. (2013). The diagnosis of Some Lung Diseases in a Prolog Expert System. *International Journal of Computers and Applications, 78*(15), 37–40. doi:10.5120/13603-1435

Sisodia, P. S., Tiwari, V., & Kumar, A. (2014). A comparative analysis of remote sensing image classification techniques. *2014 International Conference on Advances in Computing, Communications and Informatics (ICACCI)*, 1418–1421. 10.1109/ICACCI.2014.6968245

Sitová, Z., Šeděnka, J., Yang, Q., Peng, G., Zhou, G., Gasti, P., & Balagani, K. S. (2016). HMOG: New behavioral biometric features for continuous authentication of smartphone users. *IEEE Transactions on Information Forensics and Security, 11*(5), 877–892. doi:10.1109/TIFS.2015.2506542

Sladojevic, S., Arsenovic, M., Anderla, A., Culibrk, D., & Stefanovic, D. (2016). Deep neural networks based recognition of plant diseases by leaf image classification. *Computational Intelligence and Neuroscience*. PMID:27418923

Song, Y., Hu, Z., Leng, X., Tian, H., Yang, K., & Ke, X. (2015). Friendship influence on mobile behavior of location based social network users. *Journal of Communications and Networks (Seoul), 17*(2), 126–132. doi:10.1109/JCN.2015.000026

Sørensen, T. (1948). A method of establishing groups of equal amplitude in plant sociology based on similarity of species and its application to analyses of the vegetation on Danish commons. *Biol. Skr., 5*, 1–34.

Soundarajan, S., & Hopcroft, J. (2012). Using community information to improve the precision of link prediction methods. *Proceedings of the 21st International Conference on World Wide* 10.1145/2187980.2188150

Sproule, B. A., Naranjo, C. A., & Turksen, I. B. (2002). Fuzzy pharmacology: Theory and Applications. *Trends in Pharmacological Sciences, 23*(9), 412–417. doi:10.1016/S0165-6147(02)02055-2 PMID:12237153

Srilatha, P., & Manjula, R. (2016). Similarity Index based link prediction algorithms in social networks: A survey. *Journal of Telecommunications and Information Technology.*

Srinivas, Y., Timmons, W. D., & Durkin, J. (2001). A Comparative Study of the three Expert Systems for Blood Pressure Control. *Expert Systems with Applications, 20*(3), 267–274. doi:10.1016/S0957-4174(00)00065-8

Takahashi, H., Ogura, K., Bista, B. B., & Takata, T. (2016, October). A user authentication scheme using keystrokes for smartphones while moving. In *International Symposium on Information Theory and Its Applications (ISITA)*, (pp. 310-314). IEEE.

Tang, F., Mao, C., Yu, J., & Chen, J. (2011). The implementation of information service based on social network systems. *Information Science and Service Science (NISS), 2011 5th International Conference on New Trends,* 46 – 49.

Tarbush, B., & Teytelboym, A. (2017). Social groups and social network formation. *Games and Economic Behavior, 103*, 286-312.

Tasia, C. J., Chang, T. Y., Cheng, P. C., & Lin, J. H. (2014). Two novel biometric features in keystroke dynamics authentication systems for touch screen devices. *Security and Communication Networks, 7*(4), 750–758. doi:10.1002ec.776

Teke, M., Deveci, H. S., Haliloğlu, O., Gürbüz, S. Z., & Sakarya, U. (2013, June). A short survey of hyperspectral remote sensing applications in agriculture. In *Recent Advances in Space Technologies (RAST), 2013 6th International Conference on* (pp. 171-176). IEEE. 10.1109/RAST.2013.6581194

Timmerer, C., & Rainer, B. (2014). The Social Multimedia Experience. Computer, 47(3), 67-69.

Tobagi, F. A., & Kleinrock, L. (1975). Packet Switching inRadio Channels: Part II — The Hidden Terminal Problem inCarrier Sense Multiple-Access and the Busy-Tone Solution. *IEEE Transactions on Communications, 23*(12), 1417–1433. doi:10.1109/TCOM.1975.1092767

Too, E. C., Yujian, L., Njuki, S., & Yingchun, L. (2018). A comparative study of fine-tuning deep learning models for plant disease identification. *Computers and Electronics in Agriculture.* doi:10.1016/j.compag.2018.03.032

Tornell, S. M., Calafate, C. T., Cano, J., & Manzoni, P. (2015). DTN Protocols for Vehicular Networks: An Application Oriented Overview. *IEEE Communications Surveys and Tutorials, 17*(2), 868–887. doi:10.1109/COMST.2014.2375340

Travers, J., & Milgram, S. (1969). An experimental study of the small world problem. *American Sociological Association.* Retrieved from http://www.jstor.org/stable/2786545

Trier, M., & Bobrik, A. (2009). Social Search: Exploring and Searching Social Architectures in Digital Networks. *IEEE Internet Computing, 13*(2), 51–59. doi:10.1109/MIC.2009.44

Trojahn, M., & Ortmeier, F. (2013, March). Toward mobile authentication with keystroke dynamics on mobile phones and tablets. In *27th International Conference on Advanced Information Networking and Applications Workshops (WAINA),* (pp. 697-702). IEEE. 10.1109/WAINA.2013.36

Tyagi, A. C. (2016). Towards a second green revolution. *Irrigation and Drainage, 65*(4), 388–389. doi:10.1002/ird.2076

Unnithan, S. (2004, July 19). Epic movie Mughale-Azam returns in colour cinemascope, digital sound. *India Today Magzine.* Retrieved from https://www.indiatoday.in/magazine/society-the-arts/films/story/20040719-epic-movie-mughale-azam-returns-in-colour-digital-sound-789831-2004-07-19

Vakharia, V., Kiran, M. B., Dave, N. J., & Kagathara, U. (2017). Feature extraction and classification of machined component texture images using wavelet and artificial intelligence techniques. *2017 8th International Conference on Mechanical and Aerospace Engineering (ICMAE),* 140–144. 10.1109/ICMAE.2017.8038631

Vangsted, A. J., Helm-Petersen, S., Cowland, J. B., Jensen, P. B., Gimsing, P., Barlogie, B., & Knudsen, S. (2018). Drug response prediction in high-risk multiple myeloma. *Gene, 644*, 80–86. doi:10.1016/j.gene.2017.10.071 PMID:29122646

Vatrapu, R., Mukkamala, R. R., Hussain, A., & Flesch, B. (2016). Social Set Analysis: A Set Theoretical Approach to Big Data Analytics. *IEEE Access: Practical Innovations, Open Solutions, 4*, 2542–2571. doi:10.1109/ACCESS.2016.2559584

Vegni, A. M., & Loscrí, V. (2015). A Survey on Vehicular Social Networks. *IEEE Communications Surveys and Tutorials, 17*(4), 2397–2419. doi:10.1109/COMST.2015.2453481

Vo, A. T., Tran, H. S., & Le, T. H. (2017). Advertisement image classification using convolutional neural network. *Proceedings - 2017 9th International Conference on Knowledge and Systems Engineering,* 197–202. 10.1109/KSE.2017.8119458

Wang, D., & Song, C. (2015). Impact of human mobility on social networks. Journal of Communications and Networks, 17(2), 100-109.

Wang, J., Chen, L., Zhang, J., Yuan, Y., Li, M., & Zeng, W. (2018, August). CNN Transfer Learning for Automatic Image-Based Classification of Crop. In *Image and Graphics Technologies and Applications: 13th Conference on Image and Graphics Technologies and Applications, IGTA 2018, Beijing, China, April 8–10, 2018, Revised Selected Papers (Vol. 875*, p. 319). Springer. 10.1007/978-981-13-1702-6_32

Wang, P., Xu, B.W., Wu, Y., & Zhou, X.Y. (2015). Link Prediction in social networks: The state-of-the-art. Information Sciences, 58.

Wang, W., Jiang, J., An, B., Jiang, Y., & Chen, B. (2017). Toward Efficient Team Formation for Crowdsourcing in Noncooperative Social Networks. IEEE Transactions on Cybernetics, 47(12), 4208-4222.

Wang, P., Jiang, H., & Zhuang, W. (2008). A New MAC Scheme supporting Multimedia Applications in Wireless Ad hoc networks. *IEEE Transactions on Mobile Computing, 7*(12).

Wang, Y., & Cai, W. (2015). Epidemic spreading model based on social active degree in social networks. *China Communications*, *12*(12), 101–108. doi:10.1109/CC.2015.7385518

Wang, Z., Wu, C., Sun, L., & Yang, S. (2013). Peer-Assisted Social Media Streaming with Social Reciprocity. *IEEE eTransactions on Network and Service Management*, *10*(1), 84–94. doi:10.1109/TNSM.2012.12.120244

Warthman, F. (2003). *Delay-Tolerant Networks: A Tutorial*. Academic Press.

Wasserman, S., & Faust, K. (1994). *Social Network Analysis: Methods and Applications*. Cambridge, UK: Cambridge University Press. doi:10.1017/CBO9780511815478

Weaver, C., & Marr, E. T. (2013). White vegetables: a forgotten source of nutrients: Purdue roundtable executive summary. *Advances in Nutrition*, *4*(3), 318S–326S. doi:10.3945/an.112.003566 PMID:23674800

Wilkinson, G. G. (2004). Are Remotely Sensed Image Classification Techniques Improving? Results of a Long Term Trend Analysis. *IEEE Workshop on Advances in Techniques for Analysis of Remotely Sensed Data*, 30-34.doi: 10.1109/WARSD.2003.1295169

Wilson, R. J. (1996). *Introduction to Graph Theory* (4th ed.). Prentice Hall Publication.

Wood, H. M. (1977). *The use of passwords for controlled access to computer resources*. US Department of Commerce, National Bureau of Standards.

Wu, S., Chen, H., Zhao, Z., Long, H., & Song, C. (2015). An improved remote sensing image classification based on K-means using HSV color feature. *Proceedings - 2014 10th International Conference on Computational Intelligence and Security, CIS 2014*, 201–204. 10.1109/CIS.2014.90

Wu, Y. (2016). Challenges of Mobile Social Device Caching. IEEE Access, 4, 8938-8947.

Wu, M., Tang, E., & Lin, B. (2000). Data hiding in digital binary image. *2000 IEEE International Conference on Multimedia and Expo. ICME2000. Proceedings. Latest Advances in the Fast Changing World of Multimedia (Cat. No.00TH8532)*, 393-396. 10.1109/ICME.2000.869623

Xia, F., Ahmed, A. M., Yang, L. T., Ma, J., & Rodrigues, J. J. P. C. (2014). Exploiting Social Relationship to Enable Efficient Replica Allocation in Ad-hoc Social Networks. *IEEE Transactions on Parallel and Distributed Systems*, 25(12), 3167–3176. doi:10.1109/TPDS.2013.2295805

Xu, Gerla, & Bae. (2003). Effectiveness of RTS/CTS handshake in IEEE 802.11 based ad hoc networks. *Journal of Ad Hoc Networks*, 107–123.

Xue, J., Zhang, H., & Dana, K. (2018, March). Deep Texture Manifold for Ground Terrain Recognition. In *Proceedings of the IEEE Conference on Computer Vision and Pattern Recognition* (pp. 558-567). IEEE. 10.1109/CVPR.2018.00065

Yan, Z., Feng, W., & Wang, P. (2015). Anonymous Authentication for Trustworthy Pervasive Social Networking. IEEE Transactions on Computational Social Systems, 2(3), 88-98. doi:10.1109/TCSS.2016.2519463

Yang, W., Wang, H., & Yao, Y. (2015). An immunization strategy for social network worms based on network vertex influence. *China Communications*, 12(7), 154–166. doi:10.1109/CC.2015.7188533

Ye, F., Yi, S., & Sikdar, B. (2003). Improving Spatial Reuse of IEEE 802.11. Based Ad Hoc Networks. *Proc. GLOBECOM 2003*.

Yeh, C. H., & Kuo, C. J. (2002). Image segmentation through index images. *2002 IEEE International Symposium on Circuits and Systems. Proceedings*. doi: 10.1109/ISCAS.2002.1010930

Yousefi, S., Mousavi, M. S., & Fathy, M. (2006, June). Vehicular ad hoc networks (VANETs): challenges and perspectives. In *ITS Telecommunications Proceedings, 2006 6th International Conference on* (pp. 761-766). IEEE.

Yu, D., & Ko, Y. B. (2009, February). FFRDV: fastest-ferry routing in DTN-enabled vehicular ad hoc networks. In *Advanced Communication Technology, 2009. ICACT 2009. 11th International Conference on* (Vol. 2, pp. 1410-1414). IEEE.

Yuan, M., Chen, L., Yu, P. S., & Yu, T. (2013). Protecting Sensitive Labels in Social Network Data Anonymization. *IEEE Transactions on Knowledge and Data Engineering*, 25(3), 633–647. doi:10.1109/TKDE.2011.259

Yu, C., Zhang, M., & Ren, F. (2014). Collective Learning for the Emergence of Social Norms in Networked Multiagent Systems. *IEEE Transactions on Cybernetics*, *44*(12), 2342–2355. doi:10.1109/TCYB.2014.2306919 PMID:25415942

Zachary, W. W. (1977). An information flow model for conflict and fission in small groups. *Journal of Anthropological Research*, *33*(4), 452–473. doi:10.1086/jar.33.4.3629752

Zadeh, L. A. (1975). The Concept of a Linguistic Variable and Its Application to Approximate Reasoning-I. *Information Sciences*, *8*(3), 199–249. doi:10.1016/0020-0255(75)90036-5

Zeki, T. S., Malakooti, M. V., Ataeipoor, Y., & Tabibi, S. T. (2012). An Expert System for Diabetes Diagnosis. *American Academic and Scholarly Research Journal Special Issue*, *4*(5), 1–13.

Zhang, L., Tan, J., Han, D., & Zhu, H. (2017). From machine learning to deep learning: Progress in machine intelligence for rational drug discovery. *Drug Discovery Today*, *22*(11), 1680–1685. doi:10.1016/j.drudis.2017.08.010 PMID:28881183

Zhang, L., Wang, T., Jin, Z., Su, N., Zhao, C., & He, Y. (2018). The research on social networks public opinion propagation influence models and its controllability. *China Communications*, *15*(7), 98–110. doi:10.1109/CC.2018.8424607

Zhang, S., Huang, W., & Zhang, C. (2018). Three-channel convolutional neural networks for vegetable leaf disease recognition. *Cognitive Systems Research*.

Zhang, Z., & Zhang, Q. (2007). Delay/disruption tolerant mobile ad hoc networks: Latest developments. *Wireless Communications and Mobile Computing*, *7*(10), 1219–1232. doi:10.1002/wcm.518

Zhao, H., Zhou, H., Yuan, C., Huang, Y., & Chen, J. (2015). Social Discovery: Exploring the Correlation Among Three-Dimensional Social Relationships. IEEE Transactions on Computational Social Systems, 2(3), 77-87.

Zhao, J., & Cao, G. (2008). VADD: Vehicle-assisted data delivery in vehicular ad hoc networks. *IEEE Transactions on Vehicular Technology*, *57*(3), 1910–1922. doi:10.1109/TVT.2007.901869

Zhao, W., Ammar, M., & Zegura, E. (2004, May). A message ferrying approach for data delivery in sparse mobile ad hoc networks. In *Proceedings of the 5th ACM international symposium on Mobile ad hoc networking and computing* (pp. 187-198). ACM. 10.1145/989459.989483

Zhao, Z., Yang, Q., Lu, H., Weninger, T., Cai, D., He, X., & Zhuang, Y. (2018). Social-Aware Movie Recommendation via Multimodal Network Learning. *IEEE Transactions on Multimedia, 20*(2), 430–440. doi:10.1109/TMM.2017.2740022

Zhou, T., Lü, L., & Zhang, Y. C. (2009). Predicting missing links via local information. *The European Physical Journal B, 71*(4), 623–630. doi:10.1140/epjb/e2009-00335-8

Zhu, J., Liu, Y., & Yin, X. (2017). A New Structure-Hole-Based Algorithm For Influence Maximization in Large Online Social Networks. IEEE Access, 5, 23405-23412. doi:10.1109/ACCESS.2017.2758353

Zhu, Y., Xu, B., Shi, X., & Wang, Y. (2013). A Survey of Social-Based Routing in Delay Tolerant Networks: Positive and Negative Social Effects. IEEE Communications Surveys & Tutorials, 15(1), 387-401.

Zou, T., Lu, L., & Zhang, Y. C. (2009). *Predicting Missing Links via Local Information*. EPJ.

Related References

To continue our tradition of advancing information science and technology research, we have compiled a list of recommended IGI Global readings. These references will provide additional information and guidance to further enrich your knowledge and assist you with your own research and future publications.

Adesina, K., Ganiu, O., & R., O. S. (2018). Television as Vehicle for Community Development: A Study of Lotunlotun Programme on (B.C.O.S.) Television, Nigeria. In A. Salawu, & T. Owolabi (Eds.), *Exploring Journalism Practice and Perception in Developing Countries* (pp. 60-84). Hershey, PA: IGI Global. doi:10.4018/978-1-5225-3376-4.ch004

Adigun, G. O., Odunola, O. A., & Sobalaje, A. J. (2016). Role of Social Networking for Information Seeking in a Digital Library Environment. In A. Tella (Ed.), *Information Seeking Behavior and Challenges in Digital Libraries* (pp. 272–290). Hershey, PA: IGI Global. doi:10.4018/978-1-5225-0296-8.ch013

Ahmad, M. B., Pride, C., & Corsy, A. K. (2016). Free Speech, Press Freedom, and Democracy in Ghana: A Conceptual and Historical Overview. In L. Mukhongo & J. Macharia (Eds.), *Political Influence of the Media in Developing Countries* (pp. 59–73). Hershey, PA: IGI Global. doi:10.4018/978-1-4666-9613-6.ch005

Ahmad, R. H., & Pathan, A. K. (2017). A Study on M2M (Machine to Machine) System and Communication: Its Security, Threats, and Intrusion Detection System. In M. Ferrag & A. Ahmim (Eds.), *Security Solutions and Applied Cryptography in Smart Grid Communications* (pp. 179–214). Hershey, PA: IGI Global. doi:10.4018/978-1-5225-1829-7.ch010

Akanni, T. M. (2018). In Search of Women-Supportive Media for Sustainable Development in Nigeria. In A. Salawu & T. Owolabi (Eds.), *Exploring Journalism Practice and Perception in Developing Countries* (pp. 126–149). Hershey, PA: IGI Global. doi:10.4018/978-1-5225-3376-4.ch007

Akçay, D. (2017). The Role of Social Media in Shaping Marketing Strategies in the Airline Industry. In V. Benson, R. Tuninga, & G. Saridakis (Eds.), *Analyzing the Strategic Role of Social Networking in Firm Growth and Productivity* (pp. 214–233). Hershey, PA: IGI Global. doi:10.4018/978-1-5225-0559-4.ch012

Al-Rabayah, W. A. (2017). Social Media as Social Customer Relationship Management Tool: Case of Jordan Medical Directory. In W. Al-Rabayah, R. Khasawneh, R. Abu-shamaa, & I. Alsmadi (Eds.), *Strategic Uses of Social Media for Improved Customer Retention* (pp. 108–123). Hershey, PA: IGI Global. doi:10.4018/978-1-5225-1686-6.ch006

Almjeld, J. (2017). Getting "Girly" Online: The Case for Gendering Online Spaces. In E. Monske & K. Blair (Eds.), *Handbook of Research on Writing and Composing in the Age of MOOCs* (pp. 87–105). Hershey, PA: IGI Global. doi:10.4018/978-1-5225-1718-4.ch006

Altaş, A. (2017). Space as a Character in Narrative Advertising: A Qualitative Research on Country Promotion Works. In R. Yılmaz (Ed.), *Narrative Advertising Models and Conceptualization in the Digital Age* (pp. 303–319). Hershey, PA: IGI Global. doi:10.4018/978-1-5225-2373-4.ch017

Altıparmak, B. (2017). The Structural Transformation of Space in Turkish Television Commercials as a Narrative Component. In R. Yılmaz (Ed.), *Narrative Advertising Models and Conceptualization in the Digital Age* (pp. 153–166). Hershey, PA: IGI Global. doi:10.4018/978-1-5225-2373-4.ch009

An, Y., & Harvey, K. E. (2016). Public Relations and Mobile: Becoming Dialogic. In X. Xu (Ed.), *Handbook of Research on Human Social Interaction in the Age of Mobile Devices* (pp. 284–311). Hershey, PA: IGI Global. doi:10.4018/978-1-5225-0469-6.ch013

Assay, B. E. (2018). Regulatory Compliance, Ethical Behaviour, and Sustainable Growth in Nigeria's Telecommunications Industry. In I. Oncioiu (Ed.), *Ethics and Decision-Making for Sustainable Business Practices* (pp. 90–108). Hershey, PA: IGI Global. doi:10.4018/978-1-5225-3773-1.ch006

Averweg, U. R., & Leaning, M. (2018). The Qualities and Potential of Social Media. In M. Khosrow-Pour, D.B.A. (Ed.), Encyclopedia of Information Science and Technology, Fourth Edition (pp. 7106-7115). Hershey, PA: IGI Global. doi:10.4018/978-1-5225-2255-3.ch617

Azemi, Y., & Ozuem, W. (2016). Online Service Failure and Recovery Strategy: The Mediating Role of Social Media. In W. Ozuem & G. Bowen (Eds.), *Competitive Social Media Marketing Strategies* (pp. 112–135). Hershey, PA: IGI Global. doi:10.4018/978-1-4666-9776-8.ch006

Baarda, R. (2017). Digital Democracy in Authoritarian Russia: Opportunity for Participation, or Site of Kremlin Control? In R. Luppicini & R. Baarda (Eds.), *Digital Media Integration for Participatory Democracy* (pp. 87–100). Hershey, PA: IGI Global. doi:10.4018/978-1-5225-2463-2.ch005

Bacallao-Pino, L. M. (2016). Radical Political Communication and Social Media: The Case of the Mexican #YoSoy132. In T. Deželan & I. Vobič (Eds.), *R)evolutionizing Political Communication through Social Media* (pp. 56–74). Hershey, PA: IGI Global. doi:10.4018/978-1-4666-9879-6.ch004

Baggio, B. G. (2016). Why We Would Rather Text than Talk: Personality, Identity, and Anonymity in Modern Virtual Environments. In B. Baggio (Ed.), *Analyzing Digital Discourse and Human Behavior in Modern Virtual Environments* (pp. 110–125). Hershey, PA: IGI Global. doi:10.4018/978-1-4666-9899-4.ch006

Başal, B. (2017). Actor Effect: A Study on Historical Figures Who Have Shaped the Advertising Narration. In R. Yılmaz (Ed.), *Narrative Advertising Models and Conceptualization in the Digital Age* (pp. 34–60). Hershey, PA: IGI Global. doi:10.4018/978-1-5225-2373-4.ch003

Behjati, M., & Cosmas, J. (2017). Self-Organizing Network Solutions: A Principal Step Towards Real 4G and Beyond. In D. Singh (Ed.), *Routing Protocols and Architectural Solutions for Optimal Wireless Networks and Security* (pp. 241–253). Hershey, PA: IGI Global. doi:10.4018/978-1-5225-2342-0.ch011

Bekafigo, M., & Pingley, A. C. (2017). Do Campaigns "Go Negative" on Twitter? In Y. Ibrahim (Ed.), *Politics, Protest, and Empowerment in Digital Spaces* (pp. 178–191). Hershey, PA: IGI Global. doi:10.4018/978-1-5225-1862-4.ch011

Bender, S., & Dickenson, P. (2016). Utilizing Social Media to Engage Students in Online Learning: Building Relationships Outside of the Learning Management System. In P. Dickenson & J. Jaurez (Eds.), *Increasing Productivity and Efficiency in Online Teaching* (pp. 84–105). Hershey, PA: IGI Global. doi:10.4018/978-1-5225-0347-7.ch005

Bermingham, N., & Prendergast, M. (2016). Bespoke Mobile Application Development: Facilitating Transition of Foundation Students to Higher Education. In L. Briz-Ponce, J. Juanes-Méndez, & F. García-Peñalvo (Eds.), *Handbook of Research on Mobile Devices and Applications in Higher Education Settings* (pp. 222–249). Hershey, PA: IGI Global. doi:10.4018/978-1-5225-0256-2.ch010

Bishop, J. (2017). Developing and Validating the "This Is Why We Can't Have Nice Things Scale": Optimising Political Online Communities for Internet Trolling. In Y. Ibrahim (Ed.), *Politics, Protest, and Empowerment in Digital Spaces* (pp. 153–177). Hershey, PA: IGI Global. doi:10.4018/978-1-5225-1862-4.ch010

Bolat, N. (2017). The Functions of the Narrator in Digital Advertising. In R. Yılmaz (Ed.), *Narrative Advertising Models and Conceptualization in the Digital Age* (pp. 184–201). Hershey, PA: IGI Global. doi:10.4018/978-1-5225-2373-4.ch011

Bowen, G., & Bowen, D. (2016). Social Media: Strategic Decision Making Tool. In W. Ozuem & G. Bowen (Eds.), *Competitive Social Media Marketing Strategies* (pp. 94–111). Hershey, PA: IGI Global. doi:10.4018/978-1-4666-9776-8.ch005

Brown, M. A. Sr. (2017). SNIP: High Touch Approach to Communication. In *Solutions for High-Touch Communications in a High-Tech World* (pp. 71–88). Hershey, PA: IGI Global. doi:10.4018/978-1-5225-1897-6.ch004

Brown, M. A. Sr. (2017). Comparing FTF and Online Communication Knowledge. In *Solutions for High-Touch Communications in a High-Tech World* (pp. 103–113). Hershey, PA: IGI Global. doi:10.4018/978-1-5225-1897-6.ch006

Brown, M. A. Sr. (2017). Where Do We Go from Here? In *Solutions for High-Touch Communications in a High-Tech World* (pp. 137–159). Hershey, PA: IGI Global. doi:10.4018/978-1-5225-1897-6.ch008

Brown, M. A. Sr. (2017). Bridging the Communication Gap. In *Solutions for High-Touch Communications in a High-Tech World* (pp. 1–22). Hershey, PA: IGI Global. doi:10.4018/978-1-5225-1897-6.ch001

Brown, M. A. Sr. (2017). Key Strategies for Communication. In *Solutions for High-Touch Communications in a High-Tech World* (pp. 179–202). Hershey, PA: IGI Global. doi:10.4018/978-1-5225-1897-6.ch010

Bryant, K. N. (2017). WordUp!: Student Responses to Social Media in the Technical Writing Classroom. In K. Bryant (Ed.), *Engaging 21st Century Writers with Social Media* (pp. 231–245). Hershey, PA: IGI Global. doi:10.4018/978-1-5225-0562-4.ch014

Buck, E. H. (2017). Slacktivism, Supervision, and #Selfies: Illuminating Social Media Composition through Reception Theory. In K. Bryant (Ed.), *Engaging 21st Century Writers with Social Media* (pp. 163–178). Hershey, PA: IGI Global. doi:10.4018/978-1-5225-0562-4.ch010

Bucur, B. (2016). Sociological School of Bucharest's Publications and the Romanian Political Propaganda in the Interwar Period. In A. Fox (Ed.), *Global Perspectives on Media Events in Contemporary Society* (pp. 106–120). Hershey, PA: IGI Global. doi:10.4018/978-1-4666-9967-0.ch008

Bull, R., & Pianosi, M. (2017). Social Media, Participation, and Citizenship: New Strategic Directions. In V. Benson, R. Tuninga, & G. Saridakis (Eds.), *Analyzing the Strategic Role of Social Networking in Firm Growth and Productivity* (pp. 76–94). Hershey, PA: IGI Global. doi:10.4018/978-1-5225-0559-4.ch005

Camillo, A. A., & Camillo, I. C. (2016). The Ethics of Strategic Managerial Communication in the Global Context. In A. Normore, L. Long, & M. Javidi (Eds.), *Handbook of Research on Effective Communication, Leadership, and Conflict Resolution* (pp. 566–590). Hershey, PA: IGI Global. doi:10.4018/978-1-4666-9970-0.ch030

Cassard, A., & Sloboda, B. W. (2016). Faculty Perception of Virtual 3-D Learning Environment to Assess Student Learning. In D. Choi, A. Dailey-Hebert, & J. Simmons Estes (Eds.), *Emerging Tools and Applications of Virtual Reality in Education* (pp. 48–74). Hershey, PA: IGI Global. doi:10.4018/978-1-4666-9837-6.ch003

Castellano, S., & Khelladi, I. (2017). Play It Like Beckham!: The Influence of Social Networks on E-Reputation – The Case of Sportspeople and Their Online Fan Base. In A. Mesquita (Ed.), *Research Paradigms and Contemporary Perspectives on Human-Technology Interaction* (pp. 43–61). Hershey, PA: IGI Global. doi:10.4018/978-1-5225-1868-6.ch003

Castellet, A. (2016). What If Devices Take Command: Content Innovation Perspectives for Smart Wearables in the Mobile Ecosystem. *International Journal of Handheld Computing Research*, *7*(2), 16–33. doi:10.4018/IJHCR.2016040102

Chugh, R., & Joshi, M. (2017). Challenges of Knowledge Management amidst Rapidly Evolving Tools of Social Media. In R. Chugh (Ed.), *Harnessing Social Media as a Knowledge Management Tool* (pp. 299–314). Hershey, PA: IGI Global. doi:10.4018/978-1-5225-0495-5.ch014

Cockburn, T., & Smith, P. A. (2016). Leadership in the Digital Age: Rhythms and the Beat of Change. In A. Normore, L. Long, & M. Javidi (Eds.), *Handbook of Research on Effective Communication, Leadership, and Conflict Resolution* (pp. 1–20). Hershey, PA: IGI Global. doi:10.4018/978-1-4666-9970-0.ch001

Cole, A. W., & Salek, T. A. (2017). Adopting a Parasocial Connection to Overcome Professional Kakoethos in Online Health Information. In M. Folk & S. Apostel (Eds.), *Establishing and Evaluating Digital Ethos and Online Credibility* (pp. 104–120). Hershey, PA: IGI Global. doi:10.4018/978-1-5225-1072-7.ch006

Cossiavelou, V. (2017). ACTA as Media Gatekeeping Factor: The EU Role as Global Negotiator. *International Journal of Interdisciplinary Telecommunications and Networking*, 9(1), 26–37. doi:10.4018/IJITN.2017010103

Costanza, F. (2017). Social Media Marketing and Value Co-Creation: A System Dynamics Approach. In S. Rozenes & Y. Cohen (Eds.), *Handbook of Research on Strategic Alliances and Value Co-Creation in the Service Industry* (pp. 205–230). Hershey, PA: IGI Global. doi:10.4018/978-1-5225-2084-9.ch011

Cross, D. E. (2016). Globalization and Media's Impact on Cross Cultural Communication: Managing Organizational Change. In A. Normore, L. Long, & M. Javidi (Eds.), *Handbook of Research on Effective Communication, Leadership, and Conflict Resolution* (pp. 21–41). Hershey, PA: IGI Global. doi:10.4018/978-1-4666-9970-0.ch002

Damásio, M. J., Henriques, S., Teixeira-Botelho, I., & Dias, P. (2016). Mobile Media and Social Interaction: Mobile Services and Content as Drivers of Social Interaction. In J. Aguado, C. Feijóo, & I. Martínez (Eds.), *Emerging Perspectives on the Mobile Content Evolution* (pp. 357–379). Hershey, PA: IGI Global. doi:10.4018/978-1-4666-8838-4.ch018

Davis, A., & Foley, L. (2016). Digital Storytelling. In B. Guzzetti & M. Lesley (Eds.), *Handbook of Research on the Societal Impact of Digital Media* (pp. 317–342). Hershey, PA: IGI Global. doi:10.4018/978-1-4666-8310-5.ch013

Davis, S., Palmer, L., & Etienne, J. (2016). The Geography of Digital Literacy: Mapping Communications Technology Training Programs in Austin, Texas. In B. Passarelli, J. Straubhaar, & A. Cuevas-Cerveró (Eds.), *Handbook of Research on Comparative Approaches to the Digital Age Revolution in Europe and the Americas* (pp. 371–384). Hershey, PA: IGI Global. doi:10.4018/978-1-4666-8740-0.ch022

Delello, J. A., & McWhorter, R. R. (2016). New Visual Literacies and Competencies for Education and the Workplace. In B. Guzzetti & M. Lesley (Eds.), *Handbook of Research on the Societal Impact of Digital Media* (pp. 127–162). Hershey, PA: IGI Global. doi:10.4018/978-1-4666-8310-5.ch006

Di Virgilio, F., & Antonelli, G. (2018). Consumer Behavior, Trust, and Electronic Word-of-Mouth Communication: Developing an Online Purchase Intention Model. In F. Di Virgilio (Ed.), *Social Media for Knowledge Management Applications in Modern Organizations* (pp. 58–80). Hershey, PA: IGI Global. doi:10.4018/978-1-5225-2897-5.ch003

Dixit, S. K. (2016). eWOM Marketing in Hospitality Industry. In A. Singh, & P. Duhan (Eds.), Managing Public Relations and Brand Image through Social Media (pp. 266-280). Hershey, PA: IGI Global. doi:10.4018/978-1-5225-0332-3.ch014

Duhan, P., & Singh, A. (2016). Facebook Experience Is Different: An Empirical Study in Indian Context. In S. Rathore & A. Panwar (Eds.), *Capturing, Analyzing, and Managing Word-of-Mouth in the Digital Marketplace* (pp. 188–212). Hershey, PA: IGI Global. doi:10.4018/978-1-4666-9449-1.ch011

Dunne, D. J. (2016). The Scholar's Ludo-Narrative Game and Multimodal Graphic Novel: A Comparison of Fringe Scholarship. In A. Connor & S. Marks (Eds.), *Creative Technologies for Multidisciplinary Applications* (pp. 182–207). Hershey, PA: IGI Global. doi:10.4018/978-1-5225-0016-2.ch008

DuQuette, J. L. (2017). Lessons from Cypris Chat: Revisiting Virtual Communities as Communities. In G. Panconesi & M. Guida (Eds.), *Handbook of Research on Collaborative Teaching Practice in Virtual Learning Environments* (pp. 299–316). Hershey, PA: IGI Global. doi:10.4018/978-1-5225-2426-7.ch016

Ekhlassi, A., Niknejhad Moghadam, M., & Adibi, A. (2018). The Concept of Social Media: The Functional Building Blocks. In *Building Brand Identity in the Age of Social Media: Emerging Research and Opportunities* (pp. 29–60). Hershey, PA: IGI Global. doi:10.4018/978-1-5225-5143-0.ch002

Ekhlassi, A., Niknejhad Moghadam, M., & Adibi, A. (2018). Social Media Branding Strategy: Social Media Marketing Approach. In *Building Brand Identity in the Age of Social Media: Emerging Research and Opportunities* (pp. 94–117). Hershey, PA: IGI Global. doi:10.4018/978-1-5225-5143-0.ch004

Ekhlassi, A., Niknejhad Moghadam, M., & Adibi, A. (2018). The Impact of Social Media on Brand Loyalty: Achieving "E-Trust" Through Engagement. In *Building Brand Identity in the Age of Social Media: Emerging Research and Opportunities* (pp. 155–168). Hershey, PA: IGI Global. doi:10.4018/978-1-5225-5143-0.ch007

Elegbe, O. (2017). An Assessment of Media Contribution to Behaviour Change and HIV Prevention in Nigeria. In O. Nelson, B. Ojebuyi, & A. Salawu (Eds.), *Impacts of the Media on African Socio-Economic Development* (pp. 261–280). Hershey, PA: IGI Global. doi:10.4018/978-1-5225-1859-4.ch017

Endong, F. P. (2018). Hashtag Activism and the Transnationalization of Nigerian-Born Movements Against Terrorism: A Critical Appraisal of the #BringBackOurGirls Campaign. In F. Endong (Ed.), *Exploring the Role of Social Media in Transnational Advocacy* (pp. 36–54). Hershey, PA: IGI Global. doi:10.4018/978-1-5225-2854-8.ch003

Erragcha, N. (2017). Using Social Media Tools in Marketing: Opportunities and Challenges. In M. Brown Sr., (Ed.), *Social Media Performance Evaluation and Success Measurements* (pp. 106–129). Hershey, PA: IGI Global. doi:10.4018/978-1-5225-1963-8.ch006

Ezeh, N. C. (2018). Media Campaign on Exclusive Breastfeeding: Awareness, Perception, and Acceptability Among Mothers in Anambra State, Nigeria. In A. Salawu & T. Owolabi (Eds.), *Exploring Journalism Practice and Perception in Developing Countries* (pp. 172–193). Hershey, PA: IGI Global. doi:10.4018/978-1-5225-3376-4.ch009

Fawole, O. A., & Osho, O. A. (2017). Influence of Social Media on Dating Relationships of Emerging Adults in Nigerian Universities: Social Media and Dating in Nigeria. In M. Wright (Ed.), *Identity, Sexuality, and Relationships among Emerging Adults in the Digital Age* (pp. 168–177). Hershey, PA: IGI Global. doi:10.4018/978-1-5225-1856-3.ch011

Fayoyin, A. (2017). Electoral Polling and Reporting in Africa: Professional and Policy Implications for Media Practice and Political Communication in a Digital Age. In N. Mhiripiri & T. Chari (Eds.), *Media Law, Ethics, and Policy in the Digital Age* (pp. 164–181). Hershey, PA: IGI Global. doi:10.4018/978-1-5225-2095-5.ch009

Fayoyin, A. (2018). Rethinking Media Engagement Strategies for Social Change in Africa: Context, Approaches, and Implications for Development Communication. In A. Salawu & T. Owolabi (Eds.), *Exploring Journalism Practice and Perception in Developing Countries* (pp. 257–280). Hershey, PA: IGI Global. doi:10.4018/978-1-5225-3376-4.ch013

Fechine, Y., & Rêgo, S. C. (2018). Transmedia Television Journalism in Brazil: Jornal da Record News as Reference. In R. Gambarato & G. Alzamora (Eds.), *Exploring Transmedia Journalism in the Digital Age* (pp. 253–265). Hershey, PA: IGI Global. doi:10.4018/978-1-5225-3781-6.ch015

Feng, J., & Lo, K. (2016). Video Broadcasting Protocol for Streaming Applications with Cooperative Clients. In D. Kanellopoulos (Ed.), *Emerging Research on Networked Multimedia Communication Systems* (pp. 205–229). Hershey, PA: IGI Global. doi:10.4018/978-1-4666-8850-6.ch006

Fiore, C. (2017). The Blogging Method: Improving Traditional Student Writing Practices. In K. Bryant (Ed.), *Engaging 21st Century Writers with Social Media* (pp. 179–198). Hershey, PA: IGI Global. doi:10.4018/978-1-5225-0562-4.ch011

Fleming, J., & Kajimoto, M. (2016). The Freedom of Critical Thinking: Examining Efforts to Teach American News Literacy Principles in Hong Kong, Vietnam, and Malaysia. In M. Yildiz & J. Keengwe (Eds.), *Handbook of Research on Media Literacy in the Digital Age* (pp. 208–235). Hershey, PA: IGI Global. doi:10.4018/978-1-4666-9667-9.ch010

Gambarato, R. R., Alzamora, G. C., & Tárcia, L. P. (2018). 2016 Rio Summer Olympics and the Transmedia Journalism of Planned Events. In R. Gambarato & G. Alzamora (Eds.), *Exploring Transmedia Journalism in the Digital Age* (pp. 126–146). Hershey, PA: IGI Global. doi:10.4018/978-1-5225-3781-6.ch008

Ganguin, S., Gemkow, J., & Haubold, R. (2017). Information Overload as a Challenge and Changing Point for Educational Media Literacies. In R. Marques & J. Batista (Eds.), *Information and Communication Overload in the Digital Age* (pp. 302–328). Hershey, PA: IGI Global. doi:10.4018/978-1-5225-2061-0.ch013

Gao, Y. (2016). Reviewing Gratification Effects in Mobile Gaming. In X. Xu (Ed.), *Handbook of Research on Human Social Interaction in the Age of Mobile Devices* (pp. 406–428). Hershey, PA: IGI Global. doi:10.4018/978-1-5225-0469-6.ch017

Gardner, G. C. (2017). The Lived Experience of Smartphone Use in a Unit of the United States Army. In F. Topor (Ed.), *Handbook of Research on Individualism and Identity in the Globalized Digital Age* (pp. 88–117). Hershey, PA: IGI Global. doi:10.4018/978-1-5225-0522-8.ch005

Giessen, H. W. (2016). The Medium, the Content, and the Performance: An Overview on Media-Based Learning. In B. Khan (Ed.), *Revolutionizing Modern Education through Meaningful E-Learning Implementation* (pp. 42–55). Hershey, PA: IGI Global. doi:10.4018/978-1-5225-0466-5.ch003

Giltenane, J. (2016). Investigating the Intention to Use Social Media Tools Within Virtual Project Teams. In G. Silvius (Ed.), *Strategic Integration of Social Media into Project Management Practice* (pp. 83–105). Hershey, PA: IGI Global. doi:10.4018/978-1-4666-9867-3.ch006

Golightly, D., & Houghton, R. J. (2018). Social Media as a Tool to Understand Behaviour on the Railways. In S. Kohli, A. Kumar, J. Easton, & C. Roberts (Eds.), *Innovative Applications of Big Data in the Railway Industry* (pp. 224–239). Hershey, PA: IGI Global. doi:10.4018/978-1-5225-3176-0.ch010

Goovaerts, M., Nieuwenhuysen, P., & Dhamdhere, S. N. (2016). VLIR-UOS Workshop 'E-Info Discovery and Management for Institutes in the South': Presentations and Conclusions, Antwerp, 8-19 December, 2014. In E. de Smet, & S. Dhamdhere (Eds.), E-Discovery Tools and Applications in Modern Libraries (pp. 1-40). Hershey, PA: IGI Global. doi:10.4018/978-1-5225-0474-0.ch001

Grützmann, A., Carvalho de Castro, C., Meireles, A. A., & Rodrigues, R. C. (2016). Organizational Architecture and Online Social Networks: Insights from Innovative Brazilian Companies. In G. Jamil, J. Poças Rascão, F. Ribeiro, & A. Malheiro da Silva (Eds.), *Handbook of Research on Information Architecture and Management in Modern Organizations* (pp. 508–524). Hershey, PA: IGI Global. doi:10.4018/978-1-4666-8637-3.ch023

Gundogan, M. B. (2017). In Search for a "Good Fit" Between Augmented Reality and Mobile Learning Ecosystem. In G. Kurubacak & H. Altinpulluk (Eds.), *Mobile Technologies and Augmented Reality in Open Education* (pp. 135–153). Hershey, PA: IGI Global. doi:10.4018/978-1-5225-2110-5.ch007

Gupta, H. (2018). Impact of Digital Communication on Consumer Behaviour Processes in Luxury Branding Segment: A Study of Apparel Industry. In S. Dasgupta, S. Biswal, & M. Ramesh (Eds.), *Holistic Approaches to Brand Culture and Communication Across Industries* (pp. 132–157). Hershey, PA: IGI Global. doi:10.4018/978-1-5225-3150-0.ch008

Hai-Jew, S. (2017). Creating "(Social) Network Art" with NodeXL. In S. Hai-Jew (Ed.), *Social Media Data Extraction and Content Analysis* (pp. 342–393). Hershey, PA: IGI Global. doi:10.4018/978-1-5225-0648-5.ch011

Hai-Jew, S. (2017). Employing the Sentiment Analysis Tool in NVivo 11 Plus on Social Media Data: Eight Initial Case Types. In N. Rao (Ed.), *Social Media Listening and Monitoring for Business Applications* (pp. 175–244). Hershey, PA: IGI Global. doi:10.4018/978-1-5225-0846-5.ch010

Hai-Jew, S. (2017). Conducting Sentiment Analysis and Post-Sentiment Data Exploration through Automated Means. In S. Hai-Jew (Ed.), *Social Media Data Extraction and Content Analysis* (pp. 202–240). Hershey, PA: IGI Global. doi:10.4018/978-1-5225-0648-5.ch008

Hai-Jew, S. (2017). Applied Analytical "Distant Reading" using NVivo 11 Plus. In S. Hai-Jew (Ed.), *Social Media Data Extraction and Content Analysis* (pp. 159–201). Hershey, PA: IGI Global. doi:10.4018/978-1-5225-0648-5.ch007

Hai-Jew, S. (2017). Flickering Emotions: Feeling-Based Associations from Related Tags Networks on Flickr. In S. Hai-Jew (Ed.), *Social Media Data Extraction and Content Analysis* (pp. 296–341). Hershey, PA: IGI Global. doi:10.4018/978-1-5225-0648-5.ch010

Hai-Jew, S. (2017). Manually Profiling Egos and Entities across Social Media Platforms: Evaluating Shared Messaging and Contents, User Networks, and Metadata. In V. Benson, R. Tuninga, & G. Saridakis (Eds.), *Analyzing the Strategic Role of Social Networking in Firm Growth and Productivity* (pp. 352–405). Hershey, PA: IGI Global. doi:10.4018/978-1-5225-0559-4.ch019

Hai-Jew, S. (2017). Exploring "User," "Video," and (Pseudo) Multi-Mode Networks on YouTube with NodeXL. In S. Hai-Jew (Ed.), *Social Media Data Extraction and Content Analysis* (pp. 242–295). Hershey, PA: IGI Global. doi:10.4018/978-1-5225-0648-5.ch009

Hai-Jew, S. (2018). Exploring "Mass Surveillance" Through Computational Linguistic Analysis of Five Text Corpora: Academic, Mainstream Journalism, Microblogging Hashtag Conversation, Wikipedia Articles, and Leaked Government Data. In *Techniques for Coding Imagery and Multimedia: Emerging Research and Opportunities* (pp. 212–286). Hershey, PA: IGI Global. doi:10.4018/978-1-5225-2679-7.ch004

Hai-Jew, S. (2018). Exploring Identity-Based Humor in a #Selfies #Humor Image Set From Instagram. In *Techniques for Coding Imagery and Multimedia: Emerging Research and Opportunities* (pp. 1–90). Hershey, PA: IGI Global. doi:10.4018/978-1-5225-2679-7.ch001

Hai-Jew, S. (2018). See Ya!: Exploring American Renunciation of Citizenship Through Targeted and Sparse Social Media Data Sets and a Custom Spatial-Based Linguistic Analysis Dictionary. In *Techniques for Coding Imagery and Multimedia: Emerging Research and Opportunities* (pp. 287–393). Hershey, PA: IGI Global. doi:10.4018/978-1-5225-2679-7.ch005

Han, H. S., Zhang, J., Peikazadi, N., Shi, G., Hung, A., Doan, C. P., & Filippelli, S. (2016). An Entertaining Game-Like Learning Environment in a Virtual World for Education. In S. D'Agustino (Ed.), *Creating Teacher Immediacy in Online Learning Environments* (pp. 290–306). Hershey, PA: IGI Global. doi:10.4018/978-1-4666-9995-3.ch015

Harrin, E. (2016). Barriers to Social Media Adoption on Projects. In G. Silvius (Ed.), *Strategic Integration of Social Media into Project Management Practice* (pp. 106–124). Hershey, PA: IGI Global. doi:10.4018/978-1-4666-9867-3.ch007

Harvey, K. E. (2016). Local News and Mobile: Major Tipping Points. In X. Xu (Ed.), *Handbook of Research on Human Social Interaction in the Age of Mobile Devices* (pp. 171–199). Hershey, PA: IGI Global. doi:10.4018/978-1-5225-0469-6.ch009

Harvey, K. E., & An, Y. (2016). Marketing and Mobile: Increasing Integration. In X. Xu (Ed.), *Handbook of Research on Human Social Interaction in the Age of Mobile Devices* (pp. 220–247). Hershey, PA: IGI Global. doi:10.4018/978-1-5225-0469-6.ch011

Harvey, K. E., Auter, P. J., & Stevens, S. (2016). Educators and Mobile: Challenges and Trends. In X. Xu (Ed.), *Handbook of Research on Human Social Interaction in the Age of Mobile Devices* (pp. 61–95). Hershey, PA: IGI Global. doi:10.4018/978-1-5225-0469-6.ch004

Hasan, H., & Linger, H. (2017). Connected Living for Positive Ageing. In S. Gordon (Ed.), *Online Communities as Agents of Change and Social Movements* (pp. 203–223). Hershey, PA: IGI Global. doi:10.4018/978-1-5225-2495-3.ch008

Hashim, K., Al-Sharqi, L., & Kutbi, I. (2016). Perceptions of Social Media Impact on Social Behavior of Students: A Comparison between Students and Faculty. *International Journal of Virtual Communities and Social Networking*, 8(2), 1–11. doi:10.4018/IJVCSN.2016040101

Henriques, S., & Damasio, M. J. (2016). The Value of Mobile Communication for Social Belonging: Mobile Apps and the Impact on Social Interaction. *International Journal of Handheld Computing Research*, 7(2), 44–58. doi:10.4018/IJHCR.2016040104

Hersey, L. N. (2017). CHOICES: Measuring Return on Investment in a Nonprofit Organization. In M. Brown Sr., (Ed.), *Social Media Performance Evaluation and Success Measurements* (pp. 157–179). Hershey, PA: IGI Global. doi:10.4018/978-1-5225-1963-8.ch008

Heuva, W. E. (2017). Deferring Citizens' "Right to Know" in an Information Age: The Information Deficit in Namibia. In N. Mhiripiri & T. Chari (Eds.), *Media Law, Ethics, and Policy in the Digital Age* (pp. 245–267). Hershey, PA: IGI Global. doi:10.4018/978-1-5225-2095-5.ch014

Hopwood, M., & McLean, H. (2017). Social Media in Crisis Communication: The Lance Armstrong Saga. In V. Benson, R. Tuninga, & G. Saridakis (Eds.), *Analyzing the Strategic Role of Social Networking in Firm Growth and Productivity* (pp. 45–58). Hershey, PA: IGI Global. doi:10.4018/978-1-5225-0559-4.ch003

Hotur, S. K. (2018). Indian Approaches to E-Diplomacy: An Overview. In S. Bute (Ed.), *Media Diplomacy and Its Evolving Role in the Current Geopolitical Climate* (pp. 27–35). Hershey, PA: IGI Global. doi:10.4018/978-1-5225-3859-2.ch002

Ibadildin, N., & Harvey, K. E. (2016). Business and Mobile: Rapid Restructure Required. In X. Xu (Ed.), *Handbook of Research on Human Social Interaction in the Age of Mobile Devices* (pp. 312–350). Hershey, PA: IGI Global. doi:10.4018/978-1-5225-0469-6.ch014

Iwasaki, Y. (2017). Youth Engagement in the Era of New Media. In M. Adria & Y. Mao (Eds.), *Handbook of Research on Citizen Engagement and Public Participation in the Era of New Media* (pp. 90–105). Hershey, PA: IGI Global. doi:10.4018/978-1-5225-1081-9.ch006

Jamieson, H. V. (2017). We have a Situation!: Cyberformance and Civic Engagement in Post-Democracy. In R. Shin (Ed.), *Convergence of Contemporary Art, Visual Culture, and Global Civic Engagement* (pp. 297–317). Hershey, PA: IGI Global. doi:10.4018/978-1-5225-1665-1.ch017

Jimoh, J., & Kayode, J. (2018). Imperative of Peace and Conflict-Sensitive Journalism in Development. In A. Salawu & T. Owolabi (Eds.), *Exploring Journalism Practice and Perception in Developing Countries* (pp. 150–171). Hershey, PA: IGI Global. doi:10.4018/978-1-5225-3376-4.ch008

Johns, R. (2016). Increasing Value of a Tangible Product through Intangible Attributes: Value Co-Creation and Brand Building within Online Communities – Virtual Communities and Value. In R. English & R. Johns (Eds.), *Gender Considerations in Online Consumption Behavior and Internet Use* (pp. 112–124). Hershey, PA: IGI Global. doi:10.4018/978-1-5225-0010-0.ch008

Kanellopoulos, D. N. (2018). Group Synchronization for Multimedia Systems. In M. Khosrow-Pour, D.B.A. (Ed.), Encyclopedia of Information Science and Technology, Fourth Edition (pp. 6435-6446). Hershey, PA: IGI Global. doi:10.4018/978-1-5225-2255-3.ch559

Kapepo, M. I., & Mayisela, T. (2017). Integrating Digital Literacies Into an Undergraduate Course: Inclusiveness Through Use of ICTs. In C. Ayo & V. Mbarika (Eds.), *Sustainable ICT Adoption and Integration for Socio-Economic Development* (pp. 152–173). Hershey, PA: IGI Global. doi:10.4018/978-1-5225-2565-3.ch007

Karahoca, A., & Yengin, İ. (2018). Understanding the Potentials of Social Media in Collaborative Learning. In M. Khosrow-Pour, D.B.A. (Ed.), Encyclopedia of Information Science and Technology, Fourth Edition (pp. 7168-7180). Hershey, PA: IGI Global. doi:10.4018/978-1-5225-2255-3.ch623

Karataş, S., Ceran, O., Ülker, Ü., Gün, E. T., Köse, N. Ö., Kılıç, M., ... Tok, Z. A. (2016). A Trend Analysis of Mobile Learning. In D. Parsons (Ed.), *Mobile and Blended Learning Innovations for Improved Learning Outcomes* (pp. 248–276). Hershey, PA: IGI Global. doi:10.4018/978-1-5225-0359-0.ch013

Kasemsap, K. (2016). Role of Social Media in Brand Promotion: An International Marketing Perspective. In A. Singh & P. Duhan (Eds.), *Managing Public Relations and Brand Image through Social Media* (pp. 62–88). Hershey, PA: IGI Global. doi:10.4018/978-1-5225-0332-3.ch005

Kasemsap, K. (2016). The Roles of Social Media Marketing and Brand Management in Global Marketing. In W. Ozuem & G. Bowen (Eds.), *Competitive Social Media Marketing Strategies* (pp. 173–200). Hershey, PA: IGI Global. doi:10.4018/978-1-4666-9776-8.ch009

Kasemsap, K. (2017). Professional and Business Applications of Social Media Platforms. In V. Benson, R. Tuninga, & G. Saridakis (Eds.), *Analyzing the Strategic Role of Social Networking in Firm Growth and Productivity* (pp. 427–450). Hershey, PA: IGI Global. doi:10.4018/978-1-5225-0559-4.ch021

Kasemsap, K. (2017). Mastering Social Media in the Modern Business World. In N. Rao (Ed.), *Social Media Listening and Monitoring for Business Applications* (pp. 18–44). Hershey, PA: IGI Global. doi:10.4018/978-1-5225-0846-5.ch002

Kato, Y., & Kato, S. (2016). Mobile Phone Use during Class at a Japanese Women's College. In M. Yildiz & J. Keengwe (Eds.), *Handbook of Research on Media Literacy in the Digital Age* (pp. 436–455). Hershey, PA: IGI Global. doi:10.4018/978-1-4666-9667-9.ch021

Kaufmann, H. R., & Manarioti, A. (2017). Consumer Engagement in Social Media Platforms. In *Encouraging Participative Consumerism Through Evolutionary Digital Marketing: Emerging Research and Opportunities* (pp. 95–123). Hershey, PA: IGI Global. doi:10.4018/978-1-68318-012-8.ch004

Kavoura, A., & Kefallonitis, E. (2018). The Effect of Social Media Networking in the Travel Industry. In M. Khosrow-Pour, D.B.A. (Ed.), *Encyclopedia of Information Science and Technology, Fourth Edition* (pp. 4052-4063). Hershey, PA: IGI Global. doi:10.4018/978-1-5225-2255-3.ch351

Kawamura, Y. (2018). Practice and Modeling of Advertising Communication Strategy: Sender-Driven and Receiver-Driven. In T. Ogata & S. Asakawa (Eds.), *Content Generation Through Narrative Communication and Simulation* (pp. 358–379). Hershey, PA: IGI Global. doi:10.4018/978-1-5225-4775-4.ch013

Kell, C., & Czerniewicz, L. (2017). Visibility of Scholarly Research and Changing Research Communication Practices: A Case Study from Namibia. In A. Esposito (Ed.), *Research 2.0 and the Impact of Digital Technologies on Scholarly Inquiry* (pp. 97–116). Hershey, PA: IGI Global. doi:10.4018/978-1-5225-0830-4.ch006

Khalil, G. E. (2016). Change through Experience: How Experiential Play and Emotional Engagement Drive Health Game Success. In D. Novák, B. Tulu, & H. Brendryen (Eds.), *Handbook of Research on Holistic Perspectives in Gamification for Clinical Practice* (pp. 10–34). Hershey, PA: IGI Global. doi:10.4018/978-1-4666-9522-1.ch002

Kılınç, U. (2017). Create It! Extend It!: Evolution of Comics Through Narrative Advertising. In R. Yılmaz (Ed.), *Narrative Advertising Models and Conceptualization in the Digital Age* (pp. 117–132). Hershey, PA: IGI Global. doi:10.4018/978-1-5225-2373-4.ch007

Kim, J. H. (2016). Pedagogical Approaches to Media Literacy Education in the United States. In M. Yildiz & J. Keengwe (Eds.), *Handbook of Research on Media Literacy in the Digital Age* (pp. 53–74). Hershey, PA: IGI Global. doi:10.4018/978-1-4666-9667-9.ch003

Kirigha, J. M., Mukhongo, L. L., & Masinde, R. (2016). Beyond Web 2.0. Social Media and Urban Educated Youths Participation in Kenyan Politics. In L. Mukhongo & J. Macharia (Eds.), *Political Influence of the Media in Developing Countries* (pp. 156–174). Hershey, PA: IGI Global. doi:10.4018/978-1-4666-9613-6.ch010

Krochmal, M. M. (2016). Training for Mobile Journalism. In D. Mentor (Ed.), *Handbook of Research on Mobile Learning in Contemporary Classrooms* (pp. 336–362). Hershey, PA: IGI Global. doi:10.4018/978-1-5225-0251-7.ch017

Kumar, P., & Sinha, A. (2018). Business-Oriented Analytics With Social Network of Things. In H. Bansal, G. Shrivastava, G. Nguyen, & L. Stanciu (Eds.), *Social Network Analytics for Contemporary Business Organizations* (pp. 166–187). Hershey, PA: IGI Global. doi:10.4018/978-1-5225-5097-6. ch009

Kunock, A. I. (2017). Boko Haram Insurgency in Cameroon: Role of Mass Media in Conflict Management. In N. Mhiripiri & T. Chari (Eds.), *Media Law, Ethics, and Policy in the Digital Age* (pp. 226–244). Hershey, PA: IGI Global. doi:10.4018/978-1-5225-2095-5.ch013

Labadie, J. A. (2018). Digitally Mediated Art Inspired by Technology Integration: A Personal Journey. In A. Ursyn (Ed.), *Visual Approaches to Cognitive Education With Technology Integration* (pp. 121–162). Hershey, PA: IGI Global. doi:10.4018/978-1-5225-5332-8.ch008

Lefkowith, S. (2017). Credibility and Crisis in Pseudonymous Communities. In M. Folk & S. Apostel (Eds.), *Establishing and Evaluating Digital Ethos and Online Credibility* (pp. 190–236). Hershey, PA: IGI Global. doi:10.4018/978-1-5225-1072-7.ch010

Lemoine, P. A., Hackett, P. T., & Richardson, M. D. (2016). The Impact of Social Media on Instruction in Higher Education. In L. Briz-Ponce, J. Juanes-Méndez, & F. García-Peñalvo (Eds.), *Handbook of Research on Mobile Devices and Applications in Higher Education Settings* (pp. 373–401). Hershey, PA: IGI Global. doi:10.4018/978-1-5225-0256-2.ch016

Liampotis, N., Papadopoulou, E., Kalatzis, N., Roussaki, I. G., Kosmides, P., Sykas, E. D., ... Taylor, N. K. (2016). Tailoring Privacy-Aware Trustworthy Cooperating Smart Spaces for University Environments. In A. Panagopoulos (Ed.), *Handbook of Research on Next Generation Mobile Communication Systems* (pp. 410–439). Hershey, PA: IGI Global. doi:10.4018/978-1-4666-8732-5.ch016

Luppicini, R. (2017). Technoethics and Digital Democracy for Future Citizens. In R. Luppicini & R. Baarda (Eds.), *Digital Media Integration for Participatory Democracy* (pp. 1–21). Hershey, PA: IGI Global. doi:10.4018/978-1-5225-2463-2.ch001

Mahajan, I. M., Rather, M., Shafiq, H., & Qadri, U. (2016). Media Literacy Organizations. In M. Yildiz & J. Keengwe (Eds.), *Handbook of Research on Media Literacy in the Digital Age* (pp. 236–248). Hershey, PA: IGI Global. doi:10.4018/978-1-4666-9667-9.ch011

Maher, D. (2018). Supporting Pre-Service Teachers' Understanding and Use of Mobile Devices. In J. Keengwe (Ed.), *Handbook of Research on Mobile Technology, Constructivism, and Meaningful Learning* (pp. 160–177). Hershey, PA: IGI Global. doi:10.4018/978-1-5225-3949-0.ch009

Makhwanya, A. (2018). Barriers to Social Media Advocacy: Lessons Learnt From the Project "Tell Them We Are From Here". In F. Endong (Ed.), *Exploring the Role of Social Media in Transnational Advocacy* (pp. 55–72). Hershey, PA: IGI Global. doi:10.4018/978-1-5225-2854-8.ch004

Manli, G., & Rezaei, S. (2017). Value and Risk: Dual Pillars of Apps Usefulness. In S. Rezaei (Ed.), *Apps Management and E-Commerce Transactions in Real-Time* (pp. 274–292). Hershey, PA: IGI Global. doi:10.4018/978-1-5225-2449-6.ch013

Manrique, C. G., & Manrique, G. G. (2017). Social Media's Role in Alleviating Political Corruption and Scandals: The Philippines during and after the Marcos Regime. In K. Demirhan & D. Çakır-Demirhan (Eds.), *Political Scandal, Corruption, and Legitimacy in the Age of Social Media* (pp. 205–222). Hershey, PA: IGI Global. doi:10.4018/978-1-5225-2019-1.ch009

Manzoor, A. (2016). Cultural Barriers to Organizational Social Media Adoption. In A. Goel & P. Singhal (Eds.), *Product Innovation through Knowledge Management and Social Media Strategies* (pp. 31–45). Hershey, PA: IGI Global. doi:10.4018/978-1-4666-9607-5.ch002

Manzoor, A. (2016). Social Media for Project Management. In G. Silvius (Ed.), *Strategic Integration of Social Media into Project Management Practice* (pp. 51–65). Hershey, PA: IGI Global. doi:10.4018/978-1-4666-9867-3.ch004

Marovitz, M. (2017). Social Networking Engagement and Crisis Communication Considerations. In M. Brown Sr., (Ed.), *Social Media Performance Evaluation and Success Measurements* (pp. 130–155). Hershey, PA: IGI Global. doi:10.4018/978-1-5225-1963-8.ch007

Mathur, D., & Mathur, D. (2016). Word of Mouth on Social Media: A Potent Tool for Brand Building. In S. Rathore & A. Panwar (Eds.), *Capturing, Analyzing, and Managing Word-of-Mouth in the Digital Marketplace* (pp. 45–60). Hershey, PA: IGI Global. doi:10.4018/978-1-4666-9449-1.ch003

Maulana, I. (2018). Spontaneous Taking and Posting Selfie: Reclaiming the Lost Trust. In S. Hai-Jew (Ed.), *Selfies as a Mode of Social Media and Work Space Research* (pp. 28–50). Hershey, PA: IGI Global. doi:10.4018/978-1-5225-3373-3.ch002

Mayo, S. (2018). A Collective Consciousness Model in a Post-Media Society. In M. Khosrow-Pour (Ed.), *Enhancing Art, Culture, and Design With Technological Integration* (pp. 25–49). Hershey, PA: IGI Global. doi:10.4018/978-1-5225-5023-5.ch002

Mazur, E., Signorella, M. L., & Hough, M. (2018). The Internet Behavior of Older Adults. In M. Khosrow-Pour, D.B.A. (Ed.), Encyclopedia of Information Science and Technology, Fourth Edition (pp. 7026-7035). Hershey, PA: IGI Global. doi:10.4018/978-1-5225-2255-3.ch609

McGuire, M. (2017). Reblogging as Writing: The Role of Tumblr in the Writing Classroom. In K. Bryant (Ed.), *Engaging 21st Century Writers with Social Media* (pp. 116–131). Hershey, PA: IGI Global. doi:10.4018/978-1-5225-0562-4.ch007

McKee, J. (2018). Architecture as a Tool to Solve Business Planning Problems. In M. Khosrow-Pour, D.B.A. (Ed.), Encyclopedia of Information Science and Technology, Fourth Edition (pp. 573-586). Hershey, PA: IGI Global. doi:10.4018/978-1-5225-2255-3.ch050

McMahon, D. (2017). With a Little Help from My Friends: The Irish Radio Industry's Strategic Appropriation of Facebook for Commercial Growth. In V. Benson, R. Tuninga, & G. Saridakis (Eds.), *Analyzing the Strategic Role of Social Networking in Firm Growth and Productivity* (pp. 157–171). Hershey, PA: IGI Global. doi:10.4018/978-1-5225-0559-4.ch009

McPherson, M. J., & Lemon, N. (2017). The Hook, Woo, and Spin: Academics Creating Relations on Social Media. In A. Esposito (Ed.), *Research 2.0 and the Impact of Digital Technologies on Scholarly Inquiry* (pp. 167–187). Hershey, PA: IGI Global. doi:10.4018/978-1-5225-0830-4.ch009

Melro, A., & Oliveira, L. (2018). Screen Culture. In M. Khosrow-Pour, D.B.A. (Ed.), Encyclopedia of Information Science and Technology, Fourth Edition (pp. 4255-4266). Hershey, PA: IGI Global. doi:10.4018/978-1-5225-2255-3.ch369

Merwin, G. A. Jr, McDonald, J. S., Bennett, J. R. Jr, & Merwin, K. A. (2016). Social Media Applications Promote Constituent Involvement in Government Management. In G. Silvius (Ed.), *Strategic Integration of Social Media into Project Management Practice* (pp. 272–291). Hershey, PA: IGI Global. doi:10.4018/978-1-4666-9867-3.ch016

Mhiripiri, N. A., & Chikakano, J. (2017). Criminal Defamation, the Criminalisation of Expression, Media and Information Dissemination in the Digital Age: A Legal and Ethical Perspective. In N. Mhiripiri & T. Chari (Eds.), *Media Law, Ethics, and Policy in the Digital Age* (pp. 1–24). Hershey, PA: IGI Global. doi:10.4018/978-1-5225-2095-5.ch001

Miliopoulou, G., & Cossiavelou, V. (2016). Brands and Media Gatekeeping in the Social Media: Current Trends and Practices – An Exploratory Research. *International Journal of Interdisciplinary Telecommunications and Networking*, 8(4), 51–64. doi:10.4018/IJITN.2016100105

Miron, E., Palmor, A., Ravid, G., Sharon, A., Tikotsky, A., & Zirkel, Y. (2017). Principles and Good Practices for Using Wikis within Organizations. In R. Chugh (Ed.), *Harnessing Social Media as a Knowledge Management Tool* (pp. 143–176). Hershey, PA: IGI Global. doi:10.4018/978-1-5225-0495-5.ch008

Mishra, K. E., Mishra, A. K., & Walker, K. (2016). Leadership Communication, Internal Marketing, and Employee Engagement: A Recipe to Create Brand Ambassadors. In A. Normore, L. Long, & M. Javidi (Eds.), *Handbook of Research on Effective Communication, Leadership, and Conflict Resolution* (pp. 311–329). Hershey, PA: IGI Global. doi:10.4018/978-1-4666-9970-0.ch017

Moeller, C. L. (2018). Sharing Your Personal Medical Experience Online: Is It an Irresponsible Act or Patient Empowerment? In S. Sekalala & B. Niezgoda (Eds.), *Global Perspectives on Health Communication in the Age of Social Media* (pp. 185–209). Hershey, PA: IGI Global. doi:10.4018/978-1-5225-3716-8.ch007

Mosanako, S. (2017). Broadcasting Policy in Botswana: The Case of Botswana Television. In O. Nelson, B. Ojebuyi, & A. Salawu (Eds.), *Impacts of the Media on African Socio-Economic Development* (pp. 217–230). Hershey, PA: IGI Global. doi:10.4018/978-1-5225-1859-4.ch014

Nazari, A. (2016). Developing a Social Media Communication Plan. In G. Silvius (Ed.), *Strategic Integration of Social Media into Project Management Practice* (pp. 194–217). Hershey, PA: IGI Global. doi:10.4018/978-1-4666-9867-3.ch012

Neto, B. M. (2016). From Information Society to Community Service: The Birth of E-Citizenship. In B. Passarelli, J. Straubhaar, & A. Cuevas-Cerveró (Eds.), *Handbook of Research on Comparative Approaches to the Digital Age Revolution in Europe and the Americas* (pp. 101–123). Hershey, PA: IGI Global. doi:10.4018/978-1-4666-8740-0.ch007

Noguti, V., Singh, S., & Waller, D. S. (2016). Gender Differences in Motivations to Use Social Networking Sites. In R. English & R. Johns (Eds.), *Gender Considerations in Online Consumption Behavior and Internet Use* (pp. 32–49). Hershey, PA: IGI Global. doi:10.4018/978-1-5225-0010-0.ch003

Noor, R. (2017). Citizen Journalism: News Gathering by Amateurs. In M. Adria & Y. Mao (Eds.), *Handbook of Research on Citizen Engagement and Public Participation in the Era of New Media* (pp. 194–229). Hershey, PA: IGI Global. doi:10.4018/978-1-5225-1081-9.ch012

Nwagbara, U., Oruh, E. S., & Brown, C. (2016). State Fragility and Stakeholder Engagement: New Media and Stakeholders' Voice Amplification in the Nigerian Petroleum Industry. In W. Ozuem & G. Bowen (Eds.), *Competitive Social Media Marketing Strategies* (pp. 136–154). Hershey, PA: IGI Global. doi:10.4018/978-1-4666-9776-8.ch007

Obermayer, N., Csepregi, A., & Kővári, E. (2017). Knowledge Sharing Relation to Competence, Emotional Intelligence, and Social Media Regarding Generations. In A. Bencsik (Ed.), *Knowledge Management Initiatives and Strategies in Small and Medium Enterprises* (pp. 269–290). Hershey, PA: IGI Global. doi:10.4018/978-1-5225-1642-2.ch013

Obermayer, N., Gaál, Z., Szabó, L., & Csepregi, A. (2017). Leveraging Knowledge Sharing over Social Media Tools. In R. Chugh (Ed.), *Harnessing Social Media as a Knowledge Management Tool* (pp. 1–24). Hershey, PA: IGI Global. doi:10.4018/978-1-5225-0495-5.ch001

Ogwezzy-Ndisika, A. O., & Faustino, B. A. (2016). Gender Responsive Election Coverage in Nigeria: A Score Card of 2011 General Elections. In L. Mukhongo & J. Macharia (Eds.), *Political Influence of the Media in Developing Countries* (pp. 234–249). Hershey, PA: IGI Global. doi:10.4018/978-1-4666-9613-6.ch015

Okoroafor, O. E. (2018). New Media Technology and Development Journalism in Nigeria. In A. Salawu & T. Owolabi (Eds.), *Exploring Journalism Practice and Perception in Developing Countries* (pp. 105–125). Hershey, PA: IGI Global. doi:10.4018/978-1-5225-3376-4.ch006

Olaleye, S. A., Sanusi, I. T., & Ukpabi, D. C. (2018). Assessment of Mobile Money Enablers in Nigeria. In F. Mtenzi, G. Oreku, D. Lupiana, & J. Yonazi (Eds.), *Mobile Technologies and Socio-Economic Development in Emerging Nations* (pp. 129–155). Hershey, PA: IGI Global. doi:10.4018/978-1-5225-4029-8.ch007

Ozuem, W., Pinho, C. A., & Azemi, Y. (2016). User-Generated Content and Perceived Customer Value. In W. Ozuem & G. Bowen (Eds.), *Competitive Social Media Marketing Strategies* (pp. 50–63). Hershey, PA: IGI Global. doi:10.4018/978-1-4666-9776-8.ch003

Pacchiega, C. (2017). An Informal Methodology for Teaching Through Virtual Worlds: Using Internet Tools and Virtual Worlds in a Coordinated Pattern to Teach Various Subjects. In G. Panconesi & M. Guida (Eds.), *Handbook of Research on Collaborative Teaching Practice in Virtual Learning Environments* (pp. 163–180). Hershey, PA: IGI Global. doi:10.4018/978-1-5225-2426-7.ch009

Pase, A. F., Goss, B. M., & Tietzmann, R. (2018). A Matter of Time: Transmedia Journalism Challenges. In R. Gambarato & G. Alzamora (Eds.), *Exploring Transmedia Journalism in the Digital Age* (pp. 49–66). Hershey, PA: IGI Global. doi:10.4018/978-1-5225-3781-6.ch004

Passarelli, B., & Paletta, F. C. (2016). Living inside the NET: The Primacy of Interactions and Processes. In B. Passarelli, J. Straubhaar, & A. Cuevas-Cerveró (Eds.), *Handbook of Research on Comparative Approaches to the Digital Age Revolution in Europe and the Americas* (pp. 1–15). Hershey, PA: IGI Global. doi:10.4018/978-1-4666-8740-0.ch001

Patkin, T. T. (2017). Social Media and Knowledge Management in a Crisis Context: Barriers and Opportunities. In R. Chugh (Ed.), *Harnessing Social Media as a Knowledge Management Tool* (pp. 125–142). Hershey, PA: IGI Global. doi:10.4018/978-1-5225-0495-5.ch007

Pavlíček, A. (2017). Social Media and Creativity: How to Engage Users and Tourists. In A. Kiráľová (Ed.), *Driving Tourism through Creative Destinations and Activities* (pp. 181–202). Hershey, PA: IGI Global. doi:10.4018/978-1-5225-2016-0.ch009

Pillay, K., & Maharaj, M. (2017). The Business of Advocacy: A Case Study of Greenpeace. In V. Benson, R. Tuninga, & G. Saridakis (Eds.), *Analyzing the Strategic Role of Social Networking in Firm Growth and Productivity* (pp. 59–75). Hershey, PA: IGI Global. doi:10.4018/978-1-5225-0559-4.ch004

Piven, I. P., & Breazeale, M. (2017). Desperately Seeking Customer Engagement: The Five-Sources Model of Brand Value on Social Media. In V. Benson, R. Tuninga, & G. Saridakis (Eds.), *Analyzing the Strategic Role of Social Networking in Firm Growth and Productivity* (pp. 283–313). Hershey, PA: IGI Global. doi:10.4018/978-1-5225-0559-4.ch016

Pokharel, R. (2017). New Media and Technology: How Do They Change the Notions of the Rhetorical Situations? In B. Gurung & M. Limbu (Eds.), *Integration of Cloud Technologies in Digitally Networked Classrooms and Learning Communities* (pp. 120–148). Hershey, PA: IGI Global. doi:10.4018/978-1-5225-1650-7.ch008

Popoola, I. S. (2016). The Press and the Emergent Political Class in Nigeria: Media, Elections, and Democracy. In L. Mukhongo & J. Macharia (Eds.), *Political Influence of the Media in Developing Countries* (pp. 45–58). Hershey, PA: IGI Global. doi:10.4018/978-1-4666-9613-6.ch004

Porlezza, C., Benecchi, E., & Colapinto, C. (2018). The Transmedia Revitalization of Investigative Journalism: Opportunities and Challenges of the Serial Podcast. In R. Gambarato & G. Alzamora (Eds.), *Exploring Transmedia Journalism in the Digital Age* (pp. 183–201). Hershey, PA: IGI Global. doi:10.4018/978-1-5225-3781-6.ch011

Ramluckan, T., Ally, S. E., & van Niekerk, B. (2017). Twitter Use in Student Protests: The Case of South Africa's #FeesMustFall Campaign. In M. Korstanje (Ed.), *Threat Mitigation and Detection of Cyber Warfare and Terrorism Activities* (pp. 220–253). Hershey, PA: IGI Global. doi:10.4018/978-1-5225-1938-6.ch010

Rao, N. R. (2017). Social Media: An Enabler for Governance. In N. Rao (Ed.), *Social Media Listening and Monitoring for Business Applications* (pp. 151–164). Hershey, PA: IGI Global. doi:10.4018/978-1-5225-0846-5.ch008

Rathore, A. K., Tuli, N., & Ilavarasan, P. V. (2016). Pro-Business or Common Citizen?: An Analysis of an Indian Woman CEO's Tweets. *International Journal of Virtual Communities and Social Networking*, 8(1), 19–29. doi:10.4018/IJVCSN.2016010102

Redi, F. (2017). Enhancing Coopetition Among Small Tourism Destinations by Creativity. In A. Kiráľová (Ed.), *Driving Tourism through Creative Destinations and Activities* (pp. 223–244). Hershey, PA: IGI Global. doi:10.4018/978-1-5225-2016-0.ch011

Reeves, M. (2016). Social Media: It Can Play a Positive Role in Education. In R. English & R. Johns (Eds.), *Gender Considerations in Online Consumption Behavior and Internet Use* (pp. 82–95). Hershey, PA: IGI Global. doi:10.4018/978-1-5225-0010-0.ch006

Reis, Z. A. (2016). Bring the Media Literacy of Turkish Pre-Service Teachers to the Table. In M. Yildiz & J. Keengwe (Eds.), *Handbook of Research on Media Literacy in the Digital Age* (pp. 405–422). Hershey, PA: IGI Global. doi:10.4018/978-1-4666-9667-9.ch019

Resuloğlu, F., & Yılmaz, R. (2017). A Model for Interactive Advertising Narration. In R. Yılmaz (Ed.), *Narrative Advertising Models and Conceptualization in the Digital Age* (pp. 1–20). Hershey, PA: IGI Global. doi:10.4018/978-1-5225-2373-4.ch001

Ritzhaupt, A. D., Poling, N., Frey, C., Kang, Y., & Johnson, M. (2016). A Phenomenological Study of Games, Simulations, and Virtual Environments Courses: What Are We Teaching and How? *International Journal of Gaming and Computer-Mediated Simulations, 8*(3), 59–73. doi:10.4018/IJGCMS.2016070104

Ross, D. B., Eleno-Orama, M., & Salah, E. V. (2018). The Aging and Technological Society: Learning Our Way Through the Decades. In V. Bryan, A. Musgrove, & J. Powers (Eds.), *Handbook of Research on Human Development in the Digital Age* (pp. 205–234). Hershey, PA: IGI Global. doi:10.4018/978-1-5225-2838-8.ch010

Rusko, R., & Merenheimo, P. (2017). Co-Creating the Christmas Story: Digitalizing as a Shared Resource for a Shared Brand. In I. Oncioiu (Ed.), *Driving Innovation and Business Success in the Digital Economy* (pp. 137–157). Hershey, PA: IGI Global. doi:10.4018/978-1-5225-1779-5.ch010

Sabao, C., & Chikara, T. O. (2018). Social Media as Alternative Public Sphere for Citizen Participation and Protest in National Politics in Zimbabwe: The Case of #thisflag. In F. Endong (Ed.), *Exploring the Role of Social Media in Transnational Advocacy* (pp. 17–35). Hershey, PA: IGI Global. doi:10.4018/978-1-5225-2854-8.ch002

Samarthya-Howard, A., & Rogers, D. (2018). Scaling Mobile Technologies to Maximize Reach and Impact: Partnering With Mobile Network Operators and Governments. In S. Takavarasha Jr & C. Adams (Eds.), *Affordability Issues Surrounding the Use of ICT for Development and Poverty Reduction* (pp. 193–211). Hershey, PA: IGI Global. doi:10.4018/978-1-5225-3179-1.ch009

Sandoval-Almazan, R. (2017). Political Messaging in Digital Spaces: The Case of Twitter in Mexico's Presidential Campaign. In Y. Ibrahim (Ed.), *Politics, Protest, and Empowerment in Digital Spaces* (pp. 72–90). Hershey, PA: IGI Global. doi:10.4018/978-1-5225-1862-4.ch005

Schultz, C. D., & Dellnitz, A. (2018). Attribution Modeling in Online Advertising. In K. Yang (Ed.), *Multi-Platform Advertising Strategies in the Global Marketplace* (pp. 226–249). Hershey, PA: IGI Global. doi:10.4018/978-1-5225-3114-2.ch009

Schultz, C. D., & Holsing, C. (2018). Differences Across Device Usage in Search Engine Advertising. In K. Yang (Ed.), *Multi-Platform Advertising Strategies in the Global Marketplace* (pp. 250–279). Hershey, PA: IGI Global. doi:10.4018/978-1-5225-3114-2.ch010

Senadheera, V., Warren, M., Leitch, S., & Pye, G. (2017). Facebook Content Analysis: A Study into Australian Banks' Social Media Community Engagement. In S. Hai-Jew (Ed.), *Social Media Data Extraction and Content Analysis* (pp. 412–432). Hershey, PA: IGI Global. doi:10.4018/978-1-5225-0648-5.ch013

Sharma, A. R. (2018). Promoting Global Competencies in India: Media and Information Literacy as Stepping Stone. In M. Yildiz, S. Funk, & B. De Abreu (Eds.), *Promoting Global Competencies Through Media Literacy* (pp. 160–174). Hershey, PA: IGI Global. doi:10.4018/978-1-5225-3082-4.ch010

Sillah, A. (2017). Nonprofit Organizations and Social Media Use: An Analysis of Nonprofit Organizations' Effective Use of Social Media Tools. In M. Brown Sr., (Ed.), *Social Media Performance Evaluation and Success Measurements* (pp. 180–195). Hershey, PA: IGI Global. doi:10.4018/978-1-5225-1963-8.ch009

Škorić, M. (2017). Adaptation of Winlink 2000 Emergency Amateur Radio Email Network to a VHF Packet Radio Infrastructure. In A. El Oualkadi & J. Zbitou (Eds.), *Handbook of Research on Advanced Trends in Microwave and Communication Engineering* (pp. 498–528). Hershey, PA: IGI Global. doi:10.4018/978-1-5225-0773-4.ch016

Skubida, D. (2016). Can Some Computer Games Be a Sport?: Issues with Legitimization of eSport as a Sporting Activity. *International Journal of Gaming and Computer-Mediated Simulations*, *8*(4), 38–52. doi:10.4018/IJGCMS.2016100103

Sonnenberg, C. (2016). Mobile Content Adaptation: An Analysis of Techniques and Frameworks. In J. Aguado, C. Feijóo, & I. Martínez (Eds.), *Emerging Perspectives on the Mobile Content Evolution* (pp. 177–199). Hershey, PA: IGI Global. doi:10.4018/978-1-4666-8838-4.ch010

Sonnevend, J. (2016). More Hope!: Ceremonial Media Events Are Still Powerful in the Twenty-First Century. In A. Fox (Ed.), *Global Perspectives on Media Events in Contemporary Society* (pp. 132–140). Hershey, PA: IGI Global. doi:10.4018/978-1-4666-9967-0.ch010

Sood, T. (2017). Services Marketing: A Sector of the Current Millennium. In T. Sood (Ed.), *Strategic Marketing Management and Tactics in the Service Industry* (pp. 15–42). Hershey, PA: IGI Global. doi:10.4018/978-1-5225-2475-5.ch002

Stairs, G. A. (2016). The Amplification of the Sunni-Shia Divide through Contemporary Communications Technology: Fear and Loathing in the Modern Middle East. In S. Gibson & A. Lando (Eds.), *Impact of Communication and the Media on Ethnic Conflict* (pp. 214–231). Hershey, PA: IGI Global. doi:10.4018/978-1-4666-9728-7.ch013

Stokinger, E., & Ozuem, W. (2016). The Intersection of Social Media and Customer Retention in the Luxury Beauty Industry. In W. Ozuem & G. Bowen (Eds.), *Competitive Social Media Marketing Strategies* (pp. 235–258). Hershey, PA: IGI Global. doi:10.4018/978-1-4666-9776-8.ch012

Sudarsanam, S. K. (2017). Social Media Metrics. In N. Rao (Ed.), *Social Media Listening and Monitoring for Business Applications* (pp. 131–149). Hershey, PA: IGI Global. doi:10.4018/978-1-5225-0846-5.ch007

Swiatek, L. (2017). Accessing the Finest Minds: Insights into Creativity from Esteemed Media Professionals. In N. Silton (Ed.), *Exploring the Benefits of Creativity in Education, Media, and the Arts* (pp. 240–263). Hershey, PA: IGI Global. doi:10.4018/978-1-5225-0504-4.ch012

Switzer, J. S., & Switzer, R. V. (2016). Virtual Teams: Profiles of Successful Leaders. In B. Baggio (Ed.), *Analyzing Digital Discourse and Human Behavior in Modern Virtual Environments* (pp. 1–24). Hershey, PA: IGI Global. doi:10.4018/978-1-4666-9899-4.ch001

Tabbane, R. S., & Debabi, M. (2016). Electronic Word of Mouth: Definitions and Concepts. In S. Rathore & A. Panwar (Eds.), *Capturing, Analyzing, and Managing Word-of-Mouth in the Digital Marketplace* (pp. 1–27). Hershey, PA: IGI Global. doi:10.4018/978-1-4666-9449-1.ch001

Tellería, A. S. (2016). The Role of the Profile and the Digital Identity on the Mobile Content. In J. Aguado, C. Feijóo, & I. Martínez (Eds.), *Emerging Perspectives on the Mobile Content Evolution* (pp. 263–282). Hershey, PA: IGI Global. doi:10.4018/978-1-4666-8838-4.ch014

Teurlings, J. (2017). What Critical Media Studies Should Not Take from Actor-Network Theory. In M. Spöhrer & B. Ochsner (Eds.), *Applying the Actor-Network Theory in Media Studies* (pp. 66–78). Hershey, PA: IGI Global. doi:10.4018/978-1-5225-0616-4.ch005

Tomé, V. (2018). Assessing Media Literacy in Teacher Education. In M. Yildiz, S. Funk, & B. De Abreu (Eds.), *Promoting Global Competencies Through Media Literacy* (pp. 1–19). Hershey, PA: IGI Global. doi:10.4018/978-1-5225-3082-4.ch001

Toscano, J. P. (2017). Social Media and Public Participation: Opportunities, Barriers, and a New Framework. In M. Adria & Y. Mao (Eds.), *Handbook of Research on Citizen Engagement and Public Participation in the Era of New Media* (pp. 73–89). Hershey, PA: IGI Global. doi:10.4018/978-1-5225-1081-9.ch005

Trauth, E. (2017). Creating Meaning for Millennials: Bakhtin, Rosenblatt, and the Use of Social Media in the Composition Classroom. In K. Bryant (Ed.), *Engaging 21st Century Writers with Social Media* (pp. 151–162). Hershey, PA: IGI Global. doi:10.4018/978-1-5225-0562-4.ch009

Ugangu, W. (2016). Kenya's Difficult Political Transitions Ethnicity and the Role of Media. In L. Mukhongo & J. Macharia (Eds.), *Political Influence of the Media in Developing Countries* (pp. 12–24). Hershey, PA: IGI Global. doi:10.4018/978-1-4666-9613-6.ch002

Uprety, S. (2018). Print Media's Role in Securitization: National Security and Diplomacy Discourses in Nepal. In S. Bute (Ed.), *Media Diplomacy and Its Evolving Role in the Current Geopolitical Climate* (pp. 56–82). Hershey, PA: IGI Global. doi:10.4018/978-1-5225-3859-2.ch004

Van der Merwe, L. (2016). Social Media Use within Project Teams: Practical Application of Social Media on Projects. In G. Silvius (Ed.), *Strategic Integration of Social Media into Project Management Practice* (pp. 139–159). Hershey, PA: IGI Global. doi:10.4018/978-1-4666-9867-3.ch009

van der Vyver, A. G. (2018). A Model for Economic Development With Telecentres and the Social Media: Overcoming Affordability Constraints. In S. Takavarasha Jr & C. Adams (Eds.), *Affordability Issues Surrounding the Use of ICT for Development and Poverty Reduction* (pp. 112–140). Hershey, PA: IGI Global. doi:10.4018/978-1-5225-3179-1.ch006

van Dokkum, E., & Ravesteijn, P. (2016). Managing Project Communication: Using Social Media for Communication in Projects. In G. Silvius (Ed.), *Strategic Integration of Social Media into Project Management Practice* (pp. 35–50). Hershey, PA: IGI Global. doi:10.4018/978-1-4666-9867-3.ch003

van Niekerk, B. (2018). Social Media Activism From an Information Warfare and Security Perspective. In F. Endong (Ed.), *Exploring the Role of Social Media in Transnational Advocacy* (pp. 1–16). Hershey, PA: IGI Global. doi:10.4018/978-1-5225-2854-8.ch001

Varnali, K., & Gorgulu, V. (2017). Determinants of Brand Recall in Social Networking Sites. In W. Al-Rabayah, R. Khasawneh, R. Abu-shamaa, & I. Alsmadi (Eds.), *Strategic Uses of Social Media for Improved Customer Retention* (pp. 124–153). Hershey, PA: IGI Global. doi:10.4018/978-1-5225-1686-6.ch007

Varty, C. T., O'Neill, T. A., & Hambley, L. A. (2017). Leading Anywhere Workers: A Scientific and Practical Framework. In Y. Blount & M. Gloet (Eds.), *Anywhere Working and the New Era of Telecommuting* (pp. 47–88). Hershey, PA: IGI Global. doi:10.4018/978-1-5225-2328-4.ch003

Vatikiotis, P. (2016). Social Media Activism: A Contested Field. In T. Deželan & I. Vobič (Eds.), *R)evolutionizing Political Communication through Social Media* (pp. 40–54). Hershey, PA: IGI Global. doi:10.4018/978-1-4666-9879-6.ch003

Velikovsky, J. T. (2018). The Holon/Parton Structure of the Meme, or The Unit of Culture. In M. Khosrow-Pour, D.B.A. (Ed.), Encyclopedia of Information Science and Technology, Fourth Edition (pp. 4666-4678). Hershey, PA: IGI Global. doi:10.4018/978-1-5225-2255-3.ch405

Venkatesh, R., & Jayasingh, S. (2017). Transformation of Business through Social Media. In N. Rao (Ed.), *Social Media Listening and Monitoring for Business Applications* (pp. 1–17). Hershey, PA: IGI Global. doi:10.4018/978-1-5225-0846-5.ch001

Vesnic-Alujevic, L. (2016). European Elections and Facebook: Political Advertising and Deliberation? In T. Deželan & I. Vobič (Eds.), *R)evolutionizing Political Communication through Social Media* (pp. 191–209). Hershey, PA: IGI Global. doi:10.4018/978-1-4666-9879-6.ch010

Virkar, S. (2017). Trolls Just Want to Have Fun: Electronic Aggression within the Context of E-Participation and Other Online Political Behaviour in the United Kingdom. In M. Korstanje (Ed.), *Threat Mitigation and Detection of Cyber Warfare and Terrorism Activities* (pp. 111–162). Hershey, PA: IGI Global. doi:10.4018/978-1-5225-1938-6.ch006

Wakabi, W. (2017). When Citizens in Authoritarian States Use Facebook for Social Ties but Not Political Participation. In Y. Ibrahim (Ed.), *Politics, Protest, and Empowerment in Digital Spaces* (pp. 192–214). Hershey, PA: IGI Global. doi:10.4018/978-1-5225-1862-4.ch012

Weisberg, D. J. (2016). Methods and Strategies in Using Digital Literacy in Media and the Arts. In M. Yildiz & J. Keengwe (Eds.), *Handbook of Research on Media Literacy in the Digital Age* (pp. 456–471). Hershey, PA: IGI Global. doi:10.4018/978-1-4666-9667-9.ch022

Weisgerber, C., & Butler, S. H. (2016). Debranding Digital Identity: Personal Branding and Identity Work in a Networked Age. *International Journal of Interactive Communication Systems and Technologies*, 6(1), 17–34. doi:10.4018/IJICST.2016010102

Wijngaard, P., Wensveen, I., Basten, A., & de Vries, T. (2016). Projects without Email, Is that Possible? In G. Silvius (Ed.), *Strategic Integration of Social Media into Project Management Practice* (pp. 218–235). Hershey, PA: IGI Global. doi:10.4018/978-1-4666-9867-3.ch013

Wright, K. (2018). "Show Me What You Are Saying": Visual Literacy in the Composition Classroom. In A. August (Ed.), *Visual Imagery, Metadata, and Multimodal Literacies Across the Curriculum* (pp. 24–49). Hershey, PA: IGI Global. doi:10.4018/978-1-5225-2808-1.ch002

Yang, K. C. (2018). Understanding How Mexican and U.S. Consumers Decide to Use Mobile Social Media: A Cross-National Qualitative Study. In K. Yang (Ed.), *Multi-Platform Advertising Strategies in the Global Marketplace* (pp. 168–198). Hershey, PA: IGI Global. doi:10.4018/978-1-5225-3114-2.ch007

Yang, K. C., & Kang, Y. (2016). Exploring Female Hispanic Consumers' Adoption of Mobile Social Media in the U.S. In R. English & R. Johns (Eds.), *Gender Considerations in Online Consumption Behavior and Internet Use* (pp. 185–207). Hershey, PA: IGI Global. doi:10.4018/978-1-5225-0010-0.ch012

Yao, Q., & Wu, M. (2016). Examining the Role of WeChat in Advertising. In X. Xu (Ed.), *Handbook of Research on Human Social Interaction in the Age of Mobile Devices* (pp. 386–405). Hershey, PA: IGI Global. doi:10.4018/978-1-5225-0469-6.ch016

Yarchi, M., Wolfsfeld, G., Samuel-Azran, T., & Segev, E. (2017). Invest, Engage, and Win: Online Campaigns and Their Outcomes in an Israeli Election. In M. Brown Sr., (Ed.), *Social Media Performance Evaluation and Success Measurements* (pp. 225–248). Hershey, PA: IGI Global. doi:10.4018/978-1-5225-1963-8.ch011

Yeboah-Banin, A. A., & Amoakohene, M. I. (2018). The Dark Side of Multi-Platform Advertising in an Emerging Economy Context. In K. Yang (Ed.), *Multi-Platform Advertising Strategies in the Global Marketplace* (pp. 30–53). Hershey, PA: IGI Global. doi:10.4018/978-1-5225-3114-2.ch002

Yılmaz, R., Çakır, A., & Resuloğlu, F. (2017). Historical Transformation of the Advertising Narration in Turkey: From Stereotype to Digital Media. In R. Yılmaz (Ed.), *Narrative Advertising Models and Conceptualization in the Digital Age* (pp. 133–152). Hershey, PA: IGI Global. doi:10.4018/978-1-5225-2373-4.ch008

Yusuf, S., Hassan, M. S., & Ibrahim, A. M. (2018). Cyberbullying Among Malaysian Children Based on Research Evidence. In M. Khosrow-Pour, D.B.A. (Ed.), Encyclopedia of Information Science and Technology, Fourth Edition (pp. 1704-1722). Hershey, PA: IGI Global. doi:10.4018/978-1-5225-2255-3.ch149

Zervas, P., & Alexandraki, C. (2016). Facilitating Open Source Software and Standards to Assembly a Platform for Networked Music Performance. In D. Kanellopoulos (Ed.), *Emerging Research on Networked Multimedia Communication Systems* (pp. 334–365). Hershey, PA: IGI Global. doi:10.4018/978-1-4666-8850-6.ch011

About the Contributors

Babita Pandey is an Associate Professor in Department of Computer Application at Lovely Professional University of India. Her research interests include Cognitive Neuroscience, Artificial intelligence and Neural networks, Machine learning, Pattern Recognition and Cognitive Neuropsychology. She received a doctorate degree from Banaras Hindu University, Varanasi of India.

Aditya Khamparia is serving as academician and research person from past five years. Currently, He is working as Assistant Professor of Computer Science at Lovely Professional University, Punjab, India. He was awarded PhD in Computer Science from the Lovely Professional University, India. His research area is Machine Learning, Soft Computing, Educational Technologies, IoT, Semantic Web and Ontologies. He has published more than 35 scientific research publications in reputed International/National Journals and Conferences, which are indexed in various international databases. Invited as a Faculty Resource Person/Session Chair/Reviewer/TPC member in different FDP, conferences and journals. Dr. Aditya received research excellence award in 2016, 2017 and 2018 at Lovely Professional University for his research contribution during the academic year. He is member of CSI, IET, ISTE, IAENG, ACM and IACSIT. He is also acting as reviewer and member of various renowned national and international conferences/journals.

* * *

Arundhati Arjaria has done B.Tech in Information Technology from Oriental Institute of Science & Technology, Bhopal and M.Tech from Shri Govindram Seksaria institute of Technology & Science from Indore qualified Graduate Aptitude test in Engineering in 2008. Published several national and International research papers related to Mobile ad hoc networks.

Kamaljit Singh Bhatia is serving as Assistant Professor in the Department of Electronics and Communication Engineering, Inder Kumar Gujaral Punjab Technical University, Batala Campus. He is a researcher and a prolific author. There are about more than 80 research papers and four Books of International level into his credit. He is a doctorate in the field of Optical-OFDM and wireless communication from a reputed university of India. He has guided 29 research students at M. Tech level and 02 at Ph. D. level. He has about 16 years of experience in teaching and research.

Amrita Chaturvedi is an Assistant Professor in the Department of Computer Science and Engineering at Indian Institute of Technology (BHU) Varanasi, Uttar Pradesh, India. Previously she was Assistant Professor in the Department of Information Technology at Indian Institute of Information Technology, Allahabad, Uttar Pradesh, India. She has completed her PhD from the Department of Computer Science and Engineering at Indian Institute of Technology, Kanpur, Uttar Pradesh, India. Before that, she received a Bachelor of Technology in Information Technology from Institute of Engineering and Technology (Uttar Pradesh Technical University), Lucknow, and a Master of Technology in Information Technology (specialization in Software Engineering) from Indian Institute of Information Technology (Deemed University), Allahabad. During her PhD, she was selected in the EURECA (European Research and Educational Collaboration with Asia) program to do research at Vrije University, Amsterdam, The Netherlands. She has worked in Nucleus Software Exports, Noida, Uttar Pradesh, India as a software engineer for a few months after her B.Tech. She was employed as a faculty in Institute of Engineering and Technology (Uttar Pradesh Technical University), Lucknow for a year. She has also worked in user interface design as a senior project associate in Indian Institute of Technology, Kanpur, Uttar Pradesh, India. Her area of specialization is Software Engineering, Software Architecture, Ontologies, Machine Learning and Deep Learning. Her research interests include Software Architecture and Design, Ontologies based Software Engineering and use of machine learning and artificial intelligence in software engineering and other domains. She has teaching as well as research experience and has supervised various B.Tech. and M.Tech. project thesis. She has also worked in several implementation-based projects both jointly in a team as well as independently. She has acted as a Session Chair, Program Committee member as well as research paper reviewer in various International Conferences. She has also reviewed a book on design patterns. She has given several talks and seminars as well as conference welcome notes in International Conferences and has also earned various awards. She has travelled to several European, North American, African and Asian countries for educational/conference/ research purposes. She is enthusiastic to gain as well as disperse knowledge for the melioration of humanity.

Vishal Goyal is presently working as a Professor in Department of Computer Science, Punjabi University, Punjab, India. The main research area is Cognitive Computing, Artificial Intelligence, Natural Language Processing and Machine Translation Language Technologies.The author has published papers in rated journals with indexing of SCI, Web of Science and Scopus. Moreover the author has guided number of research scholars at Doctorate level.

Navdeep Kaur is serving as Professor in the Department of Computer Science, Sri Guru Granth Sahib World University, Fatehgarh Sahib, Punjab. She is doctorate from IIT Roorkee in the field of distributed database. Her research interests are information security, mobile computing, cloud computing, Computer Networks and software engineering. She has published over 100 papers in various journals and proceedings.

Deepak Panwar works as an Assistant Professor in Computer Science and Engineering Department. The field of interest is Computational Intelligence, Software Quality Assurance.

Shabir Parah is presently working as Senior Assistant Professor in Department of Electronics & Instrumentation Technology, University of Kashmir, India. The main research area is Image Processing, Information hiding, Electronic Healthcare, Secure communications, Stegnography and watermarking, Biometrics, FPGA based Digital Signal Processing, Digital system Design Using Hardware Description Languages, Non-linear dynamics and Chaos The author has published more than 100 papers in rated journals with indexing of SCI, Web of Science and Scopus. Moreover the author has guided number of research scholars at Doctorate level.

Shaligram Prajapat has received Bachelor of Science in Electronics from Devi Ahilya University Indore in 1998, Master of Science in Computer Science in 2000 and Master of Technology in Computer Science in 2007 from School of Computer Science & IT (Formerly - The Institute of Computer Science and Electronics (I. C.S.E.)) Devi Ahilya University, Indore M.P., INDIA. He has Qualified UGC-NET (Computer Science and Applications) in 2005 and GATE(Computer Science and Engineering) in 2007 . He has worked as Reader in Pioneer Institute of Professional Studies (PIPS) Indore in MCA department and joined International Institute of Professional Studies (IIPS), Devi Ahilya University Indore, as Reader for MCA and M.Tech Courses since 2007. He worked as In-charge of Development Center at IIPS D. A. University Indore (from June 2012-26 NOV 2015). https://sites.google.com/site/shaligramiipsdavvindore/home.

Linesh Raja is currently working as Assistant Professor at Amity Institute of Information Technology, Amity University Rajasthan, India. He earned the Ph.D. in computer science from Jaipur National University, India Before that he has completed his Masters and Bachelor degree from Birla Institute of Technology, India. Dr. Linesh has published several research papers in the field of wireless communication, mobile networks security and internet of things in various reputed national and international journals. He has chaired various sessions of international conferences. Currently he is the editor of Handbook of Research on Smart Farming Technologies for Sustainable Development, IGI Global. At the same time he is also acting as a guest editor of various reputed journal publishing house, such as Taylor & Francis, Inderscience and Bentham Science. He is the member of ACM and founder member of ACM Jaipur chapter.

Mamoon Rashid is currently PHD Research Scholar in Department of Computer Science Engineering, Punjabi University, Patiala and also working as an Assistant Professor in the School of Computer Science & Engineering, Lovely Professional University, Jalandhar, India. The main area of interest is Cloud Computing, Big Data Analytics, Machine Learning and Data Sciences. The author has published several research papers in Cloud Computing, Big Data Analytics and Machine Learning indexed in Scopus and Web of Science based Journals.

Mamata Rath, M.Tech, Ph.D (Comp.Sc), has twelve years of experience in teaching as well as in research and her research interests include Mobile Adhoc Networks, Internet of Things, Ubiquitous Computing, VANET and Computer Security.

Baljit Singh Saini did his Bachelor of Technology from Guru Gobind Singh Indraprastha University, New Delhi and completed his Masters in Technology from Guru Nanak Dev University, Amritsar. He is currently pursuing his Ph,D in the field of Keystroke Dynamics from Sri Guru Granth Sahib World University, Fatehgarh Sahib, Punjab. He is currently working as Assistant Professor at Lovely Professional University, Phagwara, Punjab. He has a total teaching experience of 9 years and research experience of 4 years.

Kamal K. Sethi has received Bachelor of Engineering in Computer Science & Engineering in 1999 from Barkatullah University and Master of Technology in Computer Science from DAVV in 2001. He received Ramanujam Gold Medal for M Tech program for standing first position in University merit. He has completed PhD in Computer Engineering in area of Data Mining, particularly his work emphasis on Rule Extraction from ANN. He is working as Professor and Head, Department of Information Technology at Acropolis Institute of Technology and Research, Indore. His research interest includes eLearning, knowledge management, knowledge discovery, data mining, big data analytics and data visualization. At International level, he has authored several papers in major conferences and journals in the area of database and data mining. He is senior member of CSI, India. Prof Sethi has honored and awarded as Best Professor in Information Technology in 2012 by 20th Dewang Mehta Business School Awards, Mumbai for his leadership, development, innovation and industry interface in Education.

Utkarsh Shrivastav has done B.Tech from BBD University Lucknow and currently pursuing M.Tech from Lovely Professional University, Punjab.

Harjeet Singh is presently working as an Associate Professor in the P.G. Department of Computer Science, Mata Gujri College, Fatehgarh Sahib, Punjab, India. The author has published many papers in rated journals and guiding several research scholars at Doctorate level.

Sanjay Kumar Singh has completed his B. Tech and M. Tech from ABV-IIITM, Gwalior.

Vijander Singh is Associate Professor, Amity University Rajasthan, Jaipur, India. His previous assignment includes, Assistant Professor SBCET, Jaipur, Rajasthan India. He is UGC-NET and GATE qualified. His research interests include Mobile Ad-hoc networks, Vehicular Ad-hoc Networks, Software Engineering and High Performance Computing. He has published more than 15 research papers in various conferences and International Journals of repute. He has written several book chapters in international publications. He is Guest-Editor of the several Journals. He has organized International Conferences as organizing committee member. He is the member of editorial board and reviewer for various Journals.

Index

A

Accelerometer 64, 66, 68

algorithms 24, 55, 82, 87, 108-109, 112-114, 116-119, 129, 176, 181, 194, 197

Apache Spark 79, 83, 87

applications 6, 31-34, 51, 83-84, 93-94, 108-109, 113, 125, 129, 135, 138-140, 145-148, 153-154, 156, 158, 191, 193, 195

authentication 64-66

Autoencoder 176, 179-181

B

Biometric 65

Busy Tone 96, 99, 104

C

classical techniques 108, 129

Classification 53, 68-69, 73, 84-85, 109, 111, 125, 128-129, 162, 165, 168-169, 171, 173, 179-181, 190, 192, 194

Clustering 55, 171-173, 175, 181

Common Neighborhood 7, 16-17, 25

communication 2, 12, 30, 36, 40, 97, 136, 138, 142, 146, 150-152, 157

Connectedness 53

connectivity 53, 137, 142, 145-146, 155, 176

Convolution Neural Network (CNN) 120

Convolutional Neural Network (CNN) 110, 126

correspondence 36, 40-41

D

Dataset 6, 36, 40, 56-58, 67-68, 87, 126-127, 174, 179, 188, 198, 200-201, 203

Datasets 26, 31, 56, 59-61, 67, 79, 82-83, 85, 87, 126, 171, 179

Deep Learning 84-85, 108-114, 116-117, 123-124, 126-130, 162, 165, 175-176, 181

Deep Learning Approach 129

Diabetes 188-190, 193-194, 196-197, 201-206

diagnosed 89, 189-190, 197

Drug Discovery 80, 84-85

Drug Prediction 79-80, 82, 85-86, 88

Dtn 135-138, 140-142, 145, 149-150, 153, 156-158

E

End-To-End Delay 137-139

ERR 78

extraction 2, 26, 121, 171, 175-176, 180

F

Facebook 1-2, 31-32, 36, 40, 51, 53, 56, 59-60, 81

FAR 12, 55, 64-67, 69, 71, 73, 75, 78

Feature Selection 82

features 5-7, 26, 31, 33, 50, 56, 58, 64, 66-68, 70-75, 83, 108-111, 128-129, 136, 138, 143-144, 151, 162, 168-169, 171-173, 181, 192

Ferry 137, 156-157

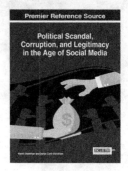

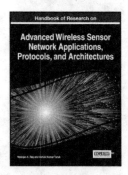

Ensure Quality Research is Introduced to the Academic Community

Become an IGI Global Reviewer for Authored Book Projects

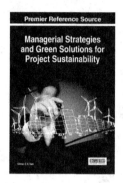

The overall success of an authored book project is dependent on quality and timely reviews.

In this competitive age of scholarly publishing, constructive and timely feedback significantly expedites the turnaround time of manuscripts from submission to acceptance, allowing the publication and discovery of forward-thinking research at a much more expeditious rate. Several IGI Global authored book projects are currently seeking highly qualified experts in the field to fill vacancies on their respective editorial review boards:

Applications may be sent to:
development@igi-global.com

Applicants must have a doctorate (or an equivalent degree) as well as publishing and reviewing experience. Reviewers are asked to write reviews in a timely, collegial, and constructive manner. All reviewers will begin their role on an ad-hoc basis for a period of one year, and upon successful completion of this term can be considered for full editorial review board status, with the potential for a subsequent promotion to Associate Editor.

If you have a colleague that may be interested in this opportunity, we encourage you to share this information with them.

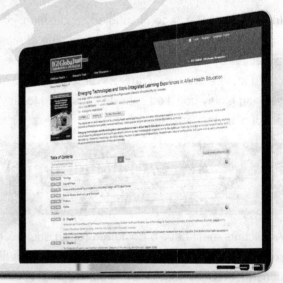